'THE WORLD'S MOST PRESTIGIOUS PRIZE'

GEIR LUNDESTAD

'*the* WORLD'S MOST
PRESTIGIOUS
PRIZE'

The Inside Story of the
NOBEL PEACE PRIZE

OXFORD
UNIVERSITY PRESS

OXFORD
UNIVERSITY PRESS

Great Clarendon Street, Oxford, OX2 6DP,
United Kingdom

Oxford University Press is a department of the University of Oxford.
It furthers the University's objective of excellence in research, scholarship,
and education by publishing worldwide. Oxford is a registered trade mark of
Oxford University Press in the UK and in certain other countries

First Edition published in 2019

Impression: 1

Published in the United States of America by Oxford University Press
198 Madison Avenue, New York, NY 10016, United States of America

British Library Cataloguing in Publication Data
Data available

Library of Congress Control Number: 2018968293

ISBN 978-0-19-884187-6

Printed and bound in Great Britain by
Clays Ltd, Elcograf S.p.A.

Preface

For twenty-five years, from 1 January 1990 to 31 December 2014, I was the Director of the Norwegian Nobel Institute and the Secretary of the Norwegian Nobel Committee. The committee, which has five members selected by the Norwegian Parliament (Storting), is responsible for awarding the Nobel Peace Prize, and the Institute is in many ways the secretariat of the committee. I enjoyed my job a great deal. That is why I chose to stay for such a long period of time.

The contact with the Peace Prize laureates was certainly the most stimulating part of my job. During my twenty-five years I met virtually all of them. I played an important role in the entire selection process, from the submission of all the many nominations for the Peace Prize, to the detailed evaluations of the most relevant names for each year, to the award ceremony on 10 December each year. During the Nobel days in December I followed in the wake of practically every step the laureates took.

The laureates were very different. Some of them belonged on the political left, somewhat fewer on the political right. However, most of them had two things in common. They had a vision of what they wanted to achieve in their lives, and most of them had shown considerable political courage in trying to make that vision a reality. Some of them faced the most difficult of circumstances. A few were not even able to come to Oslo to receive their awards.

After I left office in 2014, I wrote two books in Norwegian about the Nobel Peace Prize. The first one, *Fredens Sekretær. 25 år med Nobelprisen* (The Secretary of Peace. 25 Years with the Nobel Prize; 2015), received a great deal of attention and became a bestseller in Norway. The second, *Drømmen om fred på jord. Nobels fredspris fra 1901 til i dag* (The Dream about Peace on Earth. The Nobel Peace Prize from 1901 to Today; 2017), was more academic in nature and drew less on my own personal experiences.

This book in English draws on both these Norwegian volumes. The historical sections are primarily derived from the second. These parts are based on documents in the historical archives available in the library of the Norwegian Nobel Institute and on literature written by both historians and participants in the process, be they former committee members or the laureates themselves. The sections on the years from 1990 up to the present are derived from *Fredens Sekretær*.

As the Nobel Peace Prize has received more and more attention, many books and articles have been published about aspects of its history. Although some of these have presented useful details about the committee's work, this volume is the first real insider account of the work of the Nobel Committee. The statutes of the Nobel Foundation, which regulate the work of all the Nobel committees and all the Nobel prizes, state that the varying opinions of the committee members should not be revealed. Therefore, even in this book the views of individual committee members will not be spelled out. In most other respects I have tried to be as open as possible. The Nobel Peace Prize plays a role, however limited, in international politics in today's world. It is important that the information about the prize be as complete and as credible as possible. It is my hope that this book will represent a step forward in that respect.

I would like to thank Siân Mackie for translating the book into English, and literary agent Hans Petter Bakketeig for his work to secure other translations. Dominic Byatt, Publisher in Social Science and Humanities at Oxford University Press, has supported my work for many, many years. Celine Louasli and Sethuraman Lakshmanan at OUP, along with freelancer Joshua Hey, were most professional in transforming the manuscript into book form. I would also like to thank Bjørn Helge Vangen and Marte Salvesen at the Nobel Institute library for their technical assistance.

My wife Aase, our sons Erik and Helge, and our grandchildren Jørgen, Oscar, Alfred, Helmer, Sebastian, and Ferdinand have provided the enthusiasm which is necessary for a retired academic to continue his work even in formal retirement.

Geir Lundestad

Oslo, February 2019

Contents

I

The Nobel Peace Prize
Past and Present

'The World's Most Prestigious Prize'

On the first or second Friday of October, the chair of the Norwegian Nobel Committee, flanked by the secretary, approaches a microphone and announces who will receive that year's Peace Prize. The Grand Hall at the Nobel Institute is full of journalists from all over the world. As soon as the laureate's name is announced, leading politicians and journalists start commenting on the Nobel Committee's decision. Some will say it was a good decision, others will wonder what the committee was thinking. However, what is striking is just how interested the world is in what the committee decides.

Why does the world care about the decision of a committee of five relatively unknown Norwegians? The international press does not often devote much time to Norway. The population of Norway is less than a thousandth of the population of Earth. We are on the periphery, far to the north, far from the central parts of the world. There are probably over 300 peace prizes in the world, depending somewhat on your definition of peace. Representatives for many of these prizes have visited my office in my twenty-five years as Director of the Norwegian Nobel Institute. They all had the same two questions: why has the Nobel Peace Prize achieved such status, and how can our prize garner similar prestige?

The Nobel Peace Prize has probably never been in a stronger position than it is today. The *Oxford Dictionary of Contemporary History* describes the Peace Prize as 'the world's most prestigious prize'. American conservative writer Jay Nordlinger had a book about the Peace Prize published in 2012 entitled *Peace, They Say: A History of the Nobel Peace Prize, the Most Famous and Controversial Prize in the World.* In it, he is critical of the prize. Nordlinger's heroes, Ronald Reagan and George W. Bush, had not received the Peace Prize. Many of the recipients, including Nelson Mandela, had criticized the USA. Nevertheless, Nordlinger admired the Peace Prize and concluded that no prize, not even the Oscars, had greater prestige than the Nobel Peace Prize: 'the Nobel Peace Prize is almost certainly No. 1', he said.

There have never been more nominations for the Peace Prize, with a gradual increase in recent decades. In 1904, the first year for which a full list of the nominees is available, twenty-two people were nominated for the prize; in 1961 this number had increased to forty-two, in 1991 to seventy-nine. In 2016 there were 376 nominees. The figure increases almost every single year. It is common to have major petitions for various candidates. The record is over 700,000 signatures in support of Bishop Ruiz in South Mexico, who did not receive the prize. The number of media articles has skyrocketed. Every year in my twenty-five years as Director of the Norwegian Nobel Institute, it has taken me longer and longer to go through the growing pile of cuttings from all over the world.

For a long time, it was primarily countries in North America and Western Europe that were interested in the prize. In recent decades it has garnered attention from almost the whole world. This has been crucial for the status of the prize. It reflects the simple fact that while until 1960, or perhaps even longer, the prize was primarily a prize for individuals and organizations from North America and Western Europe, the laureates in recent decades have come from all the continents of the world (with the exception of Australia). From 1990 to the present day, ten laureates have come from Asia, eight from Africa, five from Europe, four from North America, three from the Middle East, and two from Latin America. Sixty per cent of the world's population lives in Asia, and the Norwegian Nobel Committee never forgets that this has to be reflected in the selection of laureates. The committee has been criticized for awarding the prize to so many people from the USA. Americans have undoubtedly featured prominently, but they have not been quite as numerous as many people seem to think.

There have been many high-profile laureates in the last twenty-five years. This has likely increased people's awareness of the prize. At the same time, there have been many unknown recipients. I remember the prize from 1995, when almost none of the journalists present knew anything about Józef Rotblat and the Pugwash Conferences. In 2006, the same happened with Muhammad Yunus, not to mention the Grameen Bank. Many of the journalists thought Grameen Bank was the name of a person receiving the prize alongside Yunus. Such prizes for relatively ordinary people are almost always popular in Norway. We value the 'esteemed common man', or as one journalist wrote, the 'fortuitous common man'. It is important that there are such laureates and that the committee does not give in to the temptation to always favour big, famous names. I actually think that the possibility of relative unknowns receiving the prize has also contributed to the status of the prize. We never know who will receive the prize. It was great that the relatively unknown Kailash Satyarthi was honoured in 2014 alongside the famous Malala Yousafzai. Once the journalists have sourced the relevant information, these laureates always have an important story to tell. Satyarthi certainly did.

It is sometimes claimed that the committee has greatly expanded Alfred Nobel's peace concept in the last twenty-five years. This is only partly correct. Humanitarian work was included as early as in 1901, in the first year of the prize, when it was awarded to the founder of the Red Cross, Henri Dunant. The next 'expansion' was the inclusion of human rights, and there are many potential candidates who could be considered the first laureate in this category. The first clear human rights prize went to Albert Lutuli in 1960, so this is not anything new either. What is new is that environmental work is now included in the peace concept. Several people have asked what the environment really has to do with Alfred Nobel's will. However, it is not difficult to link the two. Alfred Nobel's first criterion for the prize was 'fraternity between nations'. In my opinion, you would be hard pressed to find a clearer example of fraternity between nations than the attempts to save our planet from global warming. To do this, we all need to unite to achieve a common goal. Nobel's third criterion, 'the holding of peace congresses', can in itself also be said to be met in the form of the extensive environmental diplomacy taking place on many levels to save our planet. As I see it, this is an excellent example of how the committee responds to modern challenges while also remaining loyal to Nobel's will. Anything else would quickly contribute to the growing irrelevance of the Peace Prize.

Sometimes there is also discussion, particularly in Norway, of who should sit on the Norwegian Nobel Committee. The heated nature of these discussions might tempt some to believe that the committee is in trouble. This is simply not the case. On the contrary, there are more and more people who want a hand on the wheel. The committee has become too important for it to be left entirely to its own devices. It is a prestigious position to have. Over the years I have noted that almost all the leading Norwegian politicians at some time or other have shown an interest in being on the committee. Luckily there has not been room for very many of them.

Most peace prizes imbue elements of both the past and future. An achievement must form the basis of the award, but the committee also hopes that the prize will contribute to new results in the future. This is not anything new either. Many of the very first prizes went to peace activists with a very limited influence on the politics of their time. This was the committee's way of expressing that it hoped their ideals would be of great influence going forwards. Some people have argued that the committee should not award any prizes until the historical process, for example in the Middle East, is complete. But history has no end. It goes on and on.

Why Does the World Care about the Peace Prize?

I think there are four key reasons, and perhaps a fifth, why the Nobel Peace Prize has achieved the status it has today. First, the prize is 117 years old. The very earliest prizes garnered a fair amount of attention. This gives it a significant head start on most other peace prizes such as the Seoul Peace Prize and the Templeton Prize. Almost all of these were set up in the years following the Second World War, or even in more recent decades.

Second, the Nobel Peace Prize belongs to a family of prizes, the Nobel family. The family ties bolster all involved. The Nobel prizes have almost become a universally accepted expression of the best of what people within various professional fields can achieve. The Peace Prize also receives more attention than any of the other Nobel prizes. In fact, in some years it has garnered more attention than all the other Nobel prizes put together. We in Oslo are nevertheless extremely proud to be linked to the more scientific Nobel prizes, which are awarded in Stockholm. The Peace Prize would never have gained the status it has without the other Nobel prizes.

The Peace Prize is awarded by a Norwegian committee of five members selected by the Norwegian Parliament (Storting) in accordance with Alfred Nobel's will from 1895. Nobel did not justify this choice, but some theories are more likely than others. It is likely that Nobel visited Norway at least once, since he owned a dynamite factory here. Nobel was a very international citizen. The country he lived in for the longest was Russia. He also lived in Paris for a long time, and it was there that he wrote his will, at the

Swedish-Norwegian Club. He likely considered Norway and Sweden to be linked, which of course they were politically until 1905. So it made sense for the junior partner to award a prize as well. It is likely that Nobel, being the complex man he was, was sceptical of the Swedish hierarchy and historical war tradition, whereas the Norwegians were traditionally seen as more people- and peace-oriented. The Norwegian Parliament's interest in mediation, arbitration, and peaceful solutions to conflicts during the 1890s probably stood out in his mind. His friend Bertha von Suttner kept him well informed of such matters. It may even have had something to do with Nobel's admiration of Bjørnstjerne Bjørnson, a Norwegian author who worked as a peace activist during the 1890s.

A third reason for the prestige of the Nobel Prize is that the Norwegian Nobel Committee throughout these 117 years has established a solid record. Of course mistakes have been made—serious mistakes. Mahatma Gandhi is in a class of his own among the omissions. It is of course very unfortunate that the twentieth century's leading spokesman for non-violence never received the Peace Prize. It is likely that the committee had decided that Gandhi would be awarded the prize in 1948, but then he was shot, which was of course problematic, even though posthumous prizes were possible back then. Dag Hammarskjöld received the prize posthumously in 1961. The statutes were subsequently amended so that this was no longer possible, and this was undoubtedly the right decision. Assessing the qualifications of the living is work enough without bringing the dead into it as well. Of course we all have our favourites on the list of the 130 people and organizations that have received the Peace Prize, and on a corresponding list of names of people and organizations who should perhaps have received it—a topic that will be discussed in more detail later in this book. Even for an outspoken Northern Norwegian committee secretary, this is a touchy subject. Everyone makes mistakes. What we have to bear is mind is that very few truly significant mistakes have been made.

The fourth reason is that the prize has proven to be relatively flexible. As mentioned, the peace concept has been expanded and the prize has gradually become more global, even though this has taken too long. It was only in the 1970s that the prize really became global. Eventually women were increasingly recognized as well, and sixteen women have now received the Nobel Peace Prize. There is still a way to go, but sixteen women (compared to eighty-seven men and twenty-seven organizations) remains a better figure than for the other Nobel prizes. Nine of these sixteen women have received the Nobel Peace Prize in the last twenty-five years.

Finally, some would perhaps claim that the large sum of prize money contributes to the status of the Nobel prizes. But the sum of the prize money—in recent years ten million Swedish krona—has not always been so high. As of 2012, the prize money was reduced to eight million Swedish krona as a result of poor finances after the recession in 2008/2009. There are also peace prizes that offer greater sums of prize money than the Nobel Peace Prize. The American Templeton Prize even states in its statutes that the sum of the prize money must always be higher than it is for the Nobel prizes. Another, the Hilton Prize, offered a significantly higher sum before they reduced it to a million dollars. In a manner most un-American, they award the prize to organizations and institutions, not to individuals. This limits the media attention substantially.

Why Has It Done So Well?

The answer to the question of why the Norwegian Nobel Committee has not made more serious mistakes than it actually has can be sought on a structural level. I think it is difficult to point to the individual contributions of committee chairs, committee members, or even committee secretaries as the decisive factor. There have of course been competent people at all of these levels, but there has also not been a lack of people with limited insight. The selection of committee members has also often been somewhat coincidental.

The primary explanation can therefore probably be found on a more structural level, in the Norwegian and Scandinavian approach to international politics. Both Norwegian and Scandinavian politics come across as 'somewhat left-wing' to the rest of the world. This is where the Peace Prize should be. It should represent a mixture of idealism and realism. The prize has to aim for a better world without losing touch with the world as it is now. One school of political science says: 'where you stand depends on where you sit.' A peace prize awarded in the USA, in India, in Russia, or in Saudi Arabia would of course be completely different to the prize awarded in Norway.

Idealism is pronounced in Norway's modern history, with a focus on democracy and human rights, on humanitarian aid and disarmament, and, not least, on international cooperation. The overflow from our national values is clear. Human rights are firmly established in Norway. Norway has achieved its independence and other peoples should achieve theirs, apart from, in a Scandinavian context, the Sami people. They are better off in the existing nation states. Anti-colonialism as an attitude is hugely popular since we have never had colonies. The Norwegian Arctic Ocean imperialism and the enormous expansion of our territorial waters were all about resources, not people. Social democracy and Christianity have bolstered our responsibility for those who have least, both nationally and internationally. Disarmament makes sense for a small country with superpowers for neighbours. It has become particularly important for us to seek an end to the weapons that we ourselves do not have: atomic weapons. Law, justice, and international cooperation have long been small nations' way of limiting the influence of superpowers in international politics.

That is why there has been such a big focus on international cooperation, whether it centred on the Inter-Parliamentary Union before the First World War, the League of Nations after the First World War, or the United Nations after the Second World War. The struggle for a better organized world is a recurrent theme through the history of the Peace Prize. Others include the emphasis on democracy and human rights, something that has gone from strength to strength. Humanitarian aid has been another focus in the history of the prize, originating as far back as the first prize awarded to Henry Dunant in 1901. Disarmament and arms control, particularly in connection with the fight against atomic weapons, is something that the Norwegian Nobel Committee kept coming back to again and again.

At the same time, this idealism has been tempered by Norway's experiences as a nation state. Idealism did not save Norway from unions with Sweden and Denmark, or from being occupied by Germany during the Second World War, or from conflict with the Soviet Union during the Cold War.

If there is one concept that Norwegian politicians love, it is the concept of building bridges. Norway came to belong to the Western bloc even as it was busy building bridges to the East. Norway became gradually more affluent in the North but wanted to build bridges to poorer countries in the South. For a long time Norway was a very pro-Israel country, but eventually became more involved with Arabs in general and the Palestinians in particular. Our being both inside and outside blocs might sound a bit confusing, but it is actually a good basis for awarding the Peace Prize.

In Scandinavia, where conflicts, at least in more recent times, have been few and relatively minor, we have an unwavering faith that organization and democracy are the way to peace both nationally and internationally. The world should be like Scandinavia: well organized (hence all the prizes awarded to champions of the Inter-Parliamentary Union, the League of

Nations, and the UN) and democratic (hence the steadily increasing number of human rights prizes) with social justice (hence the prizes for those combating poverty) and a will to put an end to atomic weapons, which we ourselves do not have (hence all the prizes for opponents of atomic weapons).

Everything is so simple here, which is why we also tend to think of everything as quite simple out in the wider world. Of course this is a somewhat naïve view, but the Peace Prize needs a dose of naïvety. It is when the Peace Prize has looked to realpolitik that problems have often arisen. I mention this in relation to the prizes awarded to Theodore Roosevelt (1906), Henry Kissinger and Lê Đức Thọ (1973), Menachem Begin and Anwar Sadat (1978), and Yasser Arafat, Shimon Peres, and Yitzhak Rabin (1994), even though there are significant differences between these prizes as well. It is quite something to think that the same prize has been awarded to Mother Teresa and to Yasser Arafat. That is not to say that such realpolitik prizes should be completely avoided.

Of course this liberal–idealistic tradition is not just Norwegian or Scandinavian. If that were the case, the Peace Prize would quickly have taken on a provincial air. This tradition, often referred to in English as *liberal internationalism*, has held a strong position in many other Western countries, particularly in the USA and the United Kingdom. This is one of the main reasons why these two countries in particular are in a class of their own when it comes to their number of peace prizes. The USA has twenty-two Peace Prize laureates, and the United Kingdom has fourteen. Only five prizes have been awarded to Germany and to France, and only two to the Soviet Union/Russia (Andrei Sakharov and Mikhail Gorbachev). Democracy and human rights have spread to more and more parts of the world, just as the Peace Prize has.

On the other hand, the prize has challenged totalitarian and authoritarian regimes, whether it be in Germany (Carl von Ossietzky), the Soviet Union (Sakharov, Lech Wałęsa), or China (Dalai Lama, Liu Xiaobo). When it comes to the USA, it was entirely within reason to award the prize to conservative heroes such as Theodore Roosevelt and Henry Kissinger, particularly since they were both popular even among those who did not incline towards the right. Still, the prize more often than not went to representatives of liberal internationalism such as presidents Woodrow Wilson, Jimmy Carter, and Barack Obama. Sometimes the prize also challenges the American rulers (as it did somewhat when awarded to Martin Luther King and more recently to landmine activist Jody Williams, and in particular when it went to nuclear activist Linus Pauling, who had long been blacklisted in the USA).

The strength of the Nobel Peace Prize is therefore that it has rested on a foundation that is Norwegian and Scandinavian, but also international. There were probably several reasons why Gandhi did not receive the Peace Prize, but one of them may have been Norway's close connection to the United Kingdom, particularly during the 1930s. After the Second World War, and after India had gained its independence, this was less of a problem. Another reason may have been the distance from something so alien and apparently anti-modern as Gandhi's politics, including his absolute principle of non-violence (perhaps particularly after Norway itself had just fought against Nazi Germany). Gandhi was on the so-called shortlist five times, and as such he could have received the prize in 1948 in particular. Several other factors likely contributed as well: his being shot, the killing of hundreds of thousands of people in connection with the Partition of India into India and Pakistan in 1946/47, the (unfounded) uncertainty at one point as to whether Gandhi had modified his philosophy of non-violence. At a very basic level, Gandhi not receiving the prize can be explained by our very Eurocentric world view. Until 1960, only one representative of what started to be referred to as 'the third world' received the prize. This was Argentina's foreign minister Carlos Saavedra Lamas, who mediated an end to the so-called Chaco War between Paraguay and Bolivia. Gandhi's true greatness only really became clear later.

The Norwegians proved themselves to be very provincial in one area: when it came to European integration. During the interwar period the Nobel Committee awarded several prizes to contributors to Franco-German reconciliation. After 1945, when this phenomenon really gained political significance and came to include the reconciliation between Western and Eastern Europe as well, no such prizes were awarded, apart from the prize that went to Willy Brandt (1971), though he primarily received it for his *Ostpolitik*. Everyone knew why: a prize for European integration would divide the Norwegian Nobel Committee. No one wanted such an encumbrance, even though there could be no real doubt about the EU's peace-promoting effect. In 2012 the Norwegian Nobel Committee finally made up for this second-most significant omission in their history after failing to award the prize to Gandhi.

What Influence Has the Peace Prize Had?

There are several international experts who think that the Peace Prize is of great significance as a setter of standards. This is particularly evident within the constructivist school of political science, which focuses on the constant development of international standards that might prove to be of great significance. Democracy and human rights are gaining ground, certain types of weapons are losing international legitimacy, supranational institutions are forming, diplomacy and negotiations are becoming more and more significant, etc. The Norwegian Nobel Committee has allegedly played an important role in this context. Other researchers, particularly within the school of realism, reject this. In their view, the Peace Prize is not in a position to precipitate changes around the world. In a chaotic world where security interests are in focus, each country has to secure its needs as best it can. Regimes might even be bolstered rather than weakened when exposed to criticism from the committee.

In my opinion, many people have somewhat exaggerated notions of the role of the Peace Prize. The Nobel Committee rarely discusses, or never in any detail, the effects that the Peace Prize might have, but its work is based on a presumption that the prize is significant without the effects necessarily being that obvious. However, we can conclude that it is first and foremost a great honour to receive the Nobel Peace Prize. This is perhaps the most certain thing we can say about the effects of the prize. Those who receive it are without exception happy and proud, even though the prize can also be a burden. For twenty-five years I was tasked with informing the laureates that the committee chair would announce they would be awarded the prize for the year in half an hour or so. It was not always possible to get in touch with everyone in advance. And we did not always try to reach everyone. If a person was the overwhelming favourite to receive the prize and was also well known, the committee sometimes would not call for fear that the name would leak and the announcement would be something of an anti-climax. This is what happened in the case of the prize to Wangari Maathai in 2004 when the Norwegian ambassador in Kenya, after giving us Maathai's telephone number, hurried to call her to offer congratulations without checking whether she was alone. She was not. She was in the countryside surrounded by press. Very soon the news that Maathai would receive the prize for the year was disseminated worldwide. At the official announcement shortly afterwards it was clear that all the journalists already knew who would receive the prize. This was not an experience we wanted to repeat.

I cannot remember a single example of a laureate expressing any kind of disappointment over receiving the Peace Prize, apart from Lê Đức Thọ, who turned it down. However, even he did not rule out receiving the prize at a later date when there was peace in Vietnam.

The strangest conversation I ever had during one of these phone calls was undoubtedly with the laureate for 1995, Józef Rotblat. He had trouble believing he had actually won. He had read the speculation in the British newspapers about who would receive the prize. They had Prime Minister John Major down as a favourite, probably because of his work to bring about peace in Northern Ireland. I had to spend some time convincing Józef that we were indeed going to announce that he and the organization to which he dedicated so much time, the Pugwash Conferences on Science and World Affairs, would receive the prize 'for their efforts to diminish the part played by nuclear arms in international politics and, in the longer run, to eliminate such arms'.

When the prize was announced and the world press flocked to the Pugwash office in London, Józef was nowhere to be seen. He had gone for a walk to put his thoughts in order. However, when he finally returned, he was ready to answer all of the press' questions, and to answer them well, as we often watched him do later. He bore his 87 years well. As the only scientist who had left the Manhattan Project for reasons of conscience to devote his life to the fight against nuclear weapons, he really did have a story to tell.

The committee did not need to inform either Kofi Annan or Barack Obama. They were able to handle the situation without any advance warning from the Nobel Committee. It was impossible to inform Liu Xiaobo since he was in prison in Northeast China. But there was a long list of very pleased recipients. I was told that Elie Wiesel was one of them, but that was before my time as committee secretary. During the years I was there, Kim Dae-jung was undoubtedly among the most pleased. It was clear that he had had the prize in his sights for a long time.

I will never forget Jimmy Carter's joy. He really ought to have received the Peace Prize in 1978 along with Menachem Begin and Anwar Sadat for the Camp David Accords, but unlike the other two, he was not nominated before the deadline passed following the first committee meeting. There would have been no agreement between Egypt and Israel without Carter, even though the parties to the agreement almost always bore the primary responsibility—or received the credit—for there being any peace treaty at all. So he had waited and waited. Every year he was asked whether he was disappointed that he had not received the prize. Every year he defended the committee's choice of laureate. But then, twenty-four years later, he finally received it himself. It was not that easy to get in touch with a former US president when it was the middle of the night in America, but with help from the Secret Service, we managed it. When Carter called us, committee chair Gunnar Berge asked him to call back in five minutes. This request came as something of a surprise to me, and I did not understand the point of keeping him hanging. Carter must have wondered what was going on. But then when he called back, he was finally told—and he was thrilled.

It was impressive and touching that nineteen heads of state and government came to Oslo to celebrate the Peace Prize to the EU in 2012. This was at the initiative of Angela Merkel. Protocol put her next to President of France François Hollande at City Hall during the award ceremony. It was an important moment when they stood up to acknowledge the applause of those present. Only a Peace Prize ceremony could have brought so many EU leaders to Oslo at the same time.

Many of the laureates have spoken about the effect that the Peace Prize has had on their position. Muhammad Yunus perhaps paints the best picture: 'before I received the Peace Prize, I shouted but no one heard me. Now I whisper and everyone hears what I have to say.' For the better known laureates, presumably the Peace Prize did not have much of an effect in terms of being heard, but those who were lesser known undoubtedly experienced an enormous change. It should be noted at this point that the Peace Prize was unable to prevent Yunus from entering into a major conflict with Sheikh Hasina, the Prime Minister of Bangladesh. This ended with Yunus losing control of Grameen Bank, which he had built up over a long time. It is even rumoured that one aspect of the feud between them was that Yunus had received the Nobel Peace Prize while the Prime Minister had not, even though it was obvious that she was very interested in the prize. While Bangladesh was more or less closed for a couple of days due to the jubilation when Yunus received the Peace Prize, not even the prize could stop his life's work from being seized by the government.

The Nobel Peace Prize is also an effective door-opener for the laureates. Desmond Tutu has written about how he wanted to meet Ronald Reagan to tell him about the negative effects of the apartheid policy. He was not able to do this. Then Tutu received the Nobel Peace Prize in 1984. Soon Reagan, being the polite man he was, invited Tutu to the White House where he met both the President and his closest foreign policy advisers.

But Tutu's prize and his condemnation of apartheid at the White House did not have that much of an effect on Reagan's policy. In Tutu's view, it remained too forgiving of the apartheid regime.

Tawakkol Karman from Yemen, perhaps the least well known of all of the laureates after 1990, was also received by many heads of state when she set out on tour after she, along with Ellen Johnson Sirleaf and Leymah Gbowee, received the Peace Prize for 2011. Some doors, for example to the White House, nevertheless remained closed. The Dalai Lama was a highly respected figure in large parts of the world before he received the Peace Prize in 1989. The prize that year served to bolster his position even further. He met one US president after another even though several of them tried to mitigate the effect such a meeting would undoubtedly have on the Chinese authorities. It was fascinating which leaders wanted to meet the Dalai Lama and which did not. When the Dalai Lama made one of his many visits to Norway in 2014, the discussion about his visit in the Norwegian Parliament demonstrated that he was not even guaranteed a decent reception in the homeland of the Peace Prize.

After the prize to Liu Xiaobo in 2010 led to Chinese sanctions against Norway, no members of the Norwegian government would meet with the Dalai Lama. The discussion in the Norwegian Parliament about whom he would meet, where, and in which room was both disgraceful and comical.

Adolfo Pérez Esquivel was not only permitted to continue his work for human rights in Argentina after he received the prize in 1980, but he also received a pension from the military regime every month. This was among the more paradoxical effects of the Nobel Peace Prize. Argentina had earlier decided to honour their Nobel laureates further back in time, so now it also had to be effected for an oppositional laureate.

The prize has also occasionally served as a protection mechanism. Andrei Sakharov and Lech Wałęsa have spoken about this. Aung San Suu Kyi may also have been somewhat protected by her Peace Prize. Looking further back in time, Carl von Ossietzky was transferred to a private sanatorium after he received the Peace Prize for 1935 and thereby found himself in better circumstances, but by then his health was already so poor that he died seventeen months later. Shirin Ebadi, the laureate from 2003, was received as a hero when she returned to Tehran after the award ceremony, but her relationship with the authorities became increasingly strained. This ended with death threats and a life in exile. The authorities also imposed a significant penalty tax on the prize money and confiscated her Nobel medal for a time. Liu Xiaobo's circumstances in prison were hard both before and after he received the Nobel Peace Prize in 2010.

The US President is undoubtedly the world's most powerful person. But as we have seen again and again, even the power of the President can be limited by both Congress and the courts. In foreign policy, there are many different international conditions that circumscribe the influence of the President. After departing from office, many presidents have complained that they had far less power than they had thought they would have. It is with this in mind that it becomes obvious that 'five unknown Norwegians' on the Nobel Committee cannot have decisive influence over what happens and does not happen in international politics.

Very occasionally, when the circumstances are right for it, the Peace Prize can actually change international politics. The best example of this is probably the 1996 Peace Prize awarded to Bishop Carlos Belo and José Ramos-Horta. They were both convinced that the Peace Prize would lead to independence for East Timor. Many of us tried to lower their expectations. I was among those people. The Peace Prize could not magic away the Indonesian army. In 2002 East Timor was nevertheless granted its independence, and the Norwegian Nobel Committee has received significant recognition in connection with this. The main reason for the independence was still Indonesia's political and economic collapse in 1997/98 with the introduction of democracy, but the Peace Prize is an important additional explanation for this surprising development. Indonesia knew it had to give this area its independence.

The Peace Prize is usually one among many factors that affect broad historical processes. This applies in relation to the successful struggle against apartheid in South Africa, the strengthening of democracy and human rights in many different parts of the world, the landmine ban, and, with a lesser degree of success, the struggle against atomic weapons and the peace negotiations in the Middle East.

Lech Wałęsa has stated again and again that without the Nobel Peace Prize he would never have been in a position to achieve what he did in Poland in the spring of 1989. The free elections in Poland in June the same year were crucial for the development of democracy in the rest of Central and Eastern Europe, in the miraculous six months from the elections in Poland to the fall of Nicolae Ceaușescu in Romania in December.

And why has China shown such bitterness towards the Peace Prize awarded to Liu Xiaobo in 2010 if the prize has no influence? It would have been easy to just not care what a small Norwegian committee had decided. Instead the Chinese leadership decided to do what it could to lessen the significance of the prize. Even the term 'empty chair', with reference to Liu's absence from the award ceremony, was banned from use.

What is astounding, therefore, is not the Peace Prize's many limitations, but rather what I would call the two great wonders. First, that the world cares about the Nobel Peace Prize, and second, that occasionally the prize can actually be something more than just a great honour for the laureates.

2

Alfred Nobel and His Will

It seems that Alfred Nobel lived a very successful life. As an inventor he held over 350 patents in widely varying areas. In particular, his inventions relating to dynamite were of significant practical use for both civil and military purposes. Nobel also had a lot of success as an entrepreneur. The 1860s and 1870s were financially very good for Nobel, and he eventually became one of the wealthiest men of the era. In addition to his native languages, Swedish and Russian, he spoke English, German, and French fluently. He had the opportunity to meet and converse with many of the era's most important men.

There are a number of photographs of Alfred Nobel, but we only know of one in which he is smiling. Nobel was not a happy man. He was at his most content in his laboratory with his inventions. The fact that he was not married and had no children was probably a significant reason why he decided that most of his enormous fortune should be used for the Nobel prizes. Even so, the fame that these would bring him was likely far beyond what he could have imagined or what he probably wanted, considering how modest he was.

During several periods of his life, Alfred Nobel suffered from depression, particularly in the late 1880s and the early 1890s. Nobel was exhausted after his hard work and was often visited by 'the spirits of Niflheim' (as he referred to his depression). He was also involved in many arduous court cases and became sceptical of lawyers. That is why he did not seek their help when writing his will. His mother was his closest relative; he usually visited her in Stockholm on her birthday. His health improved somewhat in the final years of his life, and even though his mother died in 1889, he maintained contact with Sweden. Even so, he is thought to have slept with a gun under his pillow when spending his summers at his Björkborn estate during the 1890s.

Nobel liked to refer to himself as a social democrat, 'but with modifications'. The modifications were fairly major, because he was neither social nor a democrat. Nobel was not a fan of universal or women's suffrage; he did not believe in the common sense of the masses, in a parliamentary system of government, or in democracy. However, he was a big fan of education for all and made sure the workers in his many factories were reasonably well looked after and that his servants were well treated, even though he had no personal relationship with his subordinates.

Alfred Nobel's ideas about politics were complicated. Particularly as a young man he was inspired by the English poet Percy Bysshe Shelley and his interest in peace, although Nobel's ideas about peace were more practical than Shelley's utopianism. Nobel was against war and became interested in the peace movement through his contact with Bertha von Suttner (born Countess Kinsky, 1843–1914). Alfred and Bertha met only three times. The first time was in 1875, in Paris, when she applied to be a member of his household. This contact only lasted a week and was cut off when Nobel went to visit one of his factories and Bertha went back to her great love, Arthur Gundaccar Suttner. Alfred and Bertha liked each other; Alfred actually liked her so much that he asked for her hand in marriage. But she was spoken for. The second time they met was during the winter of 1886/87, again in Paris, and the third time was in Bern and Zürich in 1892. After their final meeting, and after attending a peace congress as an observer, Nobel wrote to von Suttner: 'I am quite amazed by how rapidly the number of competent and serious delegates working for peace is increasing, but also by the many absurd and despicable braggarts who manage to obstruct even the best of intentions.'

Bertha undoubtedly strengthened Alfred's interest in peace. He even became a member of the Austrian Peace Society that she chaired. Alfred admired her book *Die Waffen Nieder!* (*Lay Down Your Arms!*) from 1889. In his last letter to Bertha he wrote: 'I am very happy to see that the pacifist movement is gaining ground, thanks to the civilization of the masses and above all thanks to the fighters against prejudice and darkness, among whom you hold a prominent position.'

Von Suttner stood at the heart of the peace movement and shared the general ideology of the movement. Nevertheless, her approach was open. She proclaimed that there are 'as many roads to peace as there are to war' and advocated for extensive European cooperation, even an international army, to preserve European fraternity. As early as in 1905 she favoured a decision to award the Peace Prize to Theodore Roosevelt, primarily for his interest in arbitration and the peaceful resolution of conflicts. She also defended the awarding of the 1901 prize to Henri Dunant, which many in the peace movement were sceptical of.

Von Suttner had an unwavering faith that the peace movement would be successful. 'Peace is a condition that the progress of civilization will bring about by necessity. [...] It is a mathematical certainty that in the course of centuries the warlike spirit will witness a progressive decline.'

Alfred Nobel mentioned the Peace Prize for the first time in his initial will from 1893. In this he wrote that the prize should only be awarded six times (once every five years), 'for if we have not managed to reform the international system within 30 years, the world will be headed straight back to barbarism'. In response to this, von Suttner argued 'I firmly believe that this will happen within seven years, if not sooner, but in any case I am quite certain that we will not draw a line under the 19th century and retain this state of anarchy and barbarism that exists between nations today.' Truly this was the dream for peace on earth.

So peace was to be realized before 1900. Nobel had a different perspective: 'You must have an acceptable plan to lay before the governments. To demand disarmament is ridiculous and will gain nothing. By calling for the immediate establishment of a court of arbitration, you hurl yourself against a thousand prejudices. To succeed, you have to proceed [...] with legislative bills you cannot be certain will be accepted.'

Nobel was never an uncritical supporter of the peace movement. To Bertha he wrote: 'Perhaps my factories will put an end to war sooner than your congresses: on the day that two army corps can mutually annihilate each other in a second, all civilized nations will surely recoil with horror and disband their troops.' He later became even more dramatic. Peace would only be ensured once the weapons became chemical and therefore able to wipe out the entire civilian population. This was about as far away from the ideology of the peace movement as he could get.

While working on various versions of his will, Nobel acquired Bofors, the biggest arms manufacturer in Sweden, in 1894. He thought it folly to close it down, as many peace activists thought he should, while the Swedish arms industry was as competitive as it was. Instead he looked forward to Sweden being able to name itself among the major European players in the arms industry. These nations also needed physical strength to safeguard internal law and justice. On this point Nobel was conservative and had limited faith in the masses.

A system of law and order that limited violence gradually emerged within these nation states. Many people, particularly in the peace movement, thought the same should be the case on an international level—that the nations should refer contentious issues to international courts. Then the nations would be obliged to bow to the decision reached by the court. As we know, arbitration was very important to the peace movement. The movement was convinced that this was the way forward in terms of resolving international conflicts.

However, Nobel had limited faith in arbitration. He thought that many governments would hesitate to sign permanent arbitration agreements. Perhaps the governments would accept fixed-term agreements instead: moratoria. If these proved to be effective, they could be made more long-term. Both parties would be prohibited from going to war as long as the moratorium applied.

We see from his extensive correspondence, particularly with Bertha, that Nobel's support for the notion of collective security gradually increased. Agreements had to be worded so that nations would unite against an aggressor. Sanctions ought to be directed at the aggressor. In this way specific rules could be developed to prevent war. A kind of international organization would coordinate the various interests. As a notion it was only partially formed, but here Nobel was ahead of his time. This was an idea that the world would revisit via the League of Nations and the United Nations. Among other things, Nobel suggested that the parties to a conflict should be given time to think in case they might change their minds, but he gave up on this idea when a Turkish diplomat in his employ pointed out the benefits to be reaped by the party that mobilized and attacked first.

The Will and Bertha von Suttner's Influence

So we see that Alfred Nobel had a somewhat complex attitude to the international issues of the era. Even so, the wording of the section on the Peace Prize in his will seems to be influenced by the thoughts of others, allegedly those of Bertha von Suttner and the peace movement. This is likely the case, but this influence may not have been as strong and unequivocal as several people have claimed, because the wording of the will was somewhat ambiguous.

Nobel's three criteria for the Peace Prize were promoting 'fraternity between nations', working towards 'the abolition or reduction' of standing armies, and 'the holding and promotion' of peace congresses. The first criterion, 'fraternity between nations', is nicely put, but what precisely he meant is unclear. 'Fraternity' in terms of the notion of preventing war and promoting solidarity and international law and justice was shared by many people. It is unclear what more Nobel really meant by this and how this wording related to his other primary views. Since 'fraternity' was a some-what general notion, there did not need to be any conflict here between his personal views and the wording in his will. The 'abolition' of standing armies was a goal of which Nobel had been sceptical. It therefore makes sense that he adds 'reduction' to this point. This made it something in which Nobel could believe. Complete disarmament was not a realistic goal to him. There were many 'peace congresses', from those held by the Great Powers following 1815 to the many meetings held by the peace movement in the 1890s. It is not a given that Nobel was only thinking of the latter. His reservations and the realpolitik aspects of his complicated thinking could not have been addressed in a brief will.

It is difficult to glean much more from it than this. Nobel was undoubt-edly influenced by Bertha von Suttner when he wrote his final will in 1895, but it seems he also had a broader goal than that of Bertha and the peace movement. Bertha was never sure where Nobel really stood on the matter. Was his attitude to the peace movement primarily determined by his feel-ings for her? She was keen for him to commit himself to their cause, not just to her. The concise nature of his will does not really help clarify Nobel's complicated thoughts on the issue of peace.

It should be added that the peace movement during the 1890s was con-siderably more complex than many would think. Some people, such as the Quakers and other Christian groups, were absolute pacifists. However, most of them were supporters of defensive war. Even though the goal was undoubtedly disarmament, many of them supported the betterment of their national defence. This was definitely the case for many of the Norwegian peace activists in the 1890s. Norway needed a strong defence to gain its independence from Sweden. The 1890s had demonstrated that importunity without a strong defence got you nowhere.

The focus on arbitration, mediation, and the peaceful resolution of con-flicts united the peace movement even though there was a lot of disagreement about which issues should be subject to these solutions. Most people thought that issues concerning national sovereignty and security could not be settled in this manner. In Norway, Bjørnstjerne Bjørnson was even open to the issue of the union with Sweden being resolved through arbitration, but historian Halvdan Koht and most others thought that this type of existential issue could not be resolved in such a manner.

Most people who have written about Alfred Nobel have emphasized the complexity of his personality and of his approach to the issue of peace. Some authors, Fredrik Heffermehl in particular, have described Nobel's will as exclusively a product of his contact with the peace movement and nothing more. Gone is the Nobel who was able to express doubt about how realistic the movement's agenda was, who acquired Bofors, and who supported collective security. Heffermehl's Nobel is a person without all the complications that made Nobel the man he was.

Even though Nobel and von Suttner only met three times, there is extensive correspondence between them. However, it was not balanced. She wrote considerably more letters to him than he did to her, and she generally replied much quicker to his letters than he did to hers. Sometimes he waited almost a year to reply. She had a clear reason for writing the letters: she wanted money.

Alfred sent money to Bertha several times, but before he would consider sending more significant sums, Bertha had to work out an agenda for her activities. Alfred was sceptical of the fancy speeches and grandiose dinners at the peace meetings. However, she never produced such a grand plan. Bertha often invited Alfred to visit her in Vienna. He never did. He visited Vienna several times, but then he was either busy attending to his finances or seeing his very young friend, Sofie Hess (1856–1919), who was 20 when they first met in 1876. They had a very complicated but non-political relationship until Alfred cut ties with her a few years before his death. By then she had had a child and married a Hungarian nobleman.

When Nobel died in December 1896, this came as a surprise to Bertha, even though she had known he was in poor health. It seemed she was most interested in whether the substantial contribution she had sought from Alfred would now result from his will. It did not, at least not at first.

Alfred Nobel and the Norwegian Nobel Committee

In his will, Alfred Nobel decided that the Peace Prize should be awarded by a committee of five people appointed by the Norwegian Parliament. Nobel did not explain why a Norwegian committee should award the Peace

Prize when all the other prizes were to be awarded by Swedish scientific institutions. We are not entirely sure why he wanted it that way. But some theories are more credible than others.

Firstly, Norway and Sweden were in a union when Nobel wrote his will in 1895 at the Swedish-Norwegian Club in Paris. In this context, it made sense for Nobel to include the junior partner in the union, Norway. During the 1890s, Sweden was much more scientifically advanced than Norway and had institutions that could attend to the awarding of the other prizes: the Royal Swedish Academy of Sciences, the Karolinska Institute, and the Swedish Academy in Stockholm. This left the Peace Prize for the Norwegians.

This seems plausible, but we cannot know for certain that this was the case. It is likely that Nobel visited Norway at least once, since he had a factory there. He did not have many assets there. Most of his assets were located, in order of value, in France, Germany, Sweden, Russia, Scotland, England, Italy, Austria, and Norway.

It has often been said that Nobel gave the Peace Prize to Norway because the peace movement had a prominent position in Norway, which he probably knew from information obtained from Bertha von Suttner. We cannot be absolutely certain of this either. Although some things seem to support such an interpretation, even within Scandinavia, it was not in Norway that the peace movement started. The Danish Peace Society was founded in 1882, the Swedish in 1883, and the Norwegian only in 1895. There were attempts to found a Norwegian society during the 1880s, inspired by the other two, but nothing with any solid foundation was established until 1895.

This was not impressive. It is unclear how many members the Norwegian Peace Society actually had. The society's own estimation of 3000 to 5000 members is clearly too high. New estimates indicate that the society never had more than 800 active members either before or after 1905.

In any case, the interest the Norwegian Parliament displayed in inter-parliamentary work was probably of greater significance to von Suttner and Nobel. In February 1890, the Norwegian Parliament presented the king with an address in support of arbitration. This referred to it being an instrument that was gaining ground internationally. There were allegedly more than fifty examples in 'this century' of nations resolving conflicts through arbitration; there were no examples of nations going back on such decisions.

The address garnered significant support in the Norwegian Parliament even though Prime Minister Emil Stang said that they should proceed with caution. The Ministry for Foreign Affairs in Stockholm was unenthusiastic

and stated, following a survey, that no country would be willing to sign a
general arbitration agreement. After the USA and the United Kingdom
signed an arbitration agreement in 1897, the Norwegian Parliament reopened
the case. This did not lead to any further initiative in Stockholm either.

However, meetings of the Inter-Parliamentary Union (IPU) were held
from 1889 and almost every year during the 1890s. The number of countries
represented rose from nine in 1889 to twenty-four in 1906. It did not go
unnoticed that the Norwegian Parliament was always represented at these
meetings, and by three people. What garnered a lot more attention was
that the Norwegian Parliament actually awarded grants to these Norwegian
representatives for participating in meetings for what was formally a private
organization. This was a scheme the peace activists wanted introduced in
other countries as well. The IPU's meeting in 1893 was supposed to be held
in Christiania, or Oslo, but due to the tension of the union conflict between
Norway and Sweden, this meeting was cancelled and rearranged no sooner
than in 1899.

At the initiative of Swede Klas Pontus Arnoldson (Peace Prize laureate
in 1908), who had been on a peace tour in Norway, in 1890 the Norwegian
Parliament also established the Norwegian Parliament's Peace Association,
with widespread participation from the members of Parliament. The
International Peace Bureau (IPB), a federation of national peace societies,
was founded in 1892. Switzerland was the only country that gave money
to the organization, something that is easily explainable considering it
was headquartered in Bern. In 1896, a proposal that Norway also support
the IPB financially was voted down in the Norwegian Parliament, but
only a year later they decided that Norway would provide financial support after all. This amounted to 500 kroner, something for which the IPB
expressed deep gratitude and which from then on became a permanent
item in the budget.

It is well known that Nobel was a great admirer of Norwegian author
Bjørnstjerne Bjørnson, something he expressed among other things to
Ragnar Sohlman's Norwegian wife (Sohlman was Nobel's young assistant
who executed his will). Bjørnson's willingness to enter into an arbitration
agreement with Sweden at the height of the union conflict during the
1890s impressed Bertha von Suttner. Bjørnson was also a topic of interest
in the correspondence between von Suttner and Nobel. It cannot therefore be entirely ruled out that Nobel's admiration for Bjørnson was also a
factor when Nobel decided that a Norwegian committee should award
the Peace Prize.

All in all, it is therefore likely that the Norwegian Parliament's interest in international peace work significantly influenced Nobel's decision to have a committee appointed by the Norwegian Parliament award the Peace Prize. Central Norwegian peace activists, both within and outside of the Nobel Committee, also credited the Norwegian Parliament's commitment to peace for Nobel's decision. The peace activists expressed this on many different occasions both in the Norwegian Parliament and more privately.

3

The Nobel Peace Prize, 1901–1914
Arbitration

The Norwegian Nobel Committee before 1914

In the first few years following 1901, the members of the Norwegian Nobel Committee occupied prominent national positions and were also all linked to the international peace movement to a greater or lesser extent. Minister of Foreign Affairs and subsequent Prime Minister Jørgen Løvland was chair of the committee from 1901 until 1922. He was Minister of Foreign Affairs from 1905 until 1907 and Prime Minister from 1907 until 1908, thus during the year that Norway gained its independence, 1905, and the years that immediately followed. He supported the peace movement, even though he, like many other Norwegian peace activists, had been very much for Norway arming itself against Sweden in the 1890s.

One of the committee members, John Lund, was a member of the Norwegian Parliament from 1883 until 1895 and from 1889 until 1900, and took part in the Inter-Parliamentary Union's congresses from 1890 until 1912. He was an honorary member of the union's Governing Council from 1900 until 1913. Hans Jacob Horst was a member of the Norwegian Parliament during several periods between 1889 and 1909 and was a member of the Nobel Committee from 1901 all the way up until 1931. Horst was also a judge at the Permanent Court of Arbitration in The Hague from 1906 until 1929. He was nominated to receive the Peace Prize several times, but the committee could not bring themselves to award the prize to one of their own. All these three committee members were associated with the Liberal Party.

Another member associated with the Liberal Party was the writer Bjørnstjerne Bjørnson, who received the Nobel Prize for Literature in 1903. When he was not re-elected as a committee member in 1906 due to long periods of absence and strong personal views on various matters, politician and former president of the Norwegian Parliament Carl Berner, also from the Liberal Party, joined the committee. He was a member until 1918. In 1907, former Prime Minister and top lawyer Francis Hagerup joined as well. He was a prominent exponent of international legal cooperation and as such clearly acceptable to both the rest of the committee and the peace movement, even though he was a conservative. He was a member of the committee until his death in 1921.

The Dream of Peace through Arbitration

Peace movements first emerged in the USA and the United Kingdom, and then in France. In the USA and the United Kingdom the movements were dominated by church leaders and academics, while in France the focus was anti-clerical. In the USA, forty-five new groups emerged between 1900 and 1914 alone. Arbitration through independent commissions was the issue that united the peace movement more than any other at this time. Countless resolutions were adopted at various meetings. The vast majority of the peace laureates from the first prize in 1901 up to the First World War believed in arbitration and tried to have its principles adopted at the many meetings of parliamentarians in the Inter-Parliamentary Union and of peace activists in the International Peace Bureau. Arbitration was also the topic almost all Peace Prize laureates chose to focus on in their Nobel lectures.

Arbitration dated all the way back to the Jay Treaty of 1794 between the USA and the United Kingdom on the border issue between the USA and Canada. It was born of the Anglo-American tradition of making political issues into legal issues. Arbitration was used with greater and lesser success throughout the nineteenth century. After the war between Mexico and the USA in 1848, the so-called Treaty of Guadalupe Hidalgo introduced a general clause on arbitration, the first of its kind. The *Alabama* Claims from 1871 were the most famous case. The *Alabama* was built in the United Kingdom and 'escaped' to the Southern United States during the American Civil War. There it sank more than sixty ships from the Northern United States. Representatives for the sunken ships took the United Kingdom to court after the war. The dispute about the *Alabama*, which was eventually resolved by a dedicated international court, with the United Kingdom being ordered to apologize and pay 15 million dollars to the American government, contributed to promoting arbitration as an international conflict resolution mechanism.

More than half of around 300 arbitration cases that were processed between 1794 and 1914 took place after 1890. The belief that an international mechanism equivalent to the national courts could be developed was spreading rapidly. Other traditional methods such as mediation were somewhat overshadowed by the attention being given to arbitration.

Arbitration was never about agreements into which nations had to enter. It was something that the parties had to choose themselves. Most arbitration cases had to do with trade conflicts, property disputes, cultural disputes, and other matters that were often considered to be of somewhat lesser significance. The nations did not refer their most sensitive cases for mediation and arbitration. Almost all arbitration agreements contained exceptions for cases concerning national honour or national sovereignty, or cases of an obviously political nature, such as those to do with the system of government in the countries in question.

During the 1890s there was interest in drafting more general arbitration agreements between the USA and France and the USA and the United Kingdom. These agreements would not touch upon national sovereignty either, but all the same the American Senate refused to accept them. Their opponents felt that such agreements, despite any conditions, would reduce sovereignty. Nevertheless, many other nations entered into agreements. The hope was that models would gradually be developed that could be generally accepted. Some people, Peace Prize laureates among them, thought the arbitration work would eventually result in a kind of international, or certainly European, integration, but this was controversial.

Despite opposition from the Senate, the USA also continued to resolve issues through arbitration. A case between the USA and Canada on sealing rights in the Bering Strait was resolved in 1893 in favour of the United Kingdom (Canada). There was also dispute between the two countries about Alaska's south-eastern border with Canada. This also went to arbitration and was this time resolved in favour of the USA. Then a bigger dispute arose between Venezuela and British Guiana about their shared border. When gold was found in the disputed rainforest area, the conflict escalated. The USA supported Venezuela since in their opinion the United Kingdom under the Monroe Doctrine of 1823, concerning the barring of Europeans from Latin America, really did not have the right to a colony on that continent. The case went to arbitration, which awarded the United Kingdom most of the disputed territory, but also entitled the USA to certain principal points. The resolution of this dispute led to a clear improvement in relations between the United Kingdom and the USA.

American presidents Roosevelt, Taft, and Wilson were all interested in arbitration and peaceful resolutions to international conflicts. Like many other well-known Americans, both Wilson and his Secretary of State William Jennings Bryan were members of the American Peace Society. Under Roosevelt, the USA signed twenty-five treaties where the parties agreed to refer disputes to the court in The Hague. Secretary of State Bryan negotiated thirty 'cooling-off' treaties. These declared that cases that could not be resolved by the court in The Hague should be resolved by special international commissions. Even though not all of these agreements were approved by the Senate, this was nevertheless considered a big step forward in terms of preventing future wars.

The peace movement always issued its resolutions with a call for a peaceful end to any conflicts that arose. In 1895 Élie Ducommun, who would win the Peace Prize in 1902, therefore appealed to the Belgian king to offer his services to mediate between France and Madagascar about the status of the island. The answer was obvious. France thought that Madagascar was now part of France and that mediation was therefore impossible. In 1898 the USA went to war with Spain over Cuba without any mediation. In 1913 Secretary of State Bryan voiced his support for Alfred Nobel's old idea about having a cooling-off period between parties where they were obliged to not declare war for a period of at least a year or to send their disputes for mediation instead. By 1914 Bryan had signed many such treaties, even though Theodore Roosevelt, the Peace Prize laureate for 1906, distanced himself from both Bryan and from the treaties. Roosevelt's approach to peace was very complicated.

In 1899 Ducommun sent another telegram, this time to Queen Victoria and Boer leader Kruger, calling for mediation and arbitration. The British Ministry of Foreign Affairs promptly replied to say that this was not an option. Transvaal was not an independent country and had not entered into the necessary agreements on arbitration. The reality was that the United Kingdom would not entrust decisions on its most important national interests to others. The Boer War started three days later.

When the three leading countries within the peace movement, the USA, the United Kingdom, and France, were not willing to entrust key issues relating to war and peace to mediation and arbitration, the chances of others doing so were slim. These conflicts represented a clear setback in the work of the peace movement to promote arbitration.

Neither Sweden nor Norway would entrust the issue of Norwegian independence to an international body either. Neither of the parties could risk an international decision to their detriment. The arbitration agreement that was entered into in Karlstad in 1905 only concerned the issues that were not already resolved. The Treaty of Karlstad's arbitration clause also entrusted to arbitration issues that were of such significance to the two countries' independence, integrity, and vital interests that they normally had to be withheld from arbitration. Even though this was of little practical significance, the principle of arbitration was important to Løvland, the Minister of Foreign Affairs, and it emphasized the influence of the international peace work on Norwegian diplomacy. William Randal Cremer, the Peace Prize laureate from 1903, congratulated the parties for having entered into such an agreement. Halvdan Koht noted that this was an important step on the road to the law triumphing over 'violence done'. Many people in Norway and the other Nordic countries thought that smaller countries had the special task of reinforcing international law as a means of controlling the arrogance of superpowers.

Still there were clear limits to which cases Norway would let go to arbitration. The government sometimes gave the impression that it was willing to take things quite far, but the Norwegian Parliament made sure to safeguard national interests, 'the freedom, independence and indivisibility of the realm'. These could not be subjected to arbitration. Francis Hagerup, who led the government's investigative work at this point, pointed out that the Constitution already secured these interests. Again and again Hagerup stressed that countries' internal law, Norway's included, preceded international law. Legal textbooks emphasized that nations subject to international law had a fundamental duty to give their own nation's 'honour or life interests' first priority. This seemed to be how it would have to be until international cooperation had been significantly strengthened and there was a general acceptance of arbitration.

In only one of the twenty-three treaties entered into before 1920 were all conflicts covered by the arbitration clause. In the others, the parties' vital interests were kept outside of the issues that could be settled through arbitration. The unreserved arbitration treaty between Denmark and the Netherlands of 1904, which many people hoped would be the dominating model, was therefore no longer ideal for Norwegian politics, if it ever had been. Neither the arbitration treaties entered into between Norway and Sweden in 1905 and Denmark and Norway in 1908 nor that between Denmark and Sweden in 1908 were as comprehensive as the one between Denmark and the Netherlands.

Even within the peace movement there were many issues that could not be discussed, never mind subjected to international mediation and arbitration. The Inter-Parliamentary Union had more or less banned the discussion of topical conflicts, since this would endanger continued cooperation. The International Peace Bureau was not as clear on this point, but this led to the IPB being considered more irresponsible and of lesser significance. The German delegates of the IPU refused to participate in a discussion about Alsace-Lorraine—the conquests from the war in 1870/71. The issue of whether Poland would become independent and which borders it might potentially have was all too touchy a subject and affected too many superpowers for it to be subject to mediation or arbitration. During the various conflicts in the Balkans, there were always one or more parties that did not want mediation or arbitration.

The Hague Convention of 1899 was very focused on the notion of arbitration. The parties to the Convention actually agreed to establish an international court in 1899, but in practice this just meant that they would prepare a list of people in the various countries who might be able to serve as arbitrators. All the traditional reservations still applied, with the most important cases still exempt. The issue of sanctions for those who did not comply with arbitration agreements was not even discussed, being entirely too sensitive an issue. Of course it was hoped that the parties would more or less automatically feel obliged to bow to any judgment, as was the case in the national courts. Germany in particular was completely against even this somewhat harmless arrangement. Changing this system required unanimity from all affected parties.

The Hague Convention of 1907 did not change the significance of this point. The USA presented proposals to institutionalize mandatory arbitration in all international disputes and to strengthen the Court of Arbitration's authority to force such arbitration. Norway voted in favour of this proposal, but Germany once again prevented it from becoming a reality. No permanent court of arbitration was established to replace the temporary arrangement authorized in 1899 either. In general, the Great Powers wanted to appoint permanent officials, but the smaller nations wanted to appoint judges based on a rotation system. Hagerup referred to the fact that Norway as a seafaring nation had global interests on the same level as other seafaring nations such as the USA and the United Kingdom. Norway and other small nations backed the principle of the legal equality of nations. This disagreement meant that the proposal to establish a permanent court was rejected.

Had War Been Rendered Obsolete?

During the eighteenth century, the population of a nation was generally reflected by its gross national product. The bigger the population, the greater the production. That is why China and India had the greatest production. During the nineteenth century, this changed dramatically. The European nations became the world leaders technologically, economically, politically, and in terms of military strength. Superiority could yield the most astonishing results. For example, 23,000 Sudanians lost their lives or suffered serious injuries in the Battle of Omdurman in 1898. The corresponding figure on the British side was 430. Europe was now in a position to conquer large parts of the world.

Europe's technological superiority was evident in all areas. One could cover enormous distances in a short period of time on steamboats, on trains, in cars, and eventually by air. Jules Verne travelled around the world in eighty days. This amazing progress had the potential to threaten other civilizations, but was based on peace in Europe; a war between the European superpowers could threaten the European hegemony.

The pace of globalization increased significantly during the nineteenth century. Trade was booming. Import and export constituted a rapidly increasing proportion of the nations' national product. The peace movement was clearly in favour of free trade. It would unite people and nations and thereby strengthen international cooperation and, in the latter case, peace as well.

Norman Angell was the most renowned spokesman for this optimism. His very famous book, *The Great Illusion*, was published in 1910. It was translated into more than twenty-five languages and more than two million copies were printed. The book was read by German Emperor Wilhelm II and by the king of Italy, as well as by many politicians. Angell's argument was that war had become old-fashioned. The peoples of the world were now bound to each other. The nations were economically dependent on each other. Wealth had nothing to do with size of territory. Many wealthy nations were small, and some Great Powers, such as Russia and China, were relatively poor. The surest result of starting a war was that it would destroy the economic connections between the nations affected. The belief that a war could reap great benefit was to Angell the great illusion in international politics. What was the point of starting a war if you did not reap material benefits from it?

Angell did not claim that war was an impossibility. His main point was that it made no sense to wage war. The peace movement adopted Angell's argument, and he became an extremely popular speaker and wrote many books. But none of them compared to *The Great Illusion*, which he kept publishing in new editions, at one point to protect himself from the perception that he had claimed that war was impossible just before it became a reality. He received the Nobel Peace Prize many years later in 1933.

Ivan Bloch, also known by his French name Jean de Bloch, presented similar arguments. Bloch was an extremely well-to-do Russian Jew who was a key figure in the development of the Russian railway. However, his main interest was studying war. In 1898 he collected his arguments against war in a six-volume work published in Saint Petersburg. Bloch was particularly interested in the many advantages of the defender at war. The development of defensive positions, barbed wire, and modern weapons made it difficult for the attacker to advance. The losses would be so great as to render the whole exercise useless. To win, it was said that the attacker needed an advantage of at least eight to one. Otherwise the war would almost inevitably lead to an indeterminate outcome and in turn to chaos and revolution. The war would 'result in a catastrophe which would destroy all existing political organizations'. The war also could not last longer than a few months before the dwindling labour force would have an impact on civil production.

Bloch also travelled around to present his arguments. He gave out copies of his book at the Hague Convention in 1899. His arguments became important to the peace movement even though his death in 1902 lessened his influence significantly compared to that of Angell.

A third author who worked along the same lines was Russian-born sociologist Jacques Novicow (1849–1912). He also used the interdependence that modern economics had created as a starting point. This interdependence made the notion of territorial expansion irrational. He came up with the expression 'la passion kilométrique', the eternal longing to conquer more and more territory. War was a kind of 'collective murder'. He felt that some sort of federation was the solution to this situation, but a federation could not be introduced from the outside. It had to come about in a more organic manner.

Elihu Root's Nobel Lecture

Elihu Root was one of the most impressive Peace Prize laureates before 1914. As Secretary of Defense and subsequent Secretary of State under William McKinley and Theodore Roosevelt respectively, he understood the politician's view of the world. As a very progressive international lawyer associated with the peace movement, he shared the dream of a world without war. Root's Nobel lecture from 1913 gives good insight into his thoughts on the balance between war and peace just before the First World War broke out. What had the peace movement really achieved?

Root did not doubt that war had mankind firmly in its clutches. The sheer number of wars that had been waged demonstrated that peace propaganda in itself was not enough to put an end to war. 'It is much like treating the symptoms of disease instead of ascertaining and dealing with the cause of the symptoms' was one of the points with which he started the lecture. The starting point had to be admitting that modern civilization only represented 'a partial, incomplete, and, to a great extent, superficial modification of barbarism'. Changing the nature of mankind was a slow process that might take generations or centuries. People were not ready to accept a parliament of humankind to monitor the behaviour of nations. Such a system would mean that a nation was prepared to let others make decisions on its behalf. Only this majority of alien powers would be able to decide when nations could go to war. 'An attempt to prevent war in this way would breed war, for it would destroy local self-government and drive nations to war for liberty.' No nation in the world was prepared to accept a proposal that was so contradictory to national pride and self-determination.

After this somewhat realpolitik-esque introduction, Root went on to discuss the measures that could be taken to lead humankind into a more peaceful world. The peaceful resolution of conflicts through arbitration was the first thing to which he called attention. Attempts to resolve conflicts peacefully had been made from time immemorial, but it was the Hague

Convention in 1899 that had taken the initiative to develop an effective international system of arbitration. The Convention for the Peaceful Adjustment of International Differences and its associated court had been met with a lot of mockery and scorn. But the Convention and the court expressed a new international standard 'that the more advanced nations welcomed and the more backward nations would be ashamed to reject'. Following the drafting of the Convention, 113 mandatory treaties had been entered into on arbitration between nations that had participated in the Hague Convention, and the court had processed sixteen international disputes. The mere existence of such a court would lead to nations resolving conflicts themselves to avoid being brought before the court. According to Root, the next step had to be moving from a system where mediators were appointed from case to case to a system with permanent judges who would work on cases full-time.

The second measure to which Root called attention was the application of international law in more and more areas. The two Hague Conventions had acted as legislative assemblies that had written new laws for many new areas. The Institute of International Law, the Peace Prize laureate of 1904, had also played an important part in this regard. Root argued that the Hague Conventions should be held at regular intervals without individual nations needing to take any particular initiative.

The third measure was ensuring that students and others were taught about this development of international law. An informed population would safeguard nations against the misleading propaganda that gave the impression that one's own country was always right and one's neighbours were wrong. Of course it was not possible for everyone to be taught about international law, but it was important that those who had been so instructed took charge and educated their people. When the leading lawyers from many countries came together, this would ensure the development of uniform standards.

According to Root, three important things had already happened. An international public opinion had developed over time. This opinion was distanced from unconditional aggression. It also supported the punishment of violations of the international standards. Rapidly increasing globalization had made this possible. What was happening around the world had gradually become of interest to the rest of the world as well. The fear of being condemned by international opinion was an important new force in international politics. Though this was a new development, it was such standards that would eventually become crucial to peace in addition to the policeman's truncheon.

Like so many others, Root was also a spokesman for the notion of increasing economic interdependence having major consequences for peace. War would destroy this interdependence: '[…] the prize of aggression must be rich indeed to counterbalance the injury sustained by the interference of war with both production and commerce.' The old system of exploiting colonies and monopolizing their trade had 'practically disappeared'. These were connections that were becoming clearer and clearer to more and more economists in the world.

People had finally learned to treat each other better. 'Civilized man is becoming less cruel.' And the tempo of the processes that Root described had to increase. 'Taken all in all, the clear and persistent tendencies of a slowly developing civilization justify cheerful hope.'

In 1913, Root received the prize reserved in 1912. The award ceremony was held on 10 December 1913 without Root in attendance. He agreed to hold his Nobel lecture on 8 September 1914. However, by then the war had broken out. Accordingly, the lecture had to be cancelled, but it was published by Root in 1916 without a single change to the original manuscript.

Peace Congresses and the Road to War

Historian William H. McNeill, one of my personal favourites, has argued that 'we have to […] conclude that the standard for civilized rule was the composite multi-ethnic empire.' As long as empires were historically the most common way of organizing oneself, the need for international cooperation between individual units was limited. They resolved what little need there was through traditional diplomacy, including at congresses. After the empires collapsed and the number of nation states increased, however, the issue of cooperation between nations arose in a new form. This was also the key issue for the peace movements that came about in the 1800s.

The nations had to cooperate. They had to develop mechanisms with the same function internationally that courts had internally in each nation. In addition to the traditional methods, businessmen were gripped by the ideology of free trade, while the workers emphasized solidarity within the classes across national borders.

The world was getting smaller and smaller. Awareness of the world outside one's own borders was increasing. Nevertheless, the nation state was here to stay. Few politicians intended to give up the position and power that they in part had fought so hard to achieve. Independence was important to new nation Norway. They did not want mediation and arbitration at the expense of their independence. For most people in the peace movement, not least in Norway, it was clear that the condemnation of war in general in no way included defensive war. All nations had the right to defend themselves.

The peace societies grew more numerous. The Inter-Parliamentary Union, representing the parliaments, and the International Peace Bureau, representing the peace organizations, held annual meetings, and the number of delegates increased from meeting to meeting. The number of arbitration agreements also rapidly increased. Optimism in relation to international cooperation increased correspondingly. Alfred Fried, the Peace Prize laureate for 1911, expressed the following: 'Internationalism does not preclude nationalism, but is rather its natural result, its logical development and its higher form in that it constitutes a higher form of social organization.'

Even those who were more hesitant when it came to the peace movement were feeling optimistic about the future. In his last letter to Bertha von Suttner, Alfred Nobel wrote: 'I am delighted to see that the peace movement is gaining ground.'

But they also made mistakes. The peace movement could celebrate the conventions in The Hague in 1899 and in 1907, but outside of these Great Powers allied with each other and the rate of armament increased rapidly.

You might say that the peace movement and the Hague Conventions lived their own life outside of international diplomacy. Among the historians who have written about the run-up to the First World War, William Langer claims that the Hague Convention of 1899 was of 'no significance'. A. J. P. Taylor ignored it entirely, as does Christopher Clark in his new and impressive book about the outbreak of the First World War. Among modern historians, it is primarily Margaret MacMillan who has shown an interest in the Conventions. Three smaller agreements were entered into in 1899: a moratorium on certain types of deadly gas, a ban on dumdum bullets, and a ban on throwing projectiles from balloons. The Germans only participated in the Hague Convention because they were afraid that they would be blamed for any collapse if they were not present. Emperor Wilhelm II said 'I'll go along with the conference comedy, but I'll keep my dagger at my side during the waltz.' His uncle in the United Kingdom, King Edward VII, agreed: 'This is the greatest nonsense and rubbish I ever heard.' By this point the position of royalty had been weakened in most nations, but, with a few exceptions, the key politicians who participated in the Hague Convention were of a similar opinion. The British Admiralty said that the limitations on naval forces were 'extremely impractical'. Restrictions on the development of new weapons would only benefit 'wild peoples' at the expense of those who were more civilized.

When the second Hague Convention was held in 1907, once again at Nicholas II of Russia's initiative, the atmosphere was even more negative. Root's proposal for a permanent court of arbitration was therefore rejected. The session on disarmament lasted 25 minutes, with a resolution being passed that governments should continue their 'studies' of these issues. While peace activists and diplomats pursued their intellectualism, a system of alliances was being built, with more and more new crises arising in North Africa and in the Balkans. Nations were arming themselves. The Hague Conventions were not in a position to do anything about this.

The Court of Arbitration actually settled a dozen cases before 1914. But unfortunately the optimists were wrong. Another Hague Convention was due to be held in 1913, but it was cancelled due to increasing international tension.

In this sense, the Peace Prizes awarded before the First World War were unsuccessful. The Inter-Parliamentary Union and the International Peace Bureau could do nothing about nationalism and armament. Germany and France continued to disagree about Alsace-Lorraine, Austria-Hungary was threatened by national dissolution, united Russia had just lost a war against 'the yellow man' in Japan, it was unclear what would replace 'the sick man' in the Ottoman Empire, the conflicts in North Africa and the Balkans were numerous, and even the United Kingdom was having issues with nationalism in Ireland and India. Traditionally, Great Power diplomacy had resolved many of these conflicts. Now the conflicts were too numerous, and the Powers were bound by increasingly ironclad alliances.

The peace movement was, according to Bertha von Suttner, in truth 'a delicate flower' that would not tolerate cold draughts from the conflicts of the era. The outbreak of the First World War showed that the peace movement had simply not resulted in the changes that the activists had worked towards, and that they thought they had achieved. Elihu Root could not give his Nobel lecture because of the outbreak of the First World War. Bertha von Suttner died in June 1914 after a short period of illness, avoiding the coming war; a week later Archduke Franz Ferdinand was shot in Sarajevo.

The struggle for an international legal system was in its infancy, and no one could expect dramatic results in such a short space of time. Now, over a hundred years later, we can still see how little progress we have made in establishing an international legal system. War has been waged from time immemorial. It could not have been stopped by representatives for the middle class coming together to pass resolutions. In that sense, Alfred Nobel was correct. The peace movement's work took place more or less in isolation from the armament and increasingly ironclad alliances of Great Power politics.

The British and French socialists were in principle prepared to consider all means of opposing war, from peaceful agitation to strikes and, if necessary, revolution. The Germans found it difficult to subscribe to the use of such means. The socialist parties met on a regular basis. At the Second International's meeting in Stuttgart in 1907, a resolution was passed stating that 'the International is unable to determine the precise form of the working class struggle against militarism with regard to time and place since naturally this differs from country to country.' One had to content oneself with general condemnations of the armament race and appeals for peace.

The German peace movement never had more than 10,000 members, and they came mainly from the lower middle class. The dominant political groups distanced themselves from this movement. Even the German Church agreed with the military that war was part of God's will. Basically the German socialists were prepared to strike to prevent the war and to vote against giving the government war credits. But when the Russians mobilized on 29 July 1914, the impression that Russia was the aggressor spread. Germany had to defend herself. Then the socialists voted for the proposed increases. The French socialists could have voted against increases in the defence budget. Their leader, Jean Jaurès, was in favour of general strikes and wanted to enlist the International in their work to oppose war. Then he was shot on 31 July. The socialists were in the midst of chaos.

The situation was much the same in Austria-Hungary as it was in Germany. The country was facing major challenges from the many different ethnic groups in the large kingdom. This made it inappropriate for them to consider disarming. Vienna was becoming more and more dependent on what was going on in Berlin, where their main allies were based.

There was also a divide within the peace movement. On the one side you had the middle class, which dominated the traditional movement, and on the other side you had the working class. They did not really get involved in each other's movements. The first socialist among the Peace Prize laureates before 1914 was Henri Marie La Fontaine in 1913. However, he was a very moderate socialist, more interested in social reforms than revolution. Bertha von Suttner was no admirer of the socialists, saying 'They must first overcome their coarseness.' They had to be trained before they could become satisfactory members of society. There is little doubt as to who would be in charge of this training. People like her. At the meeting in Basel in 1912, the International declared that it was finally prepared to cooperate with peace activists from the middle class. However, there was little of this. The difference in approach was too great.

The relative disinterest of the middle class movement in working together with the working class was of course detrimental to the overall case for peace. On the other hand, nationalism was much more of a united force than the peace movement assumed before 1914. The safeguards that the peace movement had tried to build were quickly brushed aside when the conflicts escalated in the Balkans and the soldiers started to march again. The working class kept their heads for the most part, but after the war broke out large parts of the middle class were seized by the fervour of war.

The peace movement had no solution to the problems of the era. The Inter-Parliamentary Union and even the International Peace Bureau still exist today, but play somewhat peripheral roles in international politics. Nevertheless, we cannot be too judgmental. The Inter-Parliamentary Union and the International Peace Bureau were as far as we could get on the road to cooperation in an otherwise very nationalistic period. The alternative was not extensive supranational cooperation. That belonged to the future, the somewhat distant future.

4

The Nobel Peace Prize,
1919–1939
The League of Nations

The Dream of Peace through
the League of Nations

How many conferences had failed to take place under the auspices of the peace movement and the governments? How much mediation, arbitration, and disarmament had been attempted? The outbreak of the First World War showed how far the world still had to go in terms of facing key challenges. Now this major tragedy had befallen mankind, these challenges would fall to a more permanent organization, the League of Nations. Its tasks would largely be the same, but the structure would be significantly more concrete and comprehensive than it had been before the enormous bloodshed.

Hopes for the future were even higher in 1919 than they had been after Napoleon was defeated in 1815. The power of the elite had been significantly reduced throughout the 1800s, and the masses had gained greater influence. Expectations are always high when you have been at war for many years and suffered huge losses. Now the enemy had been defeated, a better world had to rise from the ashes. A new and intense dream of peace on Earth emerged.

The League of Nations was the last of American President Woodrow Wilson's famous fourteen points from January 1918. Some of the points clearly required fleshing out, such as that on the standing of Poland, and others such as the point on 'a general association of nations' were more general. Wilson received most of the credit for establishing the League of Nations, but in reality the United Kingdom had done an important part of both the preparatory work, under Prime Minister David Lloyd George, and the practical follow-up, under Robert Cecil. Nevertheless, the League of Nations was a dramatic new step for the United Kingdom. It was undoubtedly Wilson's great emphasis on the organization that led the United Kingdom to so actively acquiesce to and engage in this new era.

Wilson was determined that the League of Nations would have a political structure. He was sceptical of the peace movement's focus on international law prior to 1914. A council was to be established for the Great Powers and a number of small powers in rotation. All the member states would participate in the assembly, but even here the members had veto power, although this would be limited to procedural matters and cases to which they themselves were a party. The assembly would meet only once a year. With a weak secretariat from the outset, in reality this could be considered a modern continuation of the Great Powers' old conference diplomacy. However, the secretariat turned out to be more active than many people had thought it would be when it was established. The Court of Arbitration was made permanent in 1922 and achieved a stronger position than it had had before the First World War.

To prevent this arrangement from seeming too dramatic, Washington emphasized that this would be like the inter-American conferences, which had their origins in the 1870s, but which had become gradually more established. However, this time the whole world would participate. The British for their part saw a parallel in the British Empire. In September 1918 Lloyd George therefore declared that: 'I am for a league of nations. In fact the league of nations has begun. The British Empire is a league of nations.'

If the League of Nations was to work, there needed to be close cooperation between the Great Powers and an understanding even with the smaller powers. But three of the leading powers remained on the outside. The USA decided not to participate. The Soviet Union considered the League of Nations an assembly of capitalist robber states with which it had no interest in associating. France insisted that Germany could not join until it had proven itself worthy of being a member.

At its conception in 1919, the organization had forty-five member countries. The USA's decision to remain on the outside came as the biggest surprise. The great victor Wilson had been celebrated by millions in Europe. For the two million Parisians who received him at the end of 1918 he was the 'god of peace'; in Milan he was the 'saviour of mankind' and 'Moses from the other side of the Atlantic'.

However, Wilson was unable to persuade the Senate that the USA should join. Many thought that membership would place too much of a limit on

American sovereignty. Stubbornness, not least on Wilson's part, prevented a compromise from being reached between Wilson and Chairman of the Senate Committee on Foreign Relations Henry Cabot Lodge. This defeat was very hard on Wilson. It also significantly weakened the new organization, even though it was far from only American ideas that had contributed to shaping it.

A number of other elements also indicated that the organization was weak. The choice of Sir Eric Drummond, a senior government official at the Foreign Office, rather than a politician as the organization's Secretary-General was seen as a sign of modest ambitions. Maurice Hankey, who was offered the position of Secretary-General first, said he would rather coordinate British foreign policy than lead the League of Nations. Frenchman Joseph Avenol, who took over from Drummond in 1933, became increasingly friendly with the Germans, something which was controversial in itself and contributed to weakening the position of the organization.

It was out of the question for the League of Nations to have its own forces that could be deployed against aggressive powers. The treaty had an arrangement for economic, financial, and political sanctions against nations that violated the world order. This could if necessary be supplemented with military forces from the member countries.

It is easy to forget that during the 1920s the League of Nations actually helped to resolve a number of international conflicts. During the organization's first decade, it intervened, often with Secretary-General Drummond's assistance, in seventeen international conflicts, seven or eight of which had already resulted in military hostility. The first of these was the resolution of the conflict between Sweden and Finland about the Åland Islands. None of these conflicts involved the contested sanction system, even though the parties could have been threatened with sanctions. The point was that if the Great Powers cooperated, these types of minor conflicts could be resolved. The Locarno Treaties also represented what was at least a temporary solution to the issue of Germany's place in international politics. Many of these issues could have been resolved by the Great Powers or local forces without the League of Nations' intervention, but the organization's involvement was a new way of doing things and likely contributed to making it simpler to reach a resolution. However, its success ended in the 1930s when the opposition between the Great Powers became far more obvious.

From 1920 to 1940 the average annual expenses of the League of Nations, including sub-organizations, were around GBP 5.5 million. It was impressive that they managed to keep the expenses so low. However, this did not stop the somewhat constant complaints, particularly from the United Kingdom, about the waste and misuse of funds.

The League of Nations had several important sub-organizations. Some of these would come to play an important role in the subsequent UN system as well. The most important were the International Labour Organization, the Permanent Mandates Commission, the Permanent Court of International Justice, the League's Health Organization, the Nutrition Committee, and the Committee on Intellectual Cooperation. After 1945, the latter three became the World Health Organization (WHO), the Food and Agricultural Organization of the United Nations (FAO), and the United Nations Educational, Scientific and Cultural Organization (UNESCO) respectively. For many people around the world these organizations came to play an important role as early as during the interwar years and then even more after the Second World War.

Norway's Participation

Norway had remained neutral during the First World War even though its ties with the United Kingdom gradually grew stronger during the war, hence the title of historian Olav Riste's book *The Neutral Ally*. Membership of the League of Nations would put a formal end to the country's neutrality. It would now stand together with some Great Powers against other powers which were not members. There were many objections to breaking with the policy of neutrality. The same applied by and large to Sweden, who had developed closer ties with Germany during the war.

Nevertheless, there was little doubt that Norway would join the League of Nations. The Norwegian Parliament voted 100 in favour of joining and 20 against. The lack of universality, the fact that not all the Great Powers were in the organization, was the main reason why the Labour Party with one exception voted against joining, and many others had their doubts. Since only two truly Great Powers, the United Kingdom and France, in addition to Italy and Japan, joined, it was thought that this might provoke backlash from the powers that had not joined. Even Johan Ludwig Mowinckel, who became the Liberal Party's spokesman for the League of Nations, had his doubts, but nevertheless recommended joining. The Conservative Party's foreign policy spokesman, Carl Joachim Hambro, voted against joining because he thought that the treaty did not give the smaller nations the influence that they should have. Norwegian foreign policy during the inter-war years would largely revolve around the relationship between three people: Mowinckel for the Liberal Party, Hambro for the Conservative Party, and eventually Halvdan Koht for the Labour Party. Mowinckel and Koht also came to be key members of the Nobel Committee.

The most difficult issue was the sanction obligations that accompanied membership. In the event of war and conflict, the League of Nations could back economic and, as a final resort, even military sanctions against a nation that had waged war against another. The sanctions might therefore also bring Norway into an armed conflict with another nation. There was clear tension between the neutralist undercurrent in Norwegian foreign policy and the sanction system. Every time a serious conflict was brewing, this tension reared its head. After the Manchurian Incident in 1931/32 and the unsuccessful sanctions that were then brought against Japan, Prime Minister Mowinckel started work on releasing Norway from the League of Nations' sanction obligations. This work ended in 1938 with what was more or less a return to the traditional policy of neutrality, even though Norway remained a member of the League of Nations.

The Members of the Nobel Committee during the Interwar Period

The Nobel Committee was the hub of the Norwegian Nobel system. There was great continuity between the members of the committee. Former Prime Minister Jørgen Løvland was chairman of the Nobel Committee from 1901 until his death in 1922. Professor Fredrik Stang joined the committee in 1921 and took over as chairman after Løvland's death. Stang came from one of Norway's most political families, featuring two former prime ministers. He represented the Conservative Party, but supported a policy of cooperation with the Liberal Party, which still dominated in the Nobel Committee. Long-standing members Hans Jacob Horst and Bernhard Hanssen, who were both very involved in the peace movement, continued their work through large parts of the interwar period. In 1925 Johan Ludwig Mowinckel joined the committee and for long stretches com-bined his membership with his roles as Prime Minister and Minister of Foreign Affairs. Mowinckel was undoubtedly the key foreign affairs politician in the Liberal Party, dominating not only the politics of the party, but also the country, by and large. He combined what was eventually a clear connection to the League of Nations with increasing scepticism of the sanction policy and with a deep underlying sympathy for the United Kingdom. By virtue of his personal position and the Liberal Party's strategic position in the party structure, he also bore a great deal of the responsibility for the very moderate defence budgets in Norway until the late 1930s.

Professor Halvdan Koht joined the Nobel Committee in 1919 after consulting with the committee for several years. Koht was a professor of history at the University of Oslo. He had an extremely good grasp of foreign policy. He was also closely linked to the Labour Party. This goes some way to explaining why he initially had a somewhat divergent profile when it came to his attitude to the League of Nations. Until 1934 the Labour Party voted against joining the organization. From 1935 until his departure from the committee in connection with the Ossietzky case, Koht combined his membership of the Nobel Committee with his role of Minister of Foreign Affairs. This would lead to major problems for both Koht and for the committee.

Of the key Norwegian spokesmen for foreign affairs, only the Conservative Party's Hambro was not a member of the Nobel Committee. He only joined in 1940 once the Nobel Committee could no longer play its traditional role.

The First Laureates

Twenty-one Peace Prizes were awarded from 1918 to 1939. Ten of these had a close connection to the League of Nations; three others had a somewhat weaker connection; while the eight others had a negligible or no connection to the League of Nations. There could therefore be no real doubt as to what the committee's priority was. The Inter-Parliamentary Union was still being discussed and frequently featured on the shortlist (1923, 1924, 1927, 1935, 1938), but it was obvious that the focus had now moved to the League of Nations. Within Norwegian politics, the organization represented the great hope that still existed in Norway and in many other countries that a better organized world could lead to peace and reconciliation. While all these prizes were basically about promoting structures in international politics that could contribute to peace, the prize for 1935 to Carl von Ossietzky would turn up a completely different perspective. That prize called attention to people and ideologies, not structures, as what was crucial to international politics.

The 1920s were a good period for the League of Nations, and it was during these years in particular that many of the Peace Prizes were connected to the organization. The prize for 1919 went to President Woodrow Wilson (1856–1929). As we have seen, there were various opinions on the League of Nations and Wilson in Norway. This was also the case within the Nobel Committee, but the Liberal Party contingent comprising Løvland, Horst, and Hanssen lauded him, even though Hagerup and Koht were both sceptical. As mentioned, Koht was influenced by the Labour Party's negative attitude to the League of Nations, whereas Hagerup was afraid that the organization would be dominated by the Great Powers. All the same, it was difficult to deny Wilson the prize. Even though the USA did not become a member, his name was inextricably linked to the formation of the League of Nations.

At his inauguration in 1912, Wilson had stated: 'It would be the irony of fate if my administration had to deal chiefly with foreign affairs.' Through his programme New Freedom he aimed to implement significant reforms in domestic politics. This was the first victory for the Democrats in twenty years. The party won the majority in the Senate and in the House of Representatives as well. Wilson reduced customs duties and promoted free trade. He introduced an income tax so that the state would have enough income. He also established the Federal Reserve System and controlled the power and influence of the banks. However, with his roots as they were in the Southern United States, he did nothing to improve the situation of black people in the country.

When the First World War broke out in 1914, Wilson was determined to keep America out of the war. However, the German U-boat Campaign meant that sympathy for the United Kingdom was high. German diplomacy towards Mexico, with intimations of border changes to the detriment of the USA, also stimulated a new policy. After Russia's February Revolution in 1917, when the new bourgeois regime chose to continue the war, this could now be considered a fundamental conflict between democracy and totalitarianism. In April 1917 Wilson declared war against Germany, partly as a result of the now unrestricted German U-boat Campaign. The Germans were counting on the U-boats ending the war before the Americans were able to do too much damage.

In 1918 the Republicans won back the majority in both the Senate and the House of Representatives. The distance between the two parties was far from insurmountable when it came to membership of the League of Nations. The Republican chairman of the Committee on Foreign Relations, Henry Cabot Lodge, was internationally aware. Wilson embarked on an extensive tour to influence American opinion, but he was not prepared to compromise with the Republicans. They in turn were not open to promising sanctions against an aggressor. During the tour the President had a stroke and was paralysed for life. Shortly afterwards the Republicans voted against membership of the League of Nations.

The prize for 1920 went to Frenchman Léon Bourgeois (1851–1925). As a representative of the radical socialists, he was a member of the National Assembly for thirty-five years. He was Prime Minister for a short time in 1895 and later refused offers to be Prime Minister again. He was also a very progressive lawyer. Bourgeois considered himself a defender of the legacy of the French Revolution. He was also influenced by the nineteenth-century faith in reason and science.

While Wilson was the political father of the League of Nations, Bourgeois was referred to as its spiritual father. As former leader of the French delegation at both the Hague Conventions, he represented continuity throughout the peace movement. He had worked actively to ensure that the International Court of Justice would consist of permanent judges instead of temporary arbitrators, and he himself became one of these judges. He also wanted the new organization to be able to impose mediation on conflicting parties. A dedicated force would be established to initiate military sanctions. For Bourgeois it was important to emphasize this thread back through time, something of which Wilson was very sceptical since he thought that little had been achieved before the First World War. Wilson wanted all references to this time struck from the record. To this Bourgeois was heard to say:'My life's work is wiped out!'

In many ways Bourgeois made use of his past optimism, maintaining that underlying currents seemed to be of benefit to international cooperation. In the manuscript of his Nobel lecture—he was too sick to travel to Oslo— he emphasized that education was in the process of spreading to 'nearly every corner of the globe'. Democracy's progress was 'evident in every civilized nation'. All of this would necessitate international organizations based on the same sound principles—particularly now that the League of Nations,'heralded in 1899 and 1907 by the Hague Peace Conferences', had become a reality. It was almost inconceivable how far the world had come since the dawn of time. There would be setbacks, and the peace process would take time, but 'if the road towards the final goal is clearly marked, if an organization like the League of Nations realizes its potential and achieves its purpose, the potent benefits of peace and of human solidarity will triumph over evil.' It was almost as if the First World War had not happened. In 1920, Bourgeois was unanimously elected the first President of the Council of the League of Nations. In 1923, old and almost blind, he retired from the Senate.

The prize for 1921 also had a clear connection with the League of Nations. It was shared by Swede Hjalmar Branting (1860–1925) and Norwegian Christian Lange (1869–1938). Branting was one of the leading social democrats of his time and was Prime Minister three times between 1920 and 1925. He was opposed to revolution and supported extensive reforms implemented peacefully, even though he also wanted to build bridges with the Soviet Union. Branting joined the peace movement early on. In 1885 he was involved in the founding of one of the first peace societies in Sweden. He was active in the League of Nations and in the socialist International, and was therefore one of a few who had prominent positions within both movements. As someone who favoured national independence, he supported Norway's independence from Sweden in 1905. The conflict should have been resolved through mediation, but he was prepared to resort to a general strike to prevent a war with Norway. Branting was sentenced to three years in prison for opposing the use of military force, but this sentence was later commuted to a fine. He opposed all attempts by Sweden to cosy up to Germany during the First World War, but not always with success.

Branting felt that the Treaty of Versailles was too hard on Germany, but was happy that the national right of self-determination had had the breakthrough it did. He represented Sweden in both the Council and the Assembly. The fact that the League of Nations supported Finland in the dispute over Åland, even though the population of the islands was Swedish-speaking, disappointed Branting, but his loyal support in this case only served to reinforce his international position. His greatest disappointment was that his strong interest in disarmament gave so few concrete results.

Branting considered the League of Nations the realization of Alfred Nobel's will. The organization was the embodiment of 'fraternity between nations'. The League was very involved in disarmament, and the work of the Assembly represented the fulfilment of the point on peace congresses. It was disappointing to many that some of the great powers remained outside of the League of Nations, and Branting thought that the smaller powers should play a greater role. With his practical approach, he knew that the world was not ready for a supranational organization, but as nation states had exercised their authority over the individual, the League of Nations would gradually exercise its authority over the nations of the world.

In awarding a prize to Christian Lange, the Nobel Committee awarded a prize to the historical roots of the peace movement and to themselves. Lange had been the Norwegian Nobel Committee's first secretary and the first Director of the Norwegian Nobel Institute. He introduced many of the procedures that still apply to the committee's work today. After he left in 1909, he became the committee's honorary adviser, something that also made sense bearing in mind he was a leading expert on the international peace movement. He was so well known to the committee members that they forwent the usual review of the candidate that was and still is normal for almost all serious candidates for the Peace Prize. Lange went from the Institute to the Inter-Parliamentary Union, where he became Secretary-General. Albert Gobat had been the first Secretary-General to receive the Peace Prize in 1902; Christian Lange became the second. The prize was therefore also a prize for the Inter-Parliamentary Union. Lange also perceived the tension between the national right of self-determination and internationalism. He had no faith in an international super-nation, since this would go against the national right of self-determination, and he thought the aim should be a federation of independent nations. The Hague Conventions, in which he himself had participated in 1907 as an adviser to the Norwegian delegation, was the first tentative step on this road to cooperation. The League of Nations 'marks the first serious and conscious attempt to approach that goal' of a world federation. There may have been tension between the national and the international, 'but the unity of mankind resolves this tension.'

In the IPU, it was Lange's job to keep in touch with the national member organizations through visits and publications. He moved the headquarters from Bern to Brussels. In 1914, the IPU had 4000 members from twenty-four countries. When the First World War broke out, he moved the headquarters again, this time to his home in Christiania (Oslo). Since the Scandinavian countries were neutral, this meant that he was at least able to maintain the practice of parliamentary meetings between these countries. He also kept in touch with as many of the other members as possible. He secured financing from the Carnegie Endowment. After the war he restarted the IPU, now moving the headquarters to Geneva, the seat of the League of Nations.

It was brave of the committee to give the prize for 1921 to Lange and then to give the prize to another Norwegian in 1922, Fridtjof Nansen (1861–1930). They are the only two Norwegians to have received the Peace Prize. Nansen was one of the era's most famous Norwegians, known as an Arctic explorer and scientist, the first to ski across Greenland and the man who crossed the Arctic Ocean on *Fram*. In 1905 he played an important part in promoting Norwegian independence and a Norwegian kingdom. During the First World War he negotiated an agreement with the USA to supply food to Norway. He became a strong supporter of the League of Nations and its universality, and of the notion of a permanent international court.

Nansen's humanitarian work started before he became the League of Nations' High Commissioner for Refugees. His first task was to repatriate more than half a million prisoners of war, most of them German prisoners in Western Europe and Allied prisoners in Russia and Siberia. As High Commissioner he had two main responsibilities. The first was taking care of the one and a half million Russians who had fled from the Russian Revolution and who were spread across large parts of Europe and Asia. It was also Nansen's responsibility to undertake a population exchange between Turkey and Greece after the war between the two countries. Approximately 2.5 million Greeks, Russians, Armenians, and others were exchanged. In addition to his work as High Commissioner, Nansen continued his humanitarian work in Russia after the famine in 1921.

Nansen's Nobel lecture was a long homage to the League of Nations. He himself came to participate as a delegate many times. If the world really wanted to be rid of conflict or to put an end to armament, 'the governments must [...] stake everything upon the policy of the League of Nations without thinking about any lines of retreat. [...] If they do so and if their peoples support them in the same spirit, then shall the evil monster of war be felled and our future secured for the work of peace, that of building, not tearing down.'

The Dream of Banning War

The Peace Prize for 1925 was awarded to American Vice President Charles Dawes and British Foreign Secretary Austen Chamberlain and for 1926 to French Minister of Foreign Affairs Aristide Briand and his German colleague Gustav Stresemann. French–German reconciliation was the ultimate objective, and the prize for 1927 was awarded to Ludwig Quidde and Ferdinand Buisson, who had worked for such reconciliation on a more popular level.

Within the traditional peace tradition, the prize awarded to Frank B. Kellogg (1856–1937) in 1929 was in many ways the most remarkable. Kellogg had gone from being a poor farmer on the prairie in Minnesota to being one of the USA's leading lawyers. He was elected to the Senate as a Republican from Minnesota, but was not re-elected. Despite having given up isolationism during the First World War, he nevertheless voted against joining the League of Nations. Kellogg held various diplomatic posts, including ambassador to the United Kingdom, before he became the US Secretary of State under Calvin Coolidge from 1925 until 1929.

The notion of declaring war illegal was conceived by Chicago lawyer Salmon Levinson. The basis for this was simple. When a federal court in the USA declared something illegal, this was largely respected. The world had managed to rid itself of both slavery and duels. Now it was time for war to be declared illegal. The dream of peace on earth would finally become reality in the simplest manner possible.

Kellogg's prize-winning initiative, officially entitled *The International Treaty for the Renunciation of War as an Instrument of National Policy*, only really had two articles. In article one the signatories condemned war as a means of resolving international conflicts. In article two the nations agreed that all conflicts should only be resolved through peaceful means. Defensive war would still be permitted in line with the League of Nations' point of departure.

It might be said that the proposal actually criticized the League of Nations for not being visionary enough. There would be no plan for sanctions against an aggressor. Sanctions were a recipe for war and conflict. The will of the people for peace would be enough to support the governments' declared will for peace. The people would not stand for such important agreements simply being neglected. Kellogg believed that when all was said and done it was the people who decided. In his Nobel acceptance speech he talked about 'the force of public opinion, which controls nations and peoples—that public opinion which shapes our destinies and guides the progress of human affairs'.

It was former Peace Prize laureate and French Minister of Foreign Affairs Aristide Briand who had taken the initiative towards the USA in the form of an agreement of eternal friendship between France and the USA. He was encouraged by the goodwill that Charles Lindbergh's transatlantic flight in 1927 had generated in these two countries in particular. Nevertheless, many people thought that the proposed treaty was yet another attempt from Briand and France to oblige the USA to help defend against Germany. This was something that the Americans were still set against. Under pressure from President Coolidge and inspired by a certain popular sympathy, Kellogg became increasingly focused on the project, but tried to make it multilateral so that all the key countries could sign. It was difficult for the three Peace Prize laureates Chamberlain, Stresemann, and Briand to oppose a project that seemed to be the very embodiment of good. This was Kellogg's great achievement, he himself believed, in addition to the eighty-one treaties he had signed, more than any other American Secretary of State. More than a third of these were bilateral agreements on the peaceful resolution of conflicts through mediation and arbitration.

For the Nobel Committee, the treaty was in many ways the culmination of the approach that the committee had employed since the very beginning, which focused on mediation and arbitration, preferably without sanctions of any kind. In his presentation speech for the prize to Kellogg, Prime Minister Mowinckel emphasized that peace now prevailed throughout the world and had prevailed in Europe for ten years. However, he also claimed that the Kellogg–Briand Pact, as he called it, had to be followed up by other measures. The treaty would not lead to peace entirely on its own. The fact that it was Mowinckel and not committee chair Stang who gave the speech on behalf of the committee perhaps emphasized the government's clear interest in the cause. Koht chose to stay away from the committee meetings in 1929, even though he lived in Oslo part of the time. He was clearly against the prize being awarded to Kellogg, just as he had also been against several of the League of Nations prizes.

On 27 August 1928, the treaty was signed in Paris with all due pomp and circumstance. People were largely optimistic. Many governments nevertheless made reservations, just to be on the safe side. Several nations wanted assurances that the treaty did not violate the right of self-defence or treaties they had otherwise signed such as the Locarno Treaties or the French alliances with Eastern European countries. The United Kingdom made it clear that there were 'certain regions' whose defence did not fall under the treaty. The USA gave itself a major exception in relation to the Monroe Doctrine and Latin America. In the Western Hemisphere, the dominance of the USA would continue untouched.

In the end, sixty-four nations signed the treaty. In the Senate only one single senator opposed it, while another said it was 'worthless, but perfectly harmless'. Another referred to the treaty as 'an international kiss'. The peace movement had proven to be massively in favour of it. Only Argentina, Bolivia, El Salvador, and Uruguay refused to sign. Mussolini called the treaty 'sublime', even 'transcendental'. The Japanese praised it as a 'sublime and generous treaty'. Even the Soviet Union signed it, but Stalin nevertheless stated: 'They talk about pacifism; they speak about peace among European states. [. . .] All this is nonsense.'

The Kellogg–Briand Pact lasted three years until Japan attacked Manchuria in 1931/32 and the nations, international opinion, and the League of Nations remained calm in the face of this obvious aggression. There was little that the European Great Powers could do against Japan in such a remote area. To take any action they relied on support from the USA. When it became clear that America would also limit its opposition to protests against the Japanese aggression, the League of Nations was powerless.

There was no experience to suggest that events outside of Europe would particularly affect developments within Europe. Prime Minister Mowinckel expressed to the Norwegian Parliament that a harder course of action might be required against Japan. The Scandinavian countries thought that sanctions should be initiated against Japan. However, it took a long time to formally condemn Japan; the sanctions never came. Mowinckel concluded that: 'On the whole, I think we should still pin our political hopes on the work of the League of Nations; we must not let the disappointments and setbacks overshadow our faith that the cooperation between peoples that is taking place will ultimately bear fruit. If we were to lose that hope and faith, we would not have much left.'

1935: Carl von Ossietzky

There was no unified focus behind the 1930 prize to church leader Nathan Söderblom, the 1931 prize to peace activist Jane Addams and educator Nicholas Murray Butler, and the 1933 prize to writer Norman Angell. The 1934 prize was awarded to Arthur Henderson, another League activist.

The prize for 1935 to journalist and editor Carl von Ossietzky for his work against Germany's rearmament garnered a huge amount of attention. Two of the members of the Nobel Committee, Koht and Mowinckel, withdrew when they realized that the prize would go to Ossietzky. It was unclear how long their absence would last. They did actually attend the committee's first meetings in 1937, but in June of that year the Norwegian Parliament decided quite simply that members of the current government could not be members of the Nobel Committee. King Haakon stayed away from the award ceremony for the first and only time. A heated debate started in Norway and in several other countries in Europe even before the award ceremony.

Hitler was furious about this interference in German internal affairs and prohibited any Germans from receiving a Nobel Prize, something that prevented three scientists from receiving their prizes in Stockholm in the late 1930s. The prize to Ossietzky led to tension in the relationship between Germany and Norway. Germany stopped German honorary orders being awarded to Norwegian citizens, and Norway limited its contact with the Nazi's congresses. It was only in 1939 that the relationship between the two countries normalized.

In principle, the prize for 1935 is extremely interesting. Until then the prize had almost always been awarded based on an analysis of the more structural forces that promoted peace. International cooperation and international organization were the key to a more peaceful world. Ossietzky's work was in a related yet somewhat different vein: work on disarmament. Ossietzky was not particularly interested in the role of the League of Nations, or in mediation and arbitration. The Nobel Committee was very careful not to make the prize an attack on the Nazi regime. The focus was on Ossietzky's work for peace, neither more nor less.

But Nazi Germany undoubtedly considered the prize an insult to Germany. This is probably also how the many people who led the campaign for Ossietzky to receive the prize intended it to be perceived. Willy Brandt later described the purpose of the campaign—in which he himself as a German refugee in Norway was very active—as an attempt 'to save a victim of the Brown Terror, condemn Nazism and honour the other Germany'.

The prize was therefore intended by many as a protest against the Nazi regime, and this was also the basis for the strong opinions expressed about the awarding of the prize. The focus of the prize was thus shifted from international structures to the condemnation of specific regimes and people. After the Second World War there would be several more prizes like this, against apartheid and against Soviet and Chinese communism, but up until this point the focus had been on strengthening international institutions. The prize for 1937 to Robert Cecil and for 1938 to the Nansen International Office for Refugees exemplified this. This marked a return to prizes connected to the League of Nations. Ossietzky's prize was thus definitely a one-off event in its time.

Ossietzky wrote his first articles opposing militarism as early as before the First World War. His participation as a soldier during the war reinforced his anti-militaristic conviction, and after the war he became more and more active as both a writer and a member of peace societies. In 1927 he became editor of *Die Weltbühne*, the leading mouthpiece for left-wing intellectuals in the Weimar Republic. He was affiliated with no party and also criticized the left, including the communists, whom he condemned for their 'romanticization of revolution', and the social democrats, whom he attacked for their caution and lack of initiative.

But there was no doubt that Ossietzky himself was on the left. His attacks on the right, and on the Nazis in particular, were many and vicious. In 1927 *Die Weltbühne* published an article on leading German officers who were allegedly responsible for killing political opponents. Ossietzky was sentenced to imprisonment, but escaped with a fine. Ossietzky's articles opposing Germany's secret rearmament in violation of the Treaty of Versailles garnered the most attention. The magazine revealed how the Brüning government had used the airline Lufthansa for military reconstruction in cooperation with the Soviet military. This time Ossietzky was sentenced to eighteen months in prison for revealing military secrets, a truth with major modifications since so much of what he had written was already publicly available information. Before Christmas of 1932, after seven months in prison, he was released via a general amnesty. Ossietzky resumed his anti-militaristic writing, now targeting the new Nazi establishment. After the Reichstag fire he was imprisoned along with a large number of other enemies of the regime. By the end of 1933 he was one of around 60,000 prisoners detained in sixty-five concentration camps.

Ossietzky received six nominations for the Peace Prize in 1935, from former laureates Ludwig Quidde and Jane Addams as well as Harold Laski at the London School of Economics, among others. His candidacy was discussed by the committee, but there was no inclination to give Ossietzky the prize. Committee chair Stang was the most sympathetic, but he did not argue outright that Ossietzky should receive the prize either. Minister of Foreign Affairs Koht was against the idea: 'I do not think that Ossietzky would even have been considered had he not been imprisoned by the Nazis, and for me this was proof that his actual peace work had not been significant enough to justify awarding him the prize.'

No prize was awarded in 1935, but in 1936 the committee took the opportunity to reconsider the prize that was not awarded in 1935. Things were completely different by this point. There were forty-six eligible candidates in 1936, but Ossietzky was in a class of his own. He alone was nominated eighty-six times, and this included group nominations such as the one from 100 members of the French Senate and Chamber of Deputies. All in all, more nominations were received for Ossietzky alone than for all of the other candidates combined. The leadership of the Labour Party's parliamentary group had also submitted nominations for Ossietzky. In their justification of this they wrote: 'Both the work he did while he was free and his unshakable attitude in the time since he was arrested should set an example for everyone fighting for peace. At this time no one is more entitled to the recognition to be gained from receiving the Nobel Peace Prize.' A number of famous people who were not entitled to nominate candidates to receive the Peace Prize also supported Ossietzky's candidacy. Nobel laureate in literature Knut Hamsun condemned the prize in the press on 22 November, causing a rift with authors and other intellectuals in Norway. The conservative newspapers largely supported Hamsun, while those that were more radical condemned his strong sympathies for Germany. Koht and Mowinckel could not prevent the prize from being awarded to Ossietzky by withdrawing from the committee, but they did so regardless because they did not want to be part of such a conclusion. This further strengthened Ossietzky's candidacy, because Martin Tranmæl, one of the committee's deputies, was also keen for Ossietzky to receive the prize.

As Minister of Foreign Affairs, Koht considered himself an exponent of an active foreign policy. The Treaty of Versailles had been too harsh, with the borders not being fairly drawn. Unlike former Norwegian ministers of foreign affairs, he travelled around Europe to promote Norwegian perspectives. He was also a strong advocate of disarmament, asserting that rearmament in itself was evil and could lead to war. Koht's ultimate vision was a global society based on independent nations in rational cooperation.

Koht analysed the Great Powers from a traditional small nation perspective, asserting that it was always the Great Powers which caused conflicts. He more or less disregarded the fact that some nations and politicians tend to be more aggressive than others. Capitalist nations were nevertheless by definition in competition with each other for markets and investments. This could lead to war and conflict. Koht never commented on fascism or Nazism explicitly, either publicly or privately. He kept quiet on the topic of Hitler's foreign policy ambitions both before and after he became Minister of Foreign Affairs. Of course, he was kept abreast of the internal developments in Germany, but this information never came through in his analyses of the foreign policy situation. He considered all the leading powers' state leaders as basically rational and having largely shared values. Public criticism of the Nazi regime would of course have had a negative impact on Norway's relationship with Germany, but it is indeed remarkable that Koht apparently did not have such views in private either, at least not that anyone has been able to document. Nevertheless, the main reason for this is clear: Koht saw no alternative to the Norwegian policy of neutrality. Nordic cooperation was very unlikely. Among other things, it would be impossible to defend Denmark. Strategically it was more or less already part of Germany. Finland had its particular stance on the Soviet Union. Sweden was most important to Norway, but there was no cooperation to be had here either. Alliance politics was too dramatic. The United Kingdom did not want any direct obligations towards Norway either.

Criticism of Nazi Germany would inevitably raise the issue of an alternative policy. In connection with this Koht nevertheless had the astonishing belief that he personally, through active diplomacy, could help ease tensions. In this respect the personal element *was* important. The Great Powers needed help to get out of a vicious circle of armament that might lead to a war they really did not want.

However, during the spring of 1936 many people in the Labour Party had come to a different conclusion and wanted a clearer policy on Nazi Germany. Martin Tranmæl and Haakon Lie were the foremost exponents of this view, and they also garnered some support from the government. But Koht opposed every attempt from others to get involved in his area and was if necessary willing to resign as Minister of Foreign Affairs if he did not get his way. It was at this point that the opposition within the party eased; it was also because Koht's policy was largely supported by the Norwegian Parliament. He was also backed by Mowinckel from the Liberal Party, who played a key role in shaping Norway's foreign and defence policy.

The German leadership was not sure how to deal with the debate about a prize for Ossietzky. In a radio speech, Goebbels said that it would be better for the traitor's head to be cut off during peacetime than for hundreds of Germans to lose their lives at war because of him. Hitler was of the opinion that it would be prudent to get Ossietzky out of the country, but Göring had him transferred to a private clinic where he was closely monitored. Ossietzky himself was not interested in leaving the country. The German propaganda department said that Ossietzky should travel to Oslo to receive the Peace Prize, but he was refused a passport. One of the most remarkable aspects of the whole story is that his German lawyer managed to get his hands on most of the prize money and was actually punished for this under the Nazi regime.

Committee chair Stang's presentation speech at the ceremony on 10 December 1936 was sensational. The regime in Germany was not mentioned at all. Stang was more interested in telling the audience who Ossietzky was not. The opening of his speech went as follows: 'Carl von Ossietzky, who has been awarded the Peace Prize for 1935, belongs to no political party. He is not a Communist; he is not in any sense a conservative. Indeed, one cannot easily pin on him any of the usual political tags.' Stang denied that Ossietzky had become a symbol, but he did defend the importance of symbols. Ossietzky was a peace activist on a level with all the other peace activists who had received the Peace Prize. Stang's speech therefore concluded: 'In awarding this year's Nobel Peace Prize to Carl von Ossietzky we are therefore recognizing his valuable contribution to the cause of peace—nothing more, and certainly nothing less.'

The prize was presented as a normal Peace Prize. The committee certainly wanted no special recognition for their decision. This was undoubtedly an attempt to alleviate the German reaction. In reality this award was very innovative and heralded an alternative approach to the prize: that it was not only systems and structures that were responsible for war, but also certain ideologies, regimes, and even people.

1936–1939: New Traditional Prizes

Argentinian Minister of Foreign Affairs Carlos Saavedras Lamas was announced as a laureate at the same time as Ossietzky, but they received their respective prizes for different years: Ossietzky for 1935 and Lamas for 1936. The latter garnered far less attention than the former. As mentioned, what was most remarkable about the prize to Lamas was that he was the first laureate not to come from North America or Europe. Over two decades would then pass until another laureate was selected from 'the third world'. Lamas, as Argentinian Minister of Foreign Affairs, was otherwise known in Geneva as the Argentinian representative for both the League of Nations and the International Labour Organization (ILO).

In his work to put an end to the Chaco War between Bolivia and Paraguay, which was the main reason for the prize, Lamas placed great emphasis on both the Kellogg–Briand Pact and the so-called Stimson Doctrine. The latter was written by US Secretary of State Henry Stimson after Japan invaded Manchuria in 1931, and claimed that any aggressive war should be condemned and that territorial changes that were not the result of peaceful processes should not be approved. In the autumn of 1936, Lamas had contributed to the adoption of a similar anti-war pact for South America. It was said of the Chaco War that 'Paraguay had won 20,000 square miles [...] at the cost of about three Bolivians and two Paraguayans for each square mile.'

In 1937, the man with the impressive and very noble name of Lord Edgar Algernon Robert Gascoyne-Cecil was awarded the Peace Prize. Lord Cecil came from a prominent English family which had collaborated with the Crown since the time of Elizabeth I. Cecil's father, the Marquess of Salisbury, was Prime Minister in the late 1880s and during the 1890s, at the height of the British Empire. Cecil became interested in politics early on in his life—naturally enough on the conservative side. Until the First World War, he showed little interest in foreign policy. During the war he first worked for the Red Cross and then for the British government. The war undoubtedly contributed to his subsequent commitment to peace. He was probably the best-known spokesman for international peace work during the interwar years. In the same way that he considered 'interclass cooperation' a method of combating class conflict, for him the League of Nations became the foremost instrument of combating war between nations. Cecil was involved in establishing the League of Nations and was more or less a permanent delegate, particularly during the 1920s. During the 1930s he worked to strengthen the position of the League in international politics.

This work tended to make Cecil unpopular among conservative nationalists who were still afraid that the League would restrict the United Kingdom's independence. He therefore sometimes worked with the Labour Party. From 1920 until 1922 he was appointed the League of Nations' South African delegate. He became close friends with the Norwegians who were active there, particularly Fridtjof Nansen and Christian Lange. Nansen nominated Cecil for the Peace Prize several times, claiming that no one was more deserving of it.

Cecil was head of the League of Nations Union (LNU) in the United Kingdom. In 1934/35, the LNU organized a peace ballot. Over 11 million people participated, and almost everyone agreed that the United Kingdom should still be involved in the League of Nations. More than 10 million supported the economic sanctions system to stop aggressive powers, while nearly 7 million responded that it should also be possible to take military action. Through this ballot, Cecil forced the British government to impose sanctions against Italy following its invasion of Ethiopia, though it has to be said they were somewhat half-hearted sanctions. The government subsequently tried to solve the problems with Nazi Germany through negotiations, the so-called appeasement policy.

It has often been argued that the peace movement should accept its share of the responsibility for the outbreak of the Second World War. A firm policy might have prevented Hitler's various advances; compassion and negotiation may have encouraged him to be more aggressive. This criticism had a limited effect on Cecil. He was very much in favour of economic and military sanctions—against Nazi Germany as well. The ballot showed that the British public supported this policy. Cecil felt it was the elite who had let them down, and he was particularly critical of the power and influence of the armament industry. He thought the state should seize control of the industry, but this attitude had little to no impact on developments during the 1930s. However, in Norway and Scandinavia the support for the sanctions policy was limited. The sanctions system had been used as an important argument against joining the League of Nations, which is why, when international tensions continued to increase throughout the 1930s, Norway withdrew from this system. This was probably a result of the sanctions against Japan and Italy not being enforced or proving unsuccessful by virtue of their half-heartedness. The United Kingdom and France were keen to punish the aggressor, but still cooperate with Italy. They could not do both.

Throughout all this, Norway's chief concern was that it would be sucked into a major international conflict. The neutrality policy was paramount. As such, Norwegian public policy, which also had a significant impact on the Norwegian Nobel Committee, had a detrimental effect on the League of Nations' ability to pursue an effective policy against Nazi Germany. This happened despite the fundamental connection to the League of Nations and the prize to Cecil.

Cecil's work with the International Peace Campaign was an important reason why he received the prize in 1937 in particular and not in one of the many other years for which he had been nominated. This was an attempt to instil in various peace organizations four somewhat leftist principles associated with the League of Nations and global security. The principles related to general disarmament and war profiteering, and strengthened collective security through the League of Nations. Naturally the leftist tendency was publicly known, but it was not public knowledge that communists with close links to Moscow were as central as they actually were to the practical work. This coincided with Stalin's internal purges in the Soviet Union and with Moscow's broad attempts at cooperation in international politics. The Norwegian Nobel Committee even gave somewhat modest financial assistance to Cecil and this work. In Norway, both the Labour Party and the Communist Party supported the organization's work, and committee consultant Wilhelm Keilhau was chair of the Norwegian IPC committee when he wrote his consultant statement on the organization. Over fifty Norwegian organizations, mostly on the left, were affiliated with the Norwegian committee. The attempt to establish cooperation between the Soviet Union and the Western powers was intended to strengthen the front against Germany, but the German–Soviet Nonaggression Pact in 1939 put a definitive end to such efforts.

After all the trouble with the prize to Ossietzky, the committee felt quite safe awarding the prize to Cecil. In many ways, he was the very symbol of the peace movement. In his presentation speech, committee member Christian Lange stressed that few people, if any, had done more for the League of Nations than Cecil. However, there was something of a connection between the prizes to Ossietzky and Cecil, which prompted Lange to speak of 'the dictators' menacing attack' on world peace in Africa, Spain, and the Far East. This was an unusually spirited speech from a Norwegian perspective.

There was, as there often is in times of crisis, a particularly enthusiastic debate during the autumn of 1938 about who would receive the Peace Prize. The more conservative committee members felt that the prize should be awarded to Neville Chamberlain for his efforts to prevent war with Germany via the Munich Agreement in September. The more radical committee members felt that the prize should be awarded to Edvard Benes, the President of Czechoslovakia, whose country had had to pay the price for Hitler and Chamberlain reaching an agreement by ceding territory to Germany.

However, the prize went to the Nansen International Office in Geneva. The office had been established by the League of Nations to continue the work that the first High Commissioner for Refugees, Fridtjof Nansen, had done after the First World War. The office initially focused on refugees from Armenia, an issue that had also engaged Nansen, but later also helped refugees from many different countries. It was thought the office would only be needed for a few years, since then the refugee problem would hopefully be solved. When the office received the Peace Prize in 1938, a decision had already been made to dissolve the organization. However, a new London-based office took over its work.

Halvdan Koht worked hard to ensure that the Nansen International Office would be awarded the Peace Prize. He was no longer on the committee at that point, but the foundation for the prize was in many ways laid through his long-term effort. And so it came to pass that another organization with close links to the League of Nations received the Peace Prize, the last before the Second World War broke out.

During the interwar years, the Norwegian Nobel Committee was generally firm in its belief in the League of Nations. This was most apparent from the prizes to the four politicians in 1925 and 1926, the prize to Arthur Henderson in 1934, and the prize to Robert Cecil in 1937. But for the 1935 prize, the Norwegian Nobel Committee decided to try something different: it awarded the prize to the foremost symbolic opponent of the regime in Berlin.

In retrospect, it should have been obvious that neither the peace movement nor the Norwegian Nobel Committee had any answers to the increasing totalitarian threat. The part of the movement that Cecil represented had an answer: sticking to the League of Nations' sanctions policy and, through the International Peace Campaign, being open to cooperation not only with the communists, but more indirectly, also with the Soviet Union.

Of course, no prize was awarded for 1939 after Germany invaded Poland on 1 September. This was the start of the deadliest war the world had ever seen. Around 27 million soldiers were killed, around half of them from the Soviet Union, as well as between 20 and 30 million civilians, including 6 million Jews. The explanation for the war was apparently simple: Hitler and Nazism were entirely to blame. Then came the global expansion of the war that Japan's attack on Pearl Harbor on 7 December 1941 represented. The League of Nations had proven completely unable to prevent another major war. After the war, a new and much stronger global organization was needed.

5

The Nobel Peace Prize, 1945–2018

The United Nations

The Norwegian Nobel Committee after 1945

During the Second World War, several members of the Nobel Committee fled Norway. Committee chair Stang died in 1941. The Norwegian Nazi party Nasjonal Samling attempted to assume control of both the Nobel Institute and the Peace Prize, but were stopped by Swedish intervention. The Swedish Embassy made use of some of the rooms at the Institute in order to stake the Nobel Foundation's claim.

Gunnar Jahn became the new chair of the Nobel Committee in 1942, elected by the members who were still in Norway, and he remained in that position until 1967. Jahn was a supporter of the Liberal Party and a key member of the resistance, later running important institutions such as the Bureau of Statistics and the Central Bank of Norway. From his diary we can see that he had strong views on who should and should not receive the Peace Prize.

Proportional representation elections were also introduced for the Nobel Committee from 1948, something which led to the Labour Party having a majority on the committee during virtually all of Jahn's time. However, the party's three members until the mid-1960s, Martin Tranmæl, Aase Lionæs— the first female member of the committee—and Gustav Natvig Pedersen, rarely agreed with each other. Hambro was a member of the committee until 1964. There were many strong personalities, and the committee was often divided, something which led to several awards being postponed, particularly during the 1950s.

After the Labour Party lost its majority in the Norwegian Parliament and therefore also in the Nobel Committee, the committee achieved a wider political composition than ever before, since up until that point it had been characterized by Liberal dominance and then a Labour majority. In line with the new world view, the committee became increasingly interested in making sure that the prize had a global approach. Conflicts such as the Vietnam War and in the Middle East sometimes precipitated a lot of tension within the committee, with two members leaving in 1973 after the prize was awarded to Kissinger and Lê Đức Thọ, and one member leaving in 1994 in protest against the prize awarded to Arafat, Peres, and Rabin. The dominating ideology was still the desire for a better organized world. However, the human rights prizes involving critique of various authoritarian regimes gradually increased in number, as did the disarmament prizes, particularly in connection with the fight against nuclear weapons.

The UN and the Dream of Peace on Earth

The dreams of a better organized world before the First World War fell into ruins in 1914. The League of Nations was unable to handle the increasingly tense situation throughout the 1930s. Now a new organization, the United Nations, would take on the virtually impossible task of creating peace on earth.

What could we realistically expect of an international organization like the UN? It is not difficult to find examples of grandiose notions. What is striking nevertheless is how limited the expectations of many of the people at the heart of the UN's operations were. British Gladwyn Jebb, Acting Secretary-General of the Preparatory Commission of the United Nations, emphasized right from the start that even though establishing a perfect international organization was impossible, a less than perfect organization was a lot better than no organization at all. In the long run, it might prove crucial to avoiding nuclear war. After twenty-five years of experience, he summed up the situation as follows: 'In order that mankind should not destroy itself totally in its struggles, it is essential to have some place [...] in which reason, or law, can be brought to bear on conflicts, either for preventing them or for ending them in accordance with certain generally accepted rules. [...] And when the abyss really yawns before them, I believe that this time [...] it is to the United Nations that the nations will turn.'

Dag Hammarskjöld always said that the UN was not formed to bring mankind to heaven, but to save it from hell. Brian Urquhart, who had leading positions in the UN for forty years, claimed it was an illusion to believe that the UN could act as a kind of super-government when in reality it was a treaty supported by an administrative organization run by highly competent men.

The UN has many flaws. The organization has not been very effective, it has been too bureaucratic, too dominated by the superpowers, etc. There have been very few women at the highest levels of the UN system. It is also unable only to employ the best applicants because it needs to ensure that it always balances competence with many different national considerations. Everyone needs to be heard. There is a lot to indicate that such flaws have not diminished much during the UN's history, but the UN has proven to be a last resort, a safety net, or a final resolution mechanism when leading powers find themselves on a collision course. Hammarskjöld was happy to talk about the UN's 'constant struggle to close the gap between aspiration and performance', which despite everything might mean the difference between 'civilization and chaos'.

Despite the fact that several key people did in fact have realistic expectations of the new global organization, it was only natural that there were also significant hopes for its foundation in 1945. Even more than during the Napoleonic Wars and the First World War, there were many who thought that victory over a common enemy would almost automatically lead to a better world. Germany, Japan, and Italy had been evil incarnate. Now that they had been defeated, there were many possibilities for cooperation. Almost by definition the victors had what was most important in common. They united to form an organization that would prevent similar threats from arising in the future.

The term United Nations had come to Franklin D. Roosevelt during Winston Churchill's visit to Washington and the White House in December 1941. It sounded so much better than 'associated powers', which until then was what the Allied forces were called. The term then became the name of the new organization. The organization was definitely an American invention, characterized by the enormous position of power that the USA had built up during the war and its extremely guilty conscience for not having joined the League of Nations. Churchill did not feel he had a choice when his new partner the USA was so enthusiastic about the organization. He was most interested in protecting the British Empire's role within the new system. Similar concerns applied to Stalin. Dismissing the UN would mean not cooperating with the USA. Thus it became all the more important to ensure that the organization could not do anything contrary to the Soviet Union's interests. None of the big three intended to join an organization that could make important decisions detrimental to their fundamental interests. Of course they had to have power of veto. The discussion on their power of veto only concerned the extent to which it would also apply in questions of procedure.

Franklin D. Roosevelt was always afraid that he might become the next Woodrow Wilson, an American president who advocated for the establishment of an extensive new international organization, only for the American Senate and the American people to then oppose the USA's membership. Free trade was important to the United States. Early during the Second World War there was a lot of interest in international economics and how the German and Japanese leaders would be punished after the war. What was to become the first UN-related conference was held in 1943 to discuss the food situation in Europe after the war, and eventually resulted in the establishment of the Food and Agriculture Organization of the United Nations, whose first head received the Peace Prize in 1949. When Roosevelt died on 12 April 1945, he could still not be entirely sure that things would be different after the Second World War than they were after the First World War. In Yalta in February 1945 he had stated that all American troops had to withdraw from Europe within two years. The American people would not allow them to stay any longer.

This never happened. There are still American troops in Europe, more than seventy years after the Second World War, even though their numbers have dwindled since the end of the Cold War. The USA was prepared to take on entirely different obligations, even during the occupation of Germany and Japan, in 1945 than in 1919. In 1945 only two senators voted against the USA's participation in the new global organization. It helped that the establishment of the UN and the whole UN system was largely based on American ideas and planning. The UN would build on the experiences of the League of Nations, but also had elements that originated from longer ago.

The organizational structure was like that of the League of Nations: a general assembly, a security council, and an executive secretariat. The dominance of the superpowers dated back to the congresses before the First World War. The focus was now on the three dominating powers: the USA, the United Kingdom, and the Soviet Union. France was partially elevated to a superpower because the United Kingdom needed a strong partner in continental Europe. China became one of the five due to the American dream of what China had been and might perhaps become once again in the future.

When the cooperation between the three leading powers broke down as early as in 1946/47, it became clear that the UN would not play the role that it had been hoped it would. During the Cold War, the organization was only able to function when the Soviet Union decided to withdraw from the Security Council, such as when the Korean War broke out. Attempts to get the General Assembly to play a greater role when the Security Council was obstructed by the Soviets' veto were unable to resolve the deadlocked situation.

The Norwegian UN Ideology

After 1945, the UN became the cornerstone of Norwegian foreign policy. The Norwegian Parliament agreed unanimously that Norway should join the organization. The conditions that had characterized its membership of the League of Nations were now gone, and the decision on Norwegian UN membership was made almost without debate. In addition to the chair of the Committee on Foreign Affairs and the Minister of Foreign Affairs, there was only one Member of Parliament that wanted to speak, even though participation in the UN was far more binding than membership in the League of Nations. The Security Council could in principle impose anything on the member states. The explanation for this unanimity was partly that all parties were for membership, and partly that Norway immediately after the war had many other important matters to attend to.

Norwegian foreign policy was based on its participation in the UN even after it joined NATO in 1949. NATO was extremely important to Norwegian foreign policy, but the long-term goal was still to promote global cooperation. This also had quite an influence on an idealistic-political institution such as the Norwegian Nobel Committee. Unlike many other small nations, Norway accepted the fact that the organization would be dominated by the five superpowers. It was only through cooperation with these powers that the organization could play the role it was intended to.

It became dogma in Norwegian foreign policy that international cooperation had to be based on the UN. Many countries perceived a conflict between national considerations and an effective global organization. In Norway, international cooperation after the war was considered intrinsically good, whether from the perspective of the Norwegian Parliament or the educational system. When it came to international cooperation more generally, Norway was happy to participate without reservations. Its membership of NATO, on the other hand, was based on a specifically Norwegian base and nuclear policy, and Norway remained, as we know, outside of the EU.

In 2017 former Minister of Foreign Affairs and Defence Thorvald Stoltenberg gave the following opinion of the UN in his memoirs: 'When I started working internationally in the 1950s, my faith in the UN was almost limitless. I think the same can be said of many people. In the UN we had finally achieved an organization that could put an end to war and build a fairer and better organized world. The Secretary-General of the UN was next to God.'

The Norwegian focus on the UN and the need for multilateral international cooperation was emphasized every year in key foreign policy documents. In his book *Small Country: What Now?* from 1982, Minister of Foreign Affairs Knut Frydenlund expressed the following: 'The world's crisis is the UN's crisis and vice versa. Since the lack of organization and organized cooperation between countries is a fundamental problem in the world today, work to strengthen the UN will be absolutely necessary. It is primarily small countries such as our own that are interested in strengthening the UN. A better organized world does not automatically mean a fairer or safer world. But it is a prerequisite.'

Report No. 11 to the Storting (1989/90) on development trends in the international community and the effects of these on Norwegian foreign policy was typical in this respect. The report garnered a lot of attention and was informally referred to as 'the Bible' of Norwegian foreign policy. The report emphasized that 'membership of the UN has on many occasions been referred to as a "primary cornerstone" of Norwegian foreign policy.' 'The UN is the *only truly global organization* with near universal membership and a mandate that makes it possible to raise all the political, economic, and social problems that the global community faces.' It is true that in the list of goals and instruments in Norwegian foreign policy, 'Reinforce Norway's security' and 'Secure Norway's economic foundation and employment' came first, but then came 'Contribute to the development of a better organized global community based on international law, the principle of the peaceful resolution of disputes and strengthening of the UN.'

Despite prioritizing the UN, the report made it clear that what could be achieved via international cooperation was limited: 'However, the international organizations cannot do more than the member states permit and therefore cannot exercise any collective leadership alone.' The nation state was still the most important unit in international politics. There was therefore a strong and growing disparity between the countries' growing interdependency and the fact that the nation state still constituted the most important decision-maker in the international community. This raised big questions about what international cooperation via the UN could really achieve, but these were only implied and not really discussed in the report.

The Charter of the United Nations stated in Article 2(1) that: 'the Organization is based on the principle of the sovereign equality of all its Members.' The UN would not interfere in nations' internal affairs. It also stated in the Charter's introduction that the members were obliged to 'save succeeding generations from the scourge of war'. The dream was to 'beat swords into ploughshares'.

Over the course of history, the units of human cooperation had become bigger and bigger—from family to tribe to the local to the national. The aim was almost self-evident: for the whole world to become one political unit. Constructivist Alexander Wendt has argued that 'a world state is inevitable'. But there are few signs of the nations of the world being willing to limit their sovereignty enough for this goal to become realistic. In recent decades the compromise has been a lot of talk of 'global governance', which implies a vague notion of a common goal and orientation without really shaking off the primacy of the nation state.

Many Prizes for the UN System

There was a clear idealistic component of the Norwegian Nobel Committee's mandate. International cooperation needed to be stimulated. Considering previous prizes to the Inter-Parliamentary Union, the International Peace Bureau, and the League of Nations, it was almost a given that many prizes would be awarded to organizations and individuals associated with the UN. Ninety-one Peace Prizes were awarded between 1945 and 2017. At least twenty-one of these were awarded to individuals and organizations with such a connection.

It can be difficult to define clear boundaries. Many of these twenty-one laureates have also worked for their national governments or for other organizations in addition to the UN. Conversely, there are many people in addition to these twenty-one who have also had some connection or other to the UN. Almost every year candidates associated with the UN are considered by the committee. This also applies to most of the UN's Secretary-Generals, apart from Kurt Waldheim. His lies about his activities during the Second World War made any discussion of a prize impossible.

Due to Roosevelt's fear of becoming another Wilson, he was very careful when it came to linking himself and his name to the planning of the UN. This was mostly done in secret within the US Department of State under the direction of Russian-born Leo Pasvolsky, assistant to Secretary of State Cordell Hull. Hull had been Secretary of State since Roosevelt's inauguration in 1933 and was particularly interested in free trade and Latin American matters. He was convinced that protectionism and trade conflicts went a significant way to explaining why wars broke out, and therefore dedicated much of his time to establishing international free trade. Roosevelt always called Hull the 'father' of the UN, and this was accepted by most people, including the Norwegian Nobel Committee. In his advisory report, Professor Wilhelm Keilhau wrote that 'it is almost indisputable that Cordell Hull has had as much of a hand in preparing the new peace treaty as Wilson had in preparing the treaty for the League of Nations.'

In this matter, as in almost all other central matters, there was however no doubt that Roosevelt was the key figure. Hull resigned as Secretary of State in the autumn of 1944. Roosevelt had said that Hull, even after his departure, should preside over the establishment of the UN. Although nothing came of this, he nevertheless received the Nobel Peace Prize. He was too unwell to travel to Oslo to receive the prize, but in the speech he asked the American ambassador to read at the ceremony on 10 December 1945, he lauded the establishment of the UN, though in somewhat modest terms. The UN offered the 'peace-loving nations of the world' a mechanism that could lead to peace 'if they want peace'. But, Hull continued, no mechanism could create peace on earth unless the superpowers had the will and resolve for the new organization to be a success.

The final meeting of the League of Nations was held in April 1946. There Lord Cecil, who had spoken at the first meeting in 1920, declared that: 'The League is dead; long live the United Nations.'

Despite significant optimism in the beginning, there were soon setbacks. The UN Security Council would only work if the five superpowers stood united or at least did not exercise their power of veto. The first veto came from the Soviet Union in 1946 over the situation in Syria and Lebanon, with Moscow considering the two new independent nations a continuation of French colonial rule. There would be many such vetoes after this, eighty-two in the period from 1946 to 1955, almost all of these exercised by the Soviet Union.

The Charter of the United Nations stated that a Military Staff Committee (MSC) would be established under the Security Council that would plan and implement military operations on behalf of the UN. Nothing came of this. None of the five superpowers were interested in establishing an inde-pendent military force that might intervene around the world. As soon as in 1948, the MSC therefore reported that it was not in a position to fulfil this point in the Charter.

This did not prevent the UN from experiencing more limited successes. After the State of Israel was established in 1948, war broke out between Israel and its Arab neighbours. The UN tasked Swedish Count Folke Bernadotte with mediating an armistice. He was murdered by an Israeli terrorist while doing this, after which his assistant Ralph Bunche took over as mediator. One year later, Bunche finally managed to achieve armistice agreements between Israel and Egypt, Jordan, Lebanon, and Syria.

Armistice in the Middle East was an achievement, but it was only one reason why Bunche received the Peace Prize for 1950. He was the first non-white person to do so. This was important in and of itself. Bunche had had a significant academic career and had also held important jobs in the American Department of State before he started at the UN, where he kept working as a problem-solver for the rest of his professional life, until 1971. He was also active in the fight for black rights in the USA during the 1950s and 1960s.

The Korean War was both a victory and a defeat for the UN. After North Korea attacked South Korea in June 1950, the UN Security Council *was* actually in a position to agree on a military response. This was because the Soviet Union was staying away from the UN in protest against the new People's Republic of China not being able to take China's seat in the UN at the expense of Taiwan. But in reality the military response was American, with lesser contributions from other nations. In practice, the USA considered the assignment under American command (though Supreme Commander Douglas MacArthur was not always willing to take orders, even from Washington; he was removed from command by President Truman in 1951).

The Suez Crisis in 1956 was important for the development of the UN. The Israeli/British/French invasion was met with clear resistance from the USA since President Eisenhower was not consulted before the troops advanced. The three nations had to halt the invasion, but it was difficult to secure the British/French withdrawal. Canadian Secretary of State for External Affairs Lester B. Pearson presented a solution in the form of a proposal for a UN force that would put an end to the warfare and monitor and ensure the withdrawal of troops. This plan contributed to securing the relationship between the USA and the United Kingdom and also to keeping the British Commonwealth together. The establishment of the UN force was a new development that would be copied on many subsequent occasions.

Several members of the Norwegian Nobel Committee supported the idea of awarding the UN's first Secretary-General, former Norwegian Minister of Foreign Affairs Trygve Lie, the Nobel Peace Prize. This never happened. Lie had become too controversial a figure and did not have the temperament required to lead the new organization as best as possible in trying times. Conversely, the UN's second Secretary-General, Dag Hammarskjöld, did receive the Peace Prize. He was Secretary-General from 1953 until his sudden death in a plane crash in 1961. Hammarskjöld was Secretary-General during a reform period for the organization. When the UN was established in 1945, the organization had fifty-one member states. The Cold War led to much disagreement on which new members would be accepted, but in 1962 the number exceeded 100, and in 1968 there were 119. This increase was due to decolonization, and it led to the UN's focus changing. The East–West dichotomy was still central, but the new member states wanted to increase the focus on continued decolonization and on the economic development of poor countries. This meant it was now the USA that most often exercised its power of veto in the Security Council.

Hammarskjöld, whose background was Swedish bureaucracy and economics, became an increasingly more active Secretary-General. He played an important role during the Suez Crisis in 1956 and also during the unrest in Lebanon and Jordan two years later. His role in the Congo Crisis in the early 1960s was his most difficult and brought him into conflict with both the Soviet Union and the most radical African countries, but thanks to support from most of the other countries in Africa and Asia, he was able to continue his activities. His sudden death in 1961 would contribute to his status as a hero. Hammarskjöld is the only person to have received a post-humous Nobel Peace Prize. It is doubtful whether he really wanted one. He had told the Norwegian UN ambassador that he would rather not receive a Nobel Peace Prize. Later the rules were changed so that posthumous prizes are no longer possible, something which was undoubtedly the right decision.

It soon became clear that a decent understanding of the possibilities for peace in the world was closely linked to the living conditions that the world's ever-increasing population were living under. Here the UN and its many sub-organizations could play an important role. In October 1945, the Food and Agriculture Organization (FAO) was established as the first specialist body under the UN. Lord John Boyd Orr was the obvious choice of leader since it had been his ideas that had for the most part inspired the new organization's work. He was a leading researcher within food produc-tion and also a good administrator who thought that the world's united states were the only alternative to war. He received the Peace Prize in 1949.

Léon Jouhaux, the laureate for 1951, had worked in connection with both the League of Nations and the UN, and not least with the International Labour Organization. He had had the ILO written into the Treaty of Versailles and his whole life was based on the conviction that there was a close connection between peace and social justice. Terrible living condi-tions would stimulate conflict and war, and everything possible had to be done to improve the conditions for most people. In this context, he was a strong spokesman for European integration. He was also active in the fight against communism within both the French and international trade union movement.

Of all the people who could be said to have needed help from the UN, the situation was most difficult for the world's refugees. During the interwar period, the Norwegian Nobel Committee awarded the Peace Prize to both Fridtjof Nansen and to the Nansen International Office for Refugees. In 1954, the United Nations High Commissioner for Refugees (UNHCR), established in 1950, received the Peace Prize. In 1981 the UNHCR would receive its second Peace Prize. Refugees have always existed, but it was only in the twentieth century that international institutions were established to deal with this problem. During the Second World War, the United Nations Relief and Rehabilitation Administration (UNRRA) was established, and in 1947 it was replaced by the International Refugee Organization.

When the UNHCR was established in 1950, it was for a three-year period, which was then extended to five, and then regularly extended by additional five-year periods. This demonstrated both a gross underestimation of the scope of the refugee problem and a hope that it would be solved in the cheapest and quickest manner possible.

The United Nations International Children Emergency Fund (UNICEF) was established in 1946 to help the children of Europe after the Second World War. Former US President Herbert Hoover was a key figure in its establishment after he visited thirty-eight countries and saw the dismal conditions under which children lived. Soon the focus was even more global. The need for help was enormous, even though it was easier to raise money to help children than it was generally. UNICEF received the Nobel Peace Prize in 1965. UNICEF is perhaps the most popular of the UN's sub-organizations and is often described as 'the jewel in the UN's crown'.

In many areas the UN was at the heart of developing the standards that should apply to human interaction. Hardly anything was more important than the work for human rights. It is in this regard that the prize awarded to René Cassin in 1968 is important. Cassin was seriously injured during the First World War, but had nevertheless had an illustrious legal career in France. After the Second World War he devoted his life to international work. He has often been referred to as the 'father' of the Universal Declaration of Human Rights from 1948. (Eleanor Roosevelt was often referred to as its 'mother.' Aase Lionæs, chair of the Nobel Committee from 1968 until 1978, was a Norwegian delegate to the UN in 1948 and participated in work on the declaration.) Cassin was particularly interested in combining the Western powers' emphasis on the importance of political rights with the Eastern Europeans' preference for economic, social, and cultural rights.

For the declaration to have judicial power, legally binding covenants had to be put in place. It was a long process during which the member states migrated from generally praising human rights to accepting them as norms that also applied to their own behaviour. It was only in 1966 that the UN adopted the two covenants on political and civil rights and on economic, social, and cultural rights. Another ten years would then pass before all the 121 member countries had ratified the covenants. This was completed in 1976, the year Cassin died at the age of 89.

In 1969, the Peace Prize was awarded to the International Labour Organization. The organization's roots dated back to 1920, but its work was more extensive after the Second World War. It gained more and more members and focused on an increasing number of assignments. However, its main aim was always to strengthen the cooperation between governments, employers, and workers to thereby improve social conditions. The ILO has provided significant technical help to member states and adopted a rapidly increasing number of recommendations and reports. In recent years, the ILO has increased its focus on the position of trade unions within a democratic system of government and also on children's rights.

Seán MacBride was an Irishman who worked for the Irish Republican Army (IRA) against the British rule of Ireland for twenty years, leaving just before the IRA announced its support for Adolf Hitler. It was at this point that MacBride went into politics. He was the Irish Minister of External Affairs from 1948 until 1951 and contributed to the drafting of the European Convention on Human Rights, which also established the European Court of Human Rights, an important follow-up to the UN's work in this area. MacBride then made an international career for himself. He was a founding member of Amnesty International and served as the organization's International Chairman. When he received the Peace Prize in 1974, he was President of the International Peace Bureau, the UN's High Commissioner for Namibia, and Assistant Secretary-General of the UN.

Disarmament quickly became a key topic for the UN system. The prize to Philip Noel-Baker (1959) can be considered the first prize for disarmament after 1945. As a young man he, along with Cecil, had participated in the establishment of the League of Nations and the ILO. He had also worked for the League's secretariat. He then introduced International Relations as a field of study at the University of London and published a book, *Disarmament*, in 1926. From then on, disarmament was the focus of his life. As a Labour politician, Noel-Baker worked together with Arthur Henderson. The breakdown of the League of Nations' disarmament work was a major blow to them both. When the League of Nations was dissolved, Noel-Baker said: 'Geneva was the world's first parliament. Our work is not over; it has just begun.' After the war he became a member of the British government and his book *The Arms Race: A Programme for World Disarmament* was published, garnering considerable interest.

Two major players in the work towards disarmament received the prize in 1982: Alva Myrdal and Alfonso García Robles. Myrdal was a Swedish politician and international civil servant who worked with social causes for both the UN—for a while she was the highest ranking woman within the UN system—and UNESCO. She became the Swedish government minister in charge of disarmament and the Swedish delegate for international disarmament negotiations. In 1976 she published the book *The Game of Disarmament*, with the subtitle *How the United States and Russia Run the Arms Race*.

García Robles was a Mexican diplomat who held prominent jobs with both Mexico's Secretariat of Foreign Affairs and the UN. He was in San Francisco when the UN was established and worked for eleven years as the head of the Department of Political Affairs. The Cuban Missile Crisis in 1962 led to a strong interest in making Latin America a nuclear-free zone. García Robles was primarily responsible for the text that in 1967 led to the Treaty of Tlatelolco, the first regional agreement of its kind in the world. While later representing Mexico during the UN's disarmament negotiations in Geneva, he played a part in the UN's Special Sessions on Disarmament in both 1978 and 1982.

Peacekeeping eventually became an obvious choice of area for a Peace Prize. The prize for 1988 to the UN's peacekeeping forces showed how the international climate had already changed for the better, particularly after Gorbachev had come to power in the Soviet Union in 1985. This allowed for further cooperation between the superpowers, something which in turn would lead to a dramatic increase in such operations throughout the 1990s. The very first peacekeeping operation was the observer group that the UN established in the Middle East in 1948 to monitor developments. The observers were to be unarmed and strictly impartial. These rules were drawn up in a rush by Ralph Bunche and represented an important addition to his successful mediation in order to reach an armistice agreement.

The large number of peacekeeping operations in recent years has helped stabilize development in many countries, even though in some cases this may have only frozen the existing situation. Until 1988, no more than 20,000 soldiers had been involved. During the 2000s this figure approached 100,000. Soldiers from very different countries have been in a position to collaborate effectively, although there have also been unfortunate episodes, such as in the Congo when the UN soldiers attacked civilians.

Several of these operations were successful. In El Salvador the forces contributed to ensuring both democratic elections and peace, not only in El Salvador, but across the entire region. In Mozambique the forces oversaw the transition to independence and peace and an end to the civil war in the country. In Cambodia 15,000 UN troops secured a peace treaty after more than twenty years of war and murders by the Khmer Rouge. Cyprus was an example of how peacekeeping forces could help stop the situation from deteriorating even further. There have been UN troops in Cyprus since the mid-1970s. The island still remains divided into a Greek and a Turkish part.

However, the major expansion of UN forces did not only lead to success. In Rwanda sparse UN forces could not stop almost one million people being killed within the space of 100 days. Extremist Hutu groups slaughtered Tutsi people without mercy. In Bosnia the UN had set up several so-called 'safe havens'. But not even unanimous Security Council resolutions and 400 Dutch UN forces could prevent almost 8000 Bosnian Muslims from being killed by Serbs. This was the worst massacre in Europe after the Second World War. When it was finally possible to secure peace in the area in 1995 after an extensive military campaign led by the USA, it was NATO, not the UN, that was tasked with securing peace. Major reforms were necessary to ensure that future UN operations could be carried out better than before.

The UN became more and more central to the history of the Peace Prize. When the UN and Kofi Annan received the Nobel Peace Prize in 2001, committee chair Gunnar Berge concluded that in connection with the Nobel prizes' centenary, the Norwegian Nobel Committee wanted to emphasize that which had been the main theme throughout the prize's history: 'the hope for a better organized and more peaceful world. Nothing symbolizes that hope, or represents that reality, better than the United Nations.'

Kofi Annan was the UN's seventh Secretary-General and the first since Hammarskjöld to receive the Peace Prize. Annan had spent most of his professional life within the UN system and was the first Secretary-General with such a background. Despite his bureaucratic foundations, Annan was an activist. The UN was now to do more, and the end of the Cold War laid the foundation for a more active organization. In his Nobel lecture, Annan talked about how nations' sovereignty 'must no longer be used as a shield for gross violations of human rights'. Informally this was referred to as 'The Kofi Doctrine'.

Intervention is a difficult word in a UN where article 2.7 is intended to protect the nations from attack from the outside. Nevertheless, Annan emphasized that the police intervene to prevent violence, and doctors intervene to cure patients, ergo the UN should intervene to resolve conflicts. This was the background to the work on *Responsibility to Protect*. Conflicts were to be resolved at the lowest possible level as quickly as possible, but ultimately the global community was responsible for preventing major catastrophes such as the massacres in Rwanda, in Cambodia, and in

Bosnia. Annan's commitment was reinforced by the responsibility he as the UN's Vice Secretary-General felt for both Rwanda and Bosnia.

Even though the Cold War was over and the USA and the Soviet Union/ Russia were in a position to cooperate much better than before, there was still significant conflict between the world's superpowers. The UN forces were able to act somewhat more freely in the events that led to the collapse of Yugoslavia, but the superpowers still had differing opinions on the creation of new nation Kosovo, which had separated from Serbia. Nevertheless, the new international climate made a broad cooperation between the USA and the Soviet Union and between the USA and many Arab countries possible during the Gulf War in 1991. Saddam Hussein could not simply swallow an internationally recognized country such as Kuwait. The Iraqi forces were quickly driven from the country.

Even when the UN could not play any part due to disagreement between the superpowers, the organization had nevertheless assumed a completely different role than it had had before. Interventions had to rest on a mandate from the UN. If such a mandate did not exist, this greatly weakened the legitimacy of those intervening. This became evident in 2003 when the USA wanted to declare war against Saddam Hussein's Iraq. Not only were Russia and China against this, but also close allies such as France and Germany. Though this opposition was not able to prevent the USA from actually going to war, without a mandate from the UN the legitimacy of the invasion was significantly weakened. Later as well, such as during the conflicts in Libya and in Syria after 2011, it was expected that those who were to intervene would have to have a mandate from the UN to do so. The Western powers had this in Libya, but the fact that Russia and China felt that the Western powers had overstepped their mandate there made it more difficult for the UN to play any effective part in Syria. *Responsibility to Protect*, which had long been considered the foundation for a new and more effective UN, did not become what the optimists had hoped it would in the early 2000s.

Several UN organizations received the Peace Prize during the 2000s as well. In 2005 the prize was awarded to the International Atomic Energy Agency (IAEA) and its Director General, Mohamed ElBaradei. Some of these disarmament prizes were linked to the UN, others were not. Awards being associated with the UN has been another recurring theme throughout the Peace Prize's history. However, a stronger theme in general has been work towards a better organized world. The two themes are and were often, of course, closely linked.

So we see that there are a number of different UN organizations that have been awarded the Nobel Peace Prize. This is indeed a remarkably long and clear thread back through the history of the Peace Prize. This is undoubtedly so from a wider international perspective, though perhaps less so in a Norwegian context, as the UN has always had a strong position in Norway. Where the Norwegian Nobel Committee was concerned, the road to peace on earth undoubtedly went through the UN.

The Breadth of the UN's Work

Due to rapid decolonization, the UN gradually became a completely different institution to that which was founded in 1945. When the colonial powers under British control first started the process of decolonization, the other colonial powers had to follow suit. India's independence would contribute greatly to Africa also gaining its independence, although there were few who made that connection as early as in 1947. France would fight wars in Indochina and in Algeria, but President Charles de Gaulle drew the inevitable conclusion in 1960, finally allowing the colonies to determine their own status. Portugal demonstrated it was largely a question of the will of the homeland, holding on to its colonies for the longest even though it was the weakest of all the colonial powers. However, the revolution in 1974 put an end to the dictatorship and thus also the colonies.

The transfer of funds from the rich to the poor proved more difficult to achieve. New institutions such as the UN Development Programme (UNDP) and the UN Conference on Trade and Development (UNCTAD) were established, and aid increased significantly from most wealthy countries. But the most dramatic attempts to change international power structures, such as through the New International Economic Order in the 1970s, made little headway. Scandinavians and European social democrats were on the side of the developing countries, but with Thatcher in power in London and Reagan in Washington, the times were bad for extensive international regulations. OPEC's price increases gave the oil-producing countries new wealth, but it soon transpired that much of this wealth ended up in New York and London. The liberalization of the international economy strengthened the wealthy countries, but it also contributed to fluctuations in the state of the market. There were several setbacks that in some ways made things worse than ever before.

While military interventions brought both successes and failures, the success stories were far more numerous on the civil side. That was easy to forget in the general focus on conflict in the study of international politics. In 2000 the UN General Assembly adopted the Millennium Development Goals, which were extremely ambitious targets for the next fifteen years. Goal number one was to halve poverty in the world. As recently as in 1981, 44 per cent of the world's population lived in abject poverty. Today this figure is around 10 per cent and falling. In that sense, this goal has been more than met. The UN is now aiming to eradicate poverty entirely before 2030, a goal that until recently seemed entirely illusory, but which now might actually be achievable.

Goal number two was that everyone should receive primary education. Most of the world's population had been illiterate through the nineteenth and twentieth centuries. Today 85 per cent of all adults can read, and that proportion is increasing. There has been a lot of progress in higher education as well. In many countries, including some Muslim ones, there are now far more women than men in higher education. There need not be any tension between Islam and modernization.

The major health goals that were set are all within the limits of possibility. As recently as in 1988 polio was widespread in 125 countries. Today that figure has been reduced to two countries.

Of course the UN was not the only entity, or even the primary entity, involved in reaching such major goals. The most significant efforts were actually made by the countries affected. The fact that China was in a position to bring hundreds of millions of people out of poverty was the main reason for the decline in poverty. Nevertheless, the UN contributed with awareness campaigns and considerable resources.

While the focus on prizes to the Inter-Parliamentary Union and the International Peace Bureau before the First World War were unable to prevent the First World War, and the interest in the League of Nations was unable to prevent the Second World War, the situation when it comes to the UN after 1945 is more complicated. The UN has played a much bigger role than the League of Nations was in a position to do, both in terms of military action and, even more so, among civilians.

There is an inherent tension throughout the entire UN system. Not least in Norway we have a dream that the UN will put an end to war and conflict. But at the same time, it was never the intention for the UN to be a kind of international super-government. Many nations want to distance themselves from such a vision, which is also inconsistent with the Charter of the United Nations. Nevertheless, the spotlight on this must not prevent us from appreciating what the UN has actually been in a position to achieve.

Human Rights Prizes

Until 1945, a lot of prizes were awarded to people and organizations working towards a better organized world. Before the Second World War, there was really only one clear exception to this rule, and that was the prize awarded to Carl von Ossietzky in 1935. After the Second World War there would be many such exceptions.

After 1945, it would become quite common for prizes to be awarded in praise of democracy and human rights and in protest against specific ideologies. Fighting these inclinations became important peace work. Almost all the human rights prizes awarded after 1945 criticized specific regimes. Those most frequently criticized were the regimes in South Africa, the Soviet Union, and China, but a negative light was also shone on Argentina, Burma, Guatemala, Iran, and Pakistan. Even the USA was criticized through the prizes awarded to Linus Pauling and to Martin Luther King. Dialogue between the parties had previously been the Nobel Committee's almost constant advice. Now the prize was occasionally replaced by condemnation of undemocratic regimes and people. These were to be dealt with, not negotiated with, though if possible any transition was to be secured through negotiations.

The Norwegian Nobel Committee concluded early on that there is a connection between democracy and human rights on the one hand and peace on the other. In recent decades a growing group of peace researchers and other social scientists have become more and more interested in this as well. The main focus of the prize is still the desire for a better organized world, but at times human rights have competed for attention. Both human rights and disarmament are closely linked to the more general desire for a better organized world. All three are key elements of liberal internationalism. A better organized world would promote both human rights and disarmament, eventually even a better environment. With something of an exception having been made for disarmament, particularly the prizes to Henderson and Ossietzky, this was nevertheless a new focus for the Nobel Committee after the Second World War.

The work for human rights is not directly mentioned in Nobel's will, and the regimes that have been criticized have almost always responded that awarding prizes only to rebels stimulated unrest. However, the committee considers the work for human rights to fall within Nobel's first point on 'fraternity between nations'. Peace requires different groups of people to acknowledge and respect each other. Sooner or later oppression will lead to a reaction in the form of war and conflict.

The prize awarded to Albert Lutuli in 1960 represented something new in the history of the Peace Prize. It signalled a broader global orientation on the committee's part. Previously the laureates had generally come from North America and Western Europe. Until 1960, Argentinian Minister of Foreign Affairs Carlos Saavedra Lamas was the only non-European recipient. India's liberation hero and non-violence activist Mahatma Gandhi never received the Nobel Peace Prize, which indicates clearly how Western-oriented the Peace Prize was for a long time. The prize to Lutuli was also the first wholly unambiguous human rights prize. The prizes awarded to Buisson, Ossietzky, Bunche, and Jouhaux had all had human rights aspects to them, but they all also involved other important factors.

Lutuli came from a family of Zulu leaders and was educated at mission schools. In 1935 he was elected chief of the Zulu tribe, a position that was approved by the South African government, which also paid his salary. For a long time Lutuli was not particularly interested in politics, instead focusing on combining the Zulus' traditional culture with Christian values and modern civilization. The government's increasing implementation of racial segregation in the country made Lutuli more and more politically active. He joined the African National Congress (ANC), which was founded in 1912. He soon worked his way up through the organization, something which led to him being removed as Zulu chief by the government in 1952. Shortly afterwards he was elected president of the ANC.

The number of demonstrations and strikes increased dramatically as the apartheid state continued to develop. Lutuli was imprisoned for both brief spells and longer periods. The demonstrations in Sharpeville in 1960 would mark a turning point. Sixty-nine people were killed and many others were wounded. Lutuli and many other ANC leaders burned their passes, which formed the physical basis of the racial segregation. The UN Security Council condemned the South African government for the bloody development. It was a shock to the same government when Lutuli was then awarded the

Nobel Peace Prize for 1960. They let him travel to Oslo to receive the prize, but restricted what else he could do.

Lutuli always maintained that the fight against apartheid should take place through peaceful means. It was therefore a blow to him when 'Umkhonto we Sizwe' (Spear of the Nation) was established under the leadership of Nelson Mandela, albeit formally outside of the ANC. As early as 16 December 1961, six days after the Peace Prize was awarded, an extensive sabotage campaign was launched. Lutuli was not a pacifist, but he believed in non-violent resistance and was afraid that sabotage would be followed by armed conflict.

When the Nobel Peace Prize for 1984 went to Archbishop Desmond Tutu and not to Nelson Mandela, this was because Tutu, unlike Mandela, had adhered so rigidly to a policy of non-violence. The committee made it clear that the prize once again being awarded to a black South African was 'a renewed recognition of the courage and heroism shown by black South Africans in the use of peaceful methods in the struggle against apartheid'. The South African government reacted as criticized governments often do. A newspaper commented that 'this has to be one of the strangest recipients of the Nobel Peace Prize.'

Tutu trained as a teacher before becoming a priest. He quickly rose up through the church before becoming General Secretary of the South African Council of Churches, in which all denominations participated apart from the Dutch Reformed Church. The church in South Africa and in large parts of the world had become a key driving force in the fight against apartheid. Tutu maintained a policy of non-violence in the fight for a non racial, democratic, and just society. Economic sanctions against the regime were the most important means of opposing it. Tutu's Nobel lecture emphasized that where there is no justice, there can be no peace.

When Nelson Mandela and Frederik Willem de Klerk received the Nobel Peace Prize in 1993, it was already clear that the days of the apartheid regime were numbered. De Klerk was still the State President, whereas Mandela was formally a private individual, but everyone knew it was only a matter of time before this would change. Even in the 1980s there had been a lot of talk about how it would not be possible to put an end to the apartheid regime without an armed conflict. But now it was ending under peaceful conditions. This was possible because many white people under de Klerk's leadership had realized they would have to give up their political power, while Mandela in turn was prepared to extend a hand to the majority of the white population to ensure their acceptance of non-white participation in the political process.

Prizes shared by political opponents can contribute to significant tension: Kissinger and Lê Đức Thọ and Arafat, Peres, and Rabin are examples of this. There were also clear disagreements between Mandela and de Klerk during the Nobel festivities in Oslo in December 1993, but they both knew the value of the other. They stood together in the fight to abolish apartheid and introduce a 'one man, one voice' system in South Africa.

No Peace Prize was awarded to the major communist powers during the Cold War. Stalin had established his own prize in 1949 as part of his 70th birthday celebrations. (This was later renamed the Lenin Peace Prize.) Three people, Linus Pauling, Seán MacBride, and Nelson Mandela, received both the Nobel Peace Prize and the Stalin/Lenin Peace Prize. Khrushchev had actually expressed an interest in receiving the Nobel Peace Prize, but the feelers he sent out via the Soviet ambassador in Oslo to the Nobel Committee were not well received by committee chair Gunnar Jahn and led to nothing. Neither did the notion of Khrushchev and Eisenhower potentially receiving the prize together. Quite apart from anything else, it was not entirely clear what they would receive the prize for.

Boris Pasternak received the Nobel Prize in Literature in 1958, but after initially accepting it, he then declined it, even though he remained on the list of laureates. Aleksandr Solzhenitsyn received the literature prize in 1970, to his delight. Both of these prizes sparked discontent at the Kremlin, but this discontent increased significantly when Andrei Sakharov received the Peace Prize for 1975.

Sakharov was one of the Soviet Union's leading scientists and had worked closely with Igor Tamm, who received the Nobel Prize in Physics in 1958. Sakharov played an important role in the development of the hydrogen bomb, which was considered a major victory for Soviet science. The atomic bomb had been partly based on information gained through espionage within the American project, but the hydrogen bomb was all theirs. However, Sakharov gradually became more critical of the Soviet authorities. He was initially in favour of testing nuclear weapons, but then he criticized the education of Soviet scientists before speaking out against the treatment of Soviet dissidents. In 1968 Sakharov put down his ideas in *Reflections on Progress, Peaceful Coexistence and Intellectual Freedom*. Here he showed support for a liberalization of Soviet society and cooperation between capitalist and socialist systems. Sakharov thought the two systems would converge over time. He was also in favour of disarmament and aiding poorer countries.

Sakharov only became more and more interested in politics. After his first wife died, he married Yelena Bonner in 1971. She had previously been a communist, but was now increasingly critical of the communist system. The regime introduced measures to restrict Sakharov's activism, but without success. He continued his criticism, releasing his second essay, *My Country and the World*, in 1975. Here he claimed that there could be no peace in the world before the Soviet system was opened up.

Sakharov did not risk travelling to Oslo to receive the prize. He was afraid he would not be able to return home to the Soviet Union again. Instead his wife accepted the prize and gave his lecture for him. The lecture touched on the situation of the many prisoners of conscience in the Soviet Union and gave many of their names. Committee chair Lionæs tried to curb the consequences for Norwegian–Soviet links by emphasizing that the committee operated independently of the Norwegian government and had made the decision entirely on its own. It is likely that the committee had less faith in convergence theories—the belief that communism and capitalism might come together at some point in the future—than Sakharov himself apparently did. Lionæs criticized the Soviet Union for not letting Sakharov travel to Oslo to receive the prize and directly compared this to the Hitler regime not letting Ossietzky receive his prize.

In 1980, Sakharov was sent to Gorky (today's Nizhny Novgorod) after seeking internal asylum. There he went on a hunger strike to ensure that his wife would receive cardiac treatment in the USA. When Gorbachev came to power in 1985, Sakharov's situation quickly improved. He was even elected to the Federal Assembly, where he continued his fight for pluralism and a market economy.

The prize awarded to Lech Wałęsa in 1983 also involved clear, if somewhat more indirect, criticism of the Soviet Union and of communism than the prize to Sakharov had. The Soviet Union was not mentioned in any of the formal speeches. The committee asserted that the fight for human rights was also a fight for peace. Committee chair Egil Aarvik started his presentation speech for Wałęsa by quoting from the Universal Declaration of Human Rights. The focus was now on organizational freedom, including the right to form free trade unions. Wałęsa's fight was based on a policy of non-violence, and the committee emphasized that he had tried to make progress through negotiations. Wałęsa himself was not present in Oslo either, but he too sent his wife, Danuta, to receive the prize and read his speech. Wałęsa emphasized that Poland's major problems could only be solved through a dialogue between the government and the people.

Two aspects of Wałęsa's prize garnered particular attention, one at the time, another later. Firstly, there were those within the Norwegian Confederation of Trade Unions who thought a prize to Wałęsa might destroy the cooperation they had established, despite everything, with the official Polish trade unions, but it was difficult to oppose a prize to independent trade unions. Secondly, it has subsequently transpired that Wałęsa may have initially been in contact with the Polish secret police. However, this did not prevent his fight from being a success.

The prize awarded to Mikhail Gorbachev in 1990 was both a tribute to the new Soviet Union and a criticism of the old one. Gorbachev realized that economic reforms, perestroika, would have to be implemented, first morally and then eventually also through real economic reforms. To get a conservative Communist Party to change, one needed gradually increasing doses of glasnost—openness. As regards foreign policy, Gorbachev would cut back on the enormous defence budget and promote ties between the East and the West. To achieve this, he was prepared to give Eastern Europe and East Germany their freedom, although he also hoped reform communism would catch on in these countries as well. He flirted with the notion of using violence to keep the Soviet Union together, but was not willing to use violence on a larger scale to achieve this. Several of the republics were therefore able to withdraw from the Soviet Union.

The Nobel Committee discussed whether Ronald Reagan and/or George H. W. Bush should also receive the Nobel Peace Prize, but the committee deemed Gorbachev to be the person who had undoubtedly done the most to put an end to the Cold War. Even though both Regan and Bush did their best to give Gorbachev a reception that would strengthen his reform policy even further, it was Gorbachev himself who had brought about the major concessions, disarmament, and reforms in Eastern Europe, from which the Americans could then benefit.

Eventually the list of Peace Prizes promoting human rights and democracy and more or less indirectly criticizing undemocratic regimes grew quite long. In the Nobel Committee's opinion, human rights were universal and to be respected in all countries. The committee disapproved of those who claimed that cultures differed so significantly that different regional/cultural values should be reflected by different systems of government as well. The prevailing opinion was that everyone in the world wanted to influence their political development, even though the specific shaping of the democratic institutions might of course vary somewhat.

Thus, in 1980, the Nobel Committee confronted the military dictatorship in Argentina in particular, and in Latin America in general, through the prize awarded to Adolfo Pérez Esquivel. Committee chair John Sanness accepted the accusations of various undemocratic politicians around the world that the Nobel Committee perhaps viewed the world through Norwegian glasses. This was unavoidable. But the many people around the world fighting for human rights, Esquivel among them, also considered them universal. Like most other, but not all, human rights activists, Esquivel also had a non-violent stance.

After the military coup in 1976, Argentina moved in a clearly negative direction. An estimated 20,000 to 30,000 people disappeared as a result of the actions of the military between 1976 and 1981. Esquivel, an architect, sculptor, and painter, became increasingly involved in the struggle against the military regime. His work had a broadly Latin American aim, similar to that of the organization he helped found, Servicio Paz y Justica (SERPAJ). In 1974 he became the organization's Secretary-General. Liberation theology, which was behind much of this fight, gained support, not just in Latin America, but also in Europe.

The prize awarded to Aung San Suu Kyi in 1991 represented clear criticism of the military regime in Myanmar (Burma), which had been in power since 1962. The authorities had disregarded the election results in 1990 even though it was the regime itself that had arranged the election. The committee considered Suu Kyi's campaign of opposition 'one of the most extraordinary examples of civil courage in Asia in recent decades'. In this there was clear dismissal of the existence of specifically 'Asian values' that restricted universal human rights. This was clearly an attempt by those in power to justify their own authoritarian government.

Suu Kyi was the daughter of Burmese liberation hero General Aung San, but many years passed before she became involved in the politics of her country. She spent twenty-eight years out of the country, married British Tibet expert Michael Aris, and had two children. In the spring of 1988 she had to return to Burma to care for her sick mother. Her mother died after four months, but Suu Kyi quickly became caught up in the fight against the military regime. She became leader of the opposition, and her party, the National League for Democracy (NDL), won the election in 1990 with an overwhelming majority. By this point Suu Kyi was already under house arrest. In November 2010, she was finally released after being locked up for fifteen of the preceding twenty-one years. In June 2012, she was finally able to travel to Norway to give her Nobel lecture. During the elections in 2015, she was once again overwhelmingly victorious and became the country's leading politician, even though the military still retained some key positions. Her lack of response to the Muslim Rohingya people being expelled from the country and to Bangladesh reduced her popularity in Norway and the West considerably.

When Rigoberta Menchú from Guatemala received the Nobel Peace Prize in 1992, this represented clear criticism of a large number of local Latin American military regimes, even though there were indications after 1986 that the human rights situation in the country was improving. Menchú did not have a clearly non-violent stance and was linked to revolutionary movements that practised violence. Committee chair Francis Sejersead stated: 'I don't say that each single action she has taken in itself expressed peace. She has been in so many difficult situations. It is our conclusion that her long-term goal is peace.'

There was also some controversy around Menchú's personal biography. Professor David Stoll revealed what were undoubtedly clear discrepancies in the accounts to which she had contributed, but there is no doubt that her family experienced great suffering. Even Stoll agreed that Menchú had been deserving of the Peace Prize. She had become a central spokeswoman for the large population of Mayans and other indigenous groups in her home country and, in part, elsewhere in the world. The committee deemed it significant that Menchú would receive the prize in 1992, 500 years after Columbus discovered America. There was a clear indigenous perspective behind this, that of an indigenous people whose rights were often neglected but now had to be respected. She also made a memorable trip to Finnmark to visit the indigenous Sami population after she had received the prize in Oslo.

The 1996 prize to Bishop Carlos Belo and José Ramos-Horta was awarded for a 'just and peaceful solution to the conflict in East Timor'. It was clear that the solution they envisaged would lead to independence for East Timor, something that Indonesia strongly opposed. Indonesia considered East Timor an integral part of Indonesia and had invaded the country in 1975 when the Portuguese withdrew. Catholic East Timor would not accept Muslim Indonesia seizing control in this manner. Of a population of around 800,000, perhaps as many as 150,000–200,000 people lost their lives during the Indonesian occupation due to guerrilla warfare and assaults, and the chaos that followed.

Belo was a Catholic bishop in East Timor and became the clear leader of the struggle against Indonesia. He criticized the many assaults that took place, even though he was not always supported by the Vatican. Ramos-Horta was the peace movement Fretilin's foreign policy spokesman and travelled the world to promote the country's independence. Indonesia showed some understanding of the prize to Belo, but harshly criticized the prize to Ramos-Horta.

The inhabitants of East Timor, and not least the two laureates, were convinced that the Peace Prize would eventually result in the independence of the province, something that was far from a given under the circumstances in 1996. Nevertheless, they were right, partly since the Peace Prize had honed the international reaction to Indonesia's brutal hegemony, but more so because of the major political changes in Indonesia and other countries in the region as a result of economic collapse in 1997/98.

The prize awarded to President of South Korea Kim Dae-jung in 2000 was yet another example of criticism of a former military regime and dismissal of all the talk about 'Asian values'. Kim himself had confronted such values many times, considering them a means of justifying an authoritarian regime. In December 1997, he was elected President of South Korea, something that marked a definite end to the military regime in the country. South Korea itself was a prime example of desired development: rapid economic growth that within only a few decades brought the country from African to Southern European standards of living, followed by the introduction of a democratic system of government.

This, in combination with the inter Korean summit with North Korea's Kim Jong-il in 2000, was a crucial reason why Kim Dae-jung was awarded the Peace Prize. He had been at the forefront of extensive lobbying. It later transpired that South Korean companies had paid North Korea significant sums to ensure that the summit went ahead in 2000. Many people in South Korea thought that Kim must also have bribed the Norwegian Nobel Committee. Of course this was not the case, but the accusations said a lot about the bitter political climate in the south.

There was nothing unusual about lobbying—many people were involved in such activities. In most cases it had little influence over the committee's work, but Kim's plans were more ambitious. What was nevertheless most important was what he had actually achieved, which was to introduce and consolidate democracy in South Korea and to arrange a summit with North

Korean leader Kim Jong-il via the 'Sunshine Policy'. The Sunshine Policy did not give the results that Kim Dae-jung had hoped it would, but it was in the spirit of Alfred Nobel that he tried to open up the world's most closed-off country.

Shirin Ebadi received the Peace Prize in 2003 for 'her efforts for democracy and human rights, especially the rights of women and children, in Iran and the Muslim world in general'. She was the first female judge in Iran, and the first Muslim woman to receive the Peace Prize. The Nobel Committee stated that 'at a time when Islam is being demonized in many quarters of the Western world, it was the Norwegian Nobel Committee's wish to underline how important and how valuable it is to foster dialogue between peoples and between civilizations.' There are strong and fundamental defenders of democracy and human rights in Muslim countries as well. Again, such rights are not primarily Western—they are universal. Ebadi was a devout Muslim and considered Islam a force for good. The authoritarian aspects of her country's history were not the fault of Islam, she thought, but of even more embedded authoritarian and patriarchal features.

Ebadi herself was of course critical of the authorities in Tehran, but was dismissive of criticism of Islam. Many people in Iran received the news about the prize with enthusiasm, something that was not particularly popular with the authorities, who considered the prize to be interfering in internal relations. Later their criticism of Ebadi and of the award became even harsher. After receiving death threats, she decided to go into exile in 2009.

On the whole, the position of human rights was significantly reinforced during the twentieth century. From dominating only in North America and Western Europe during the interwar period, democracy also took over in Latin America, in Eastern Europe, in parts of Asia, with India leading the way, and in several African countries. Two areas still represent the most significant exceptions. First, large parts of the Muslim world are under authoritarian rule, even though there have been signs of change, notably in Indonesia and Tunisia. The prize to Ebadi was a nod to the Muslim countries from the Nobel Committee.

Then there is China. The Norwegian Nobel Committee had already awarded a prize that had greatly affected the situation in China—the prize to the Dalai Lama in 1989. The Dalai Lama always insisted 'I am a simple Buddhist monk. No more, no less.' But of course he was much more. He was chosen as the new Dalai Lama, the leader of six million Buddhists, when he was five years old. He achieved real power when he was fifteen. In 1950 the Chinese seized control of Tibet, and in 1959 the Dalai Lama fled the country to continue his fight for religious and political freedom. He established a Tibet in exile in the city of Dharamsala in the Himalayas in India. He travelled around the world and became a popular man in many circles in the West due to his approachability, his significant sense of humour, and his firm emphasis on the principle of non-violence. In 1987/88 the Dalai Lama was willing to accept China's control of Tibet's foreign and defence policy as long as the authorities in Beijing accepted the province's religious and cultural autonomy. It was no coincidence that he was awarded the Nobel Peace Prize in 1989, the year of the student protests in China, but despite this the prize had no direct effect on the situation in China itself.

For the Norwegian Nobel Committee, there were major challenges associated with awarding the prize to a Chinese dissident. A lot was heading in the right direction in China. The country was undergoing explosive economic growth and hundreds of millions of people were being lifted out of poverty due to this successful policy. There was also no doubt that the population of the country were able to express themselves more freely than before, not least compared to during the difficult years of the Great Leap Forwards (1958–61) and the Cultural Revolution (1966–76). The committee increasingly felt that they could not award so many human rights prizes and miss China out completely. Despite its progress, the country was a one-party state where the Communist Party alone made all the important decisions about the future of the country.

In 2014, the spotlight shifted to Pakistan and India. When Malala Yousafzai from Pakistan was awarded the Peace Prize along with Kailash Satyarthi from India, this was 'for their fight against the oppression of children and adolescents, and for children's right to education'. It was also an important factor in the prize to Malala that she had opposed political and religious extremism in a Pakistan that, despite its external democracy, displayed clear characteristics of fundamentalism. She had almost died after an attempt was made on her life after she had spoken out about girls' schooling in Pakistan. Since then she has had to live in exile in the United Kingdom.

The Arab Spring in 2011 had served to indicate that fundamental changes would finally come about in the Arab countries. The prize awarded to Tawakkol Karman from Yemen in 2011 along with Ellen Johnson Sirleaf and Laymah Gbowee, both from Liberia, was an attempt by the committee to reinforce these reforms. However, the liberal powers quickly came under fire, partly from the old regimes, with the military at their head, and partly from religious fundamentalist movements. Soon much was as it was before. In Egypt, democratically elected religious fundamentalists were once again replaced by a military dictatorship. In Yemen the old regime did fall, but was eventually replaced by civil war, for which the opposing parties received support from Saudi Arabia and Iran respectively. Karman was forced to flee the country.

Tunisia, where the Arab Spring had started in 2010/11, was the only optimistic exception. Here a broad coalition between trade unions, employers' organizations, lawyers, and human rights organizations established the Tunisian National Dialogue Quartet. This group, the Peace Prize laureates for 2015, proved themselves to be in a position to maintain the reform policy and alleviate the tensions between Islamists and secular groups that had put an end to the revolutions in other Arab countries.

The Peace Prize for 2016 was awarded to President of Colombia Juan Manuel Santos. Although the prize had clear human rights aspects, it was first and foremost a nod to a classic peace treaty between two parties, the government and the FARC guerrillas, which had waged a civil war lasting more than fifty years. The prize was undoubtedly of support to the President during this peace process. Although the peace treaty was rejected by a slight majority in a referendum, in only a short time Santos managed to make changes that increased the popularity of the revised treaty.

The Peace Prize and Disarmament

The second point that Alfred Nobel mentioned in his will was 'the abolition or reduction of standing armies'. In line with this, the Norwegian Nobel Committee has awarded many prizes to the many people working to reduce the position of nuclear weapons in international politics. On a more or less regular basis the committee had returned to this topic: Philip Noel-Baker (1959), Linus Pauling (1962), Andrei Sakharov (1975), Alva Myrdal and García Robles (1982), International Physicians for the Prevention of Nuclear War (1985), Joseph Rotblat and the Pugwash Conferences on Science and World Affairs (1995), the IAEA and Mohamed ElBaradei (2005), and the International Campaign to Abolish Nuclear Weapons (ICAN) (2017). Some other prizes, everything from Albert Schweitzer in 1952 to Barack Obama in 2009, also had nuclear aspects, among many other elements. Two prizes also focused on disarmament in other areas: the International Campaign to Ban Landmines (ICBL) in 1997 and the Organisation for the Prohibition of Chemical Weapons (OPCW) in 2013.

Of course, the UN has been at the heart of much of the international work towards disarmament and arms control. However, in this area it might be unclear which of the activists were closely associated with the UN and who worked more independently. Linus Pauling's work to stop nuclear tests was something that mainly took place within his own scientific environment, though he often appealed to leading statesmen and to the UN. The work of the 1997 laureate, the International Campaign to Ban Landmines and its coordinator Jody Williams, took place largely outside of the UN. It had proven extremely difficult to achieve something that controversial through the UN system.

Nuclear weapons were used for the first and hitherto last time on Hiroshima and Nagasaki in August 1945. Even though the number of powers with nuclear weapons has increased slower than many people thought it would, more and more powers have acquired them: the Soviet Union (1949), the United Kingdom (1952), France (1960), China (1964), Israel (unclear when), India (1974), Pakistan (1998), and North Korea (2006). Some nations have actually also got rid of their nuclear weapons: South Africa, Ukraine, Belarus, and Kazakhstan—though it should be noted that the latter three did not get rid of their own nuclear weapons, but the Russian weapons that were stationed on their soil. As the stores of nuclear weapons have gradually been modernized, the number of warheads has actually decreased dramatically, particularly in the USA and in Russia. Treaties on test bans (1963) and on non-proliferation (1968) have been entered into, as have a number of agreements between the USA and the Soviet Union/Russia on reducing the number of warheads.

Since nuclear weapons have not been used for war since August 1945, several scholars have argued that an international standard against the use of nuclear weapons has evolved. If this is the case, this standard is not based on explicit agreements, but on an understanding that non-use has become standard practice. Only China and India have formally committed themselves to not being the first to use such weapons. The other nuclear nations think that they can continue to ensure their own security through the deterrence that the nuclear weapons allegedly still provide. There are realist political scientists who have argued that further proliferation of such weapons would actually contribute to reducing the risk of major conflicts. According to that logic, both Iran and Ukraine should develop their own nuclear weapons. The results when it comes to nuclear disarmament have therefore been relatively modest. Where there have been successes, there are always many different reasons for this. The potential influence of the Peace Prize cannot be isolated.

But there are nevertheless some more specific examples of influence. The fact that Linus Pauling was in a position to get more than 11,000 scientists from forty-nine countries to sign an appeal for a test ban, with proof of the genetic consequences that continued testing might have, was most likely one of the contributing factors to the Test Ban Treaty of 1963. However, it should be noted that testing continued for many years, only underground to prevent the harmful fallout. The work that Rotblat and the Pugwash Conferences did was quite likely one of the many contributing factors to the US–Soviet agreements on restrictions. Many of the most renowned scientists from both sides, as well as from many other countries, were able to come together and carry out calculations and analyses that would form the basis of such agreement out of the media spotlight. The fact that such cooperation was possible during the Cold War was remarkable in itself.

The International Atomic Energy Agency was founded in 1957. Its purpose was twofold: to promote the peaceful utilization of nuclear energy and ensure that such activities were not exploited for arms production. The duty of the five leading nuclear nations to 'reduce nuclear weapons globally with the ultimate aim of achieving a world free of nuclear weapons' was implicit in the IAEA's statutes, but was expressed even more clearly in the Treaty on the Non-Proliferation of Nuclear Weapons (NPT) from 1970. The nuclear nations would reduce the number of such weapons while other nations refrained entirely from developing them. ElBaradei thought this to be somewhat reminiscent of someone with a cigarette hanging out of their mouth telling everyone else to quit smoking.

When it came to exposing illegal nuclear programmes, the IAEA's record left much to be desired. In 1992 the organization revealed that North Korea had an extensive nuclear programme. The Gulf War had demonstrated that Saddam Hussein actually had a significant nuclear project as well. The IAEA had been thoroughly deceived. Conversely, they were right ten years later to be sceptical of the USA's accusation that Iraq still had such an arrangement. In 2002/03 the IAEA revealed that Iran had developed a nuclear programme in secret. In 2015 an agreement was finally reached between the

Western powers, Russia, China, and Iran, on a strict delimitation of this programme. The IAEA has undoubtedly played an important role as monitor of developments in the field of nuclear physics, although others have made most of the key decisions in this area. In 2018 Donald Trump abandoned the Iran agreement.

The negotiations behind the landmine treaty were special. A large number of humanitarian organizations came together for them, supported by some sympathetic governments. They were soon in a position to draw up a treaty, which was signed by 121 nations in December 1997, shortly before the Nobel days in Oslo. After a sufficient number of nations had ratified the treaty, it entered into force in March 1999. This has to be a record for the quickest preparation of a concrete disarmament treaty. When it announced the prize, the Norwegian Nobel Committee expressed the hope that the landmine ban process, 'as a model for similar processes in the future, [...] proves of decisive importance to the international effort for disarmament and peace'. This was actually indirect criticism of the UN. The fact that the entire process took place outside of the UN system was what made such speed possible. Superpowers such as the USA, Russia, China, and India were against the treaty and would have hindered progress if the negotiations had taken place within the UN. In 2007/08 much of the same story repeated itself, this time with cluster munitions. This was effectively the landmines all over again, but no Peace Prize was awarded to this campaign. The two processes were too alike, the weapons quite similar, and the governments and people involved mostly the same as before.

The use of gas in war is longstanding. The founding of the Organisation for the Prohibition of Chemical Weapons in 1997 had established a new ambitious goal. The organization was 'determined for the sake of all mankind to exclude completely the possibility of the use of chemical weapons'. In 2013, when the organization received the Nobel Peace Prize, the world had come quite close to achieving this ambitious goal. The 190 countries who were members of the OPCW represented 98 per cent of the world's population and 80 per cent of the world's chemical industry. It was a victory for the OPCW when, immediately after the prize was announced, Syria also joined the Chemical Weapons Convention, with its chemical weapons subsequently being removed from the country, even as the civil war waged on, to be destroyed. The world has thus come quite close to achieving an ambitious goal, although the remaining minority maintain their stance and in 2017 it transpired that Syria still had and was willing to use chemical weapons.

There were undoubtedly some victories, also in the area of disarmament, mostly in the non-nuclear sphere. President Obama adopted the goal that many scientists had long had: establishing a world free from nuclear weapons. However, he also said that he did not expect to see this goal achieved in his lifetime. Many Peace Prizes would be required for the world to have any chance of achieving this. As Rotblat and others have said, such an ambitious goal really required the development of a global authority which can ensure that no nations try to worm their way out of helping to achieve it. And this would likely further postpone the achievement of a world with no nuclear weapons.

The Peace Prize and the Environment

The Peace Prize has gradually taken on a wider focus. Nobel's will said nothing about protecting the environment being a criterion. Nevertheless, it is not difficult to argue that environmental considerations have a connection with his will. There is hardly any better example of 'fraternity between nations' than the fight against global warming. Saving the planet is an extreme example of global fraternity and cohesion. Modern diplomacy with environmental conferences at all levels, global to local, involving both governments and various types of organizations, might also be said to constitute a modern form of 'peace congresses'.

The connection between the environment and peace exists on many different levels. Scarcity of resources might lead to conflict, for example matters related to control of oil or water. When the polar ice caps melt, this might lead to new discussions about borders and where they will be located. Who will have power over the North Pole? Desertification may lead to people having to move and, in doing so, coming into conflict with each other. This is undoubtedly one of many factors in the numerous conflicts we have seen in recent years in the Sahel, the area of land extending from Mali to Sudan. When the sea rises, this may also result in people migrating, which may lead to new tensions, as we have seen between India and Bangladesh, for example.

Particularly in the USA there has been political debate about how serious climate changes really are and the extent to which they are man-made. Scientifically there is little doubt that the global temperature has risen.

Every year, or even every month, it seems to increase. The foremost international climate goal is now to limit that increase to 1.5–2 degrees. Despite all the debate, there is growing scientific consensus about the increasingly widespread consequences of global warming.

So far, two prizes have been awarded in connection with the environment. The first was the 2004 prize to Wangari Maathai; the second was the 2007 prize to the Intergovernmental Panel on Climate Change (IPCC) and Al Gore. As a democracy activist in Kenya and an environmental activist internationally, Maathai had a broad profile, though it was her environmental work that garnered the most interest. After all, she was the first environmental activist to receive the Nobel Peace Prize, though it could be protested that planting trees to prevent desertification, which is what she was doing, was something of a narrow focus considering the Nobel Committee was putting a new field up for consideration.

In 2007, the Intergovernmental Panel on Climate Change and Al Gore received the Nobel Peace Prize. The prize to the IPCC for its extensive scientific work to counter global warming and to Gore for his politically popular presentations based on this scientific foundation was at the heart of the climate debate.

The IPCC was established in 1988 by the United Nations Environment Programme (UNEP) and the World Meteorological Organization (WMO). The resolution adopted by the UN General Assembly states that the background to the IPCC is that the Assembly notes 'with concern that the emerging evidence indicates that continued growth in atmospheric concentrations of "greenhouse" gases could produce global warming with an eventual rise in sea levels, the effects of which could be disastrous for mankind if timely steps are not taken at all levels'. The IPCC bases its work on studies conducted by hundreds, if not thousands, of scientists around the world. Their reports indicate a growing consensus that the dangers of global warming will become increasingly clear. A rather loud minority still reject the notion of global warming. This minority now has a prominent advocate in a position of power, namely Donald Trump in the USA. Nevertheless, most countries have been willing to adopt more and more extensive programmes for limiting global warming, but it remains to be seen whether the rate at which these decisions are being made is sufficient to make a critical difference.

As with human rights and disarmament, the environmental struggle is part of liberal internationalism. They are also all more or less linked to the dream of a better organized world. These are all tasks that the world needs to work on together.

Why Has the USA Received So Many Peace Prizes?

When discussing the recurring themes of the Peace Prize extending back through its history, it is remarkable that the USA in particular has received the most prizes—twenty-two in total. The United Kingdom has also received many—fourteen—but then it is a long way down to France and Switzerland with seven and six respectively, and most of them were awarded in the earlier years of the prize. The USA's prizes are spread across the duration of the prize's history, from Theodore Roosevelt in 1906 to Barack Obama in 2009.

The USA is a large and important country with strong idealistic currents. Most of this idealism is historically linked to liberal internationalism, which has been a recurrent theme through the history of the Peace Prize. Four American presidents have received the Nobel Peace Prize. In addition to Roosevelt and Obama, it was also awarded to Wilson in 1919 and to Jimmy Carter in 2002. It is no coincidence that three of these men were Democrats, and that the other was a Republican of the liberal variety. To Norway and Norwegians it is almost as if the USA is split in two, a liberal and democratic country with which we feel solidarity and a conservative country for which we have little respect or understanding. Although some Peace Prizes have gone to those on the right, such as those to Roosevelt, Root, and Kissinger, right-wing America has had a strained relationship with the Peace Prize, as is also evidenced by Jay Nordlinger's book *Peace, They Say*. (Yet even in the White House under George W. Bush the Peace Prize awarded to Theodore Roosevelt was displayed with great pride in the Roosevelt Room just across the hall from the Oval Office.) Modern-day right-wing heroes Ronald Reagan and George W. Bush never received the Peace Prize. Even Richard Nixon was interested in the prize. The fact that Willy Brandt received the prize in 1971 was taken by some of Nixon's White House employees as a signal that even the most prominent politicians could receive the prize. Of course they were thinking about Nixon. But it was Kissinger, and not Nixon, who received it.

In addition to the four presidents, two vice presidents have received the prize, Dawes in 1925 and Al Gore in 2007. So too have five secretaries of state: Root, Kellogg, Hull, Marshall, and Kissinger. Precisely half of the American laureates, eleven of the twenty-two, therefore represented the American government.

The other half received theirs for their work for a number of different causes, but again there is little doubt that most of them were linked to liberal internationalism. Some of them were on the far left politically. When Linus Pauling received his prize for his work on stopping nuclear tests in 1962, representatives of the American government stayed away from the festivities. Pauling was quite simply too left-wing, having been accused of harbouring communist sympathies and having at the time been refused a passport to travel abroad. When Martin Luther King Jr received the prize in 1964, he was still a highly controversial figure in the USA, even though important civil rights laws were finally adopted by Congress in 1964/65. President Lyndon B. Johnson was among the many people disappointed that King was receiving the prize, even though he did his utmost to ensure that the laws would be passed. Johnson knew he would not receive any prize for abolishing racial segregation in the USA now that King had received his Peace Prize for that very reason.

The list of left-wing American activists is long: Jane Addams in 1931, Emily Greene Balch in 1946, Ralph Bunche in 1950, and Jody Williams in 1997. The latter was involved in harsh polemics with President Clinton when he did not wholeheartedly support the Mine Ban Treaty. Others were more centrally oriented, if not slightly further to the right: Butler in 1931, Borlaug in 1970, and Elie Wiesel in 1986.

Liberal internationalism has had a strong position in both the USA and the United Kingdom. However, this has not prevented an occasional major lack of internationalism in both countries. The USA's treatment of the Native Americans and the African-American population and the United Kingdom's lengthy colonial rule are examples of this. The USA also waged wars that broke with the conscience of the world, such as those in Vietnam and Iraq. But compared to other superpowers, it is nevertheless striking how far these countries, despite everything, have walked along the path of liberal internationalism. Whereas the USA and the United Kingdom have the most Peace Prize laureates, as mentioned, the former communist Soviet Union has only two: dissident Sakharov and reformer Gorbachev.

They both received their prizes for their criticism of the communist system. The same was true in China with critics the Dalai Lama and Liu Xiaobo. France had many laureates before the Second World War. Since 1945 it has had only one: René Cassin.

It was not so remarkable that small nations such as Norway supported liberal internationalism. Law and justice is not only our national ideology, it is also our way of reducing the advantage that superpowers have by virtue of their military resources. However, there were two superpowers that would likely use their military strength when required but who were also leading nations within the liberal tradition.

6

Ten Portraits, 1990–2012

Mikhail Gorbachev (1990)

I had spent much of my life as a historian studying the beginning of and, eventually, the end of the Cold War. In 1990 the Cold War was definitely just about over. Who would be lauded for this positive development? It was in this sense that my work as Director and historian collided from my very first day on the job. These were very exciting times.

On 15 October 1990, chair Gidske Anderson announced that the Peace Prize for 1990 would be awarded to Mikhail Sergeyevich Gorbachev, President of the Soviet Union and General Secretary of the Communist Party of the Soviet Union. It was a dramatic decision. During the Cold War the Soviet Union had not only been the USA and NATO's primary opponent, but the country was also considered the greatest threat to Norway's security. Now the leader of the country would receive the highest honour any Norwegian institution could offer.

Nevertheless, the arguments in favour of a prize for Gorbachev were very strong. He received the prize for 'his leading role in the peace process which today characterizes important parts of the international community'. The committee was fully aware that this process had resulted 'from several factors', but they nevertheless ended up honouring Gorbachev. The committee did not risk saying much about what had come to pass. The countries in Eastern Europe had regained their freedom, Germany was united, major disarmament treaties had been entered into, and regional conflicts such as the one in Afghanistan were, if not resolved, at least no longer causing conflict between the East and the West. The UN could now play a completely different role to the one that it had played during the Cold War. All this had already happened, but the committee only alluded to it in general terms. The change had come about almost as a bolt from the blue. There were many international foreign policy experts who, only weeks and days before the Berlin Wall fell in 1989, had predicted that basic conditions would not be affected by the changes taking place in Eastern Europe.

The committee praised Gorbachev for the openness he had also created inside the Soviet Union—for glasnost. Nevertheless, it was carefully stressed that Gorbachev was receiving the prize for his foreign policy, not his domestic policy. In her presentation speech on 10 December, committee chair Anderson made it clear that 'this is neither the time nor the place to discuss the Soviet Union's internal affairs. The Norwegian Nobel Committee has given President Gorbachev the Peace Prize for his leading role in international politics.' Gorbachev had on many occasions declared that he was still a 'communist'. His democratic record was not particularly lengthy. The committee did not say anything in particular about economic developments, but it was starting to become apparent that Gorbachev's economic reforms had not made the situation better in the Soviet Union. Quite the reverse. It eventually became clear that the economic problems under Brezhnev were mere trifles compared to the chaos that prevailed under Gorbachev.

Gorbachev had come to power in 1985. His will to reform was clear. He summarized it as follows: 'We cannot go on living like this!' In the first few years it was uncertain how far his reform policy would go. Domestic policy focused mostly on moral-political reforms. He put his foreign policy into action in a new offensive war in Afghanistan. The union in the Eastern bloc was still 'unbreakable'. The summit with US President Ronald Reagan in Geneva in November 1985 did not give any concrete results.

It eventually became apparent that Gorbachev's will to reform went far beyond morality policy. Increasingly large doses of glasnost and perestroika were required to change the course of domestic policy. From 1987, Gorbachev was prepared to make major unilateral concessions in negotiations with the USA about intermediate-range weapons, in the Soviet Union's own defence budget, and in the number of armed soldiers.

It is likely that the Norwegian Nobel Committee discussed Gorbachev's candidacy towards the end of the 1980s, but it was not easy to give such a prize to the President of the Soviet Union. Giving him the prize alone was considered a major and difficult step. Ought Ronald Reagan to be included? The American President had expressed an interest in easing tension with the Soviet Union even before Gorbachev came to power, but nothing came of this, partly because, as Reagan himself put it, the Soviet leaders 'keep dying'. Reagan was also unpopular in Norway. He was not widely praised for his shift from being a fierce condemner of communism to expressing a will to cooperate with the Soviet Union. Opinion polls showed that Gorbachev was far more popular among Norwegians. The unwillingness to award a Peace Prize to Reagan must have been substantial.

There was no lack of other good candidates during these years. The prizes to Oscar Arias in 1987 for the peace process in Central America and to the Dalai Lama for his general message of peace in 1989, which was also a difficult year for China, were both meaningful and popular far beyond Norway. Conversely, the 1988 prize to the UN's peacekeeping forces had not reinforced the same contemporary message, even though it fit well into the UN and cooperation ideology that was so important in Norway, in Scandinavia, and in liberal internationalist circles in general.

Reagan was out of the picture by 1990. George H. W. Bush had not been President long and had spent much of 1989 assessing whether Reagan's détente policy as regards the Soviet Union had gone too far. The major processes in Eastern Europe in 1989, from the elections in Poland in June to Ceaușescu's fall in Romania in December, had nevertheless taken place under Bush. His role in the unification of Germany, through his support of Helmut Kohl's ever-increasing tempo for the unification process, was only partially evident at the time.

Even though Gorbachev was the favourite to receive the prize in 1990, it was not a given from the start of the process that he would. The greatest uncertainty was what Gorbachev himself might do. Was the process in Eastern Europe irrevocable? What might happen in the Soviet Union when the demands for independence kept increasing, particularly in the Baltic countries, which in many ways were so close to the Nordic countries? It was also entirely possible that ghosts from the past might emerge. Gorbachev had been loyal to the system as early as during Stalin's time before coming to the increasingly clear conclusion during the 1980s that reforms were required. As a student at Moscow State University he had been Komsomol's (the young communists') secretary for the Faculty of Law. He was well aware what indoctrination and orthodoxy were.

Vaclav Havel was a clear alternative, but in many ways he was the local result of a process that had its roots in Gorbachev's policy. The most important local player was undoubtedly Lech Wałęsa, who had received the prize in 1983. It is also likely that former politicians on the Nobel Committee considered Havel to be first and foremost a poet and philosopher, with his competence as a politician being more uncertain. This attitude persisted throughout the 1990s and was reinforced by the dissolution of Czechoslovakia in 1992, which served to bring his limitations as a politician to light.

In 1990, with Gorbachev's eligibility still increasing, the committee decided he would receive the prize. The reactions to this decision were largely positive. Gorbachev was 'Man of the Year' in *Time Magazine*. When the prize was announced, *The New York Times* wrote: 'The man and the moment came together, and what a moment it was. As the fervor for freedom last year leaped from Poland and Hungary to Czechoslovakia and East Germany, Mikhail Gorbachev stayed the hand of those who wanted to crush it. He thereby allowed Europe to be transformed, peacefully. That alone would justify the Nobel Peace Prize he was awarded yesterday.' Gorbachev received enthusiastic congratulations from heads of state all over the world, including from all the leading Western powers. Conversely, the Chinese government condemned Gorbachev as a betrayer of communism. To them he became the very epitome of how reforms were not to be implemented. He worked for political and economic reforms in parallel. When the Chinese managed to implement extensive economic reforms without relaxing their political grip, this seemed to indicate an outlook as regards both aims and means quite different to that of Gorbachev.

Blood was shed when Soviet forces advanced on Vilnius in Lithuania in January 1991, with fourteen protesters losing their lives. There was also unrest in Riga in Latvia. Gorbachev's link to this use of force was never fully understood. When this happened, I received a phone call from *Dagbladet* at two in the morning. The newspaper wondered whether I had any comments. It was clear that the journalist now thought the Peace Prize had been awarded to Gorbachev too hastily. I was too sleepy, and too shocked, both by the events in Vilnius and by journalists calling me in the middle of the night, to give a particularly meaningful response. This would not be the last time a journalist called me in the night.

There was an outcry. The protests against the prize to Gorbachev came largely from an increasingly more independent Russia, and from the Baltic countries. They could not understand why someone who had destroyed the economy of the Soviet Union and been so dismissive of their struggle for independence would receive such a prize. Sakharov's widow, Yelena Bonner, threatened to return her husband's Peace Prize. It was unclear whether she would have returned the prize money as well. However, other family members protested against this. During a dinner that her Norwegian publisher arranged for her, I, as representative of the Nobel Committee, was given a proper dressing down. The Nobel Committee had allegedly destroyed the Peace Prize by giving Gorbachev the same prize that her husband had previously received. I had met Bonner before, so I was not unprepared for her temper.

The events in Vilnius helped establish a People's Peace Prize. It was to be awarded to Lithuanian head of state Vytautas Landsbergis. Some of those who supported this prize criticized the choice of Gorbachev, while others considered the prize to Landsbergis an additional prize. The establishment of this People's Peace Prize could nevertheless hardly be interpreted as anything other than criticism of the Nobel Committee on a level with the People's Peace Prize in the mid-1970s to Máiréad Corrígan and Betty Williams from Northern Ireland. They subsequently received the Nobel Peace Prize in 1977. Landsbergis never did. I met him at the major conference The Anatomy of Hate in Oslo in August 1990. The former music professor did not give the impression of being a significant political or moral leader, even though he supported views that were widely popular in the Baltic countries. He did not play any major role in the conference either.

Gorbachev did not come to Oslo to receive the Peace Prize in December 1990. He said that he had an important meeting in Moscow and asked whether the ceremony could be postponed. This was a delicate situation. Surely it was not difficult to postpone the ceremony for a few days? After some back and forth, the committee decided that the ceremony would go ahead as planned on 10 December. It was a smart decision. If you start negotiating with the laureates about the best date, you lose all control. If the laureate is present, great. If they are not, it goes ahead without them. Particularly in recent decades the prize has amassed such prestige that almost everyone attends. The most significant exceptions to this have been those authoritarian regimes that have not permitted the laureate to travel, or those who have feared that once they left their country, they would not be allowed back in. In this category we find Andrei Sakharov, Lech Wałęsa, and Aung San Suu Kyi. They were all represented by spouses or children.

In 2002, former Prime Minister Gro Harlem Brundtland told me that she had met Gorbachev in November 1990 during the summit on disarmament in Europe in Paris. The Soviet President told Gro that 'they' would not let him travel to Oslo to receive the Peace Prize. He did not specify who 'they' were, but it was allegedly the conservatives who came to power in the

autumn of 1990, appointed by Gorbachev himself. They were also behind
the attempted coup in August 1991.

In his memoirs, Gorbachev writes that he received the news of his prize
with 'mixed feelings'. Of course he was honoured, but the reaction in the
Soviet Union was influenced by the notion that the Nobel Prize represented Western imperial interests. The Prizes in Literature to Boris Pasternak
and Aleksandr Solzhenitsyn and the Peace Prize to Sakharov had all been
harshly condemned, and now Gorbachev would receive the same prize! It
only helped a little that the loyal Mikhail Sholokhov had received the Prize
in Literature, and that Gorbachev had made amends with Sakharov. When
it became clear that the committee would not postpone the ceremony,
Minister of Foreign Affairs Thorvald Stoltenberg got in touch with me. He
wanted to make sure that the committee presented its position as positively
as possible to avoid creating unnecessary friction between Norway and the
Soviet Union. A no should preferably sound like a yes.

First Deputy Minister for Foreign Affairs Anatoly Kovalev represented
Gorbachev at the ceremony on 10 December. Kovalev had worked with
Soviet foreign policy for several decades. He was competent, but gave the
impression of being of the old school. He stayed at the Soviet Embassy during
his visit. I was responsible for making sure he was in the right place at the
right time. Once when I came to collect him, he was still in bed. No one
had dared wake him. He was obviously a man for whom they had respect,
but when I arrived, they plucked up the courage to get him up and ready
quite quickly. I tried to talk to Kovalev about Soviet foreign policy several
times. His responses were fairly conventional. If there were interesting
nuances in what he said, I failed to notice them.

One Sunday in late 1990, before it had become clear that Gorbachev
would not come in December, I received a call from Soviet ambassador
Anatoly Tischenko, who invited me to his residence the same afternoon. So
much for the skiing I had planned. At his residence in Madserud allé, I was
received by a somewhat flustered ambassador. He was worried about
Gorbachev's visit. Did we have everything under control? I assured him that
of course we did. The foundation for such feigned confidence was shaky.
I had never been interested in staging big events and I had no relevant
experience. Nevertheless I, recent professor in Tromsø and new Director of
the Nobel Institute, assured the Soviet ambassador that there was nothing to
worry about. We had everything under control, even though everything
was new, not just to me, but also to most of the very modest staff at the

Nobel Institute. The ambassador told me he had received a significant sum from the Ministry of Foreign Affairs in Moscow to redecorate the premises before the President and party leader came to visit. But then the best thing that could have happened to the ambassador came to pass: he redecorated and Gorbachev did not come.

The ambassador was not a big fan of Gorbachev. During the attempted coup in August 1991, he was quick to take down the picture of the President. This was his way of declaring his loyalty to the new establishment. He nevertheless continued in his role as ambassador in Norway for a few more years. What I otherwise heard about the inner workings of the embassy illustrated why the Soviet Union had such major problems. Photocopying documents required the ambassador's personal signature. This was to limit any ideological infection. It was clear that such a regime would have a strained relationship with the computer technology which was becoming increasingly important in society. Imagine having the complete works of Solzhenitsyn on a floppy disc. It was dangerous!

In June 1991, Gorbachev eventually came to Norway. In connection with the visit, a discussion broke out between the Nobel Committee and the Prime Minister's office about who would stand where when we received the Soviet leader. The Prime Minister's office was convinced that the Prime Minister should be first in line, and then the chair of the Nobel Committee, who at that point was Francis Sejersted. Of course, I was equally convinced that the chair of the Nobel Committee should greet him first. It was the Nobel Committee that had invited Gorbachev, and he was coming as the Nobel Committee's guest. The Nobel Committee was by no means subordinate to government agencies. I stuck to my guns and what I thought was right. I myself would not be present in Fornebu when he arrived. To my surprise Gro relented. Francis was to greet him first!

Of course Gorbachev arrived on a government jet. As the secretary of the Nobel Committee, I had sent letters to Gorbachev detailing the practical arrangements in connection with the Nobel ceremony in Oslo, including the travel arrangements for laureates. Using previous letters as a template, I wrote that two to three seats would be reserved on an SAS flight to Oslo. Luckily this correspondence went through the Norwegian ambassador in Moscow. Of course he, the experienced Dagfinn Stenseth, picked up on this blunder. He called me and simply noted that would have been an unusual arrangement for a Soviet head of state. He was undoubtedly right. The laureate organized his own transport in the form of a separate jet.

Things had calmed considerably compared to the situation in January by the time Gorbachev came in June. There had been no more violence, and Gorbachev's popularity had consequently increased again in Norway. Even the new member of the Nobel Committee, Kåre Kristiansen, who had not been involved in the decision to award Gorbachev the prize, but who had publicly supported those opposed to Gorbachev giving a Nobel lecture, attended the events. A right-wing minority in Oslo City Council nevertheless voted against the Nobel Committee using the City Hall for the Nobel lecture. This was embarrassing. This was what convinced me that we should apply for a period of five years at a time to prevent Oslo City Council from expressing what it thought about the Nobel Committee's choice every year.

But goodness me, we were *very* excited about Gorbachev coming. The police presence was enormous. Helicopters overhead, security agents everywhere. During Gorbachev's Nobel lecture at City Hall there were nevertheless two people who got up and shrieked protests at him. This was embarrassing for us as hosts. Gorbachev was the person least affected by this. He had experienced similar before. The protesters were quickly removed from the premises. However, the worst part was when a woman wearing national costume of some description—she may have been Afghan—not only stood up with a bouquet of flowers in her hand, but almost made it all the way to the lectern before she was stopped by the many Norwegian and Soviet security agents in the hall. It turned out that the bouquet only contained flowers, but the incident was scandalous for the police. My good friend, chief of police Willy Haugli, was mortified. He did not like me bringing it up afterwards, neither then nor later on.

On the occasions when the committee met Gorbachev, we had many questions we wanted to ask him, not to criticize him, but because it was interesting to be so close to such a key figure in international politics. I, on behalf of the committee, had spent a significant amount of time studying the Soviet leader and had a lot I wanted to ask him about. It surprised me that Gorbachev gave such long answers to most questions. He never stopped talking. However, it was not particularly easy to work out exactly what he had said. This was not a man who went straight to the heart of the matter and commented concisely. It came as even more of a surprise that once he had given his response, his wife Raisa would then answer the same question as if that were the natural thing to do, even though no one had asked her about anything. This said a lot about her position not just in the family, but also in Soviet politics, as a key conversation partner and adviser to her husband.

The relationship between Raisa and Mikhail Gorbachev was special. It was touching to see them sitting together holding hands when we were driving between various events. They stood very close to each other. It was otherwise quite difficult to relate to Raisa. She had a high profile compared to most wives of party leaders, Nina Khrushcheva perhaps being an exception. A separate schedule was to be drawn up for Raisa during the visit to Oslo. Since she had received certain criticism in the Soviet Union for her active role, we thought it might be better if she kept a low profile. But when we submitted a proposal, we were told that this would not do. She ended up taking a walk through Frogner Park, with a great deal of publicity.

What was most evident from the conversations with Gorbachev was his uncertainty as regards the Baltic countries. He wanted to keep the Soviet Union together and reacted instinctively to all attempts to leave the union. He had systematically underestimated the explosive force of nationalism and expressed early on that this was a problem that communism had solved. On the other hand, he was against using force to retain the rebellious republics. A use of force would undermine his entire policy both domestically and internationally. He had no solution to this problem. It was out of his control. Gorbachev could not prevent the Baltic countries from gaining their independence.

Gorbachev's Nobel lecture made a big impression on me. Slightly overwhelmed by the atmosphere as I was, I deemed it a historic document. On closer reading, I see it was somewhat standard Gorbachev. He talked once more about the starting point in March/April 1985 and emphasized how far the Soviet Union still had to go. He reviewed the reforms, particularly the foreign policy reforms, but also the domestic reforms. The danger of global nuclear war was as good as gone. As was the Iron Curtain. Germany was united. The process could not be reversed. The world might not be rid of nuclear weapons before 2000, as Gorbachev had previously surmised, but we were getting there. The right of self-determination was a difficult topic within the Soviet Union, but he recognized that 'if a people really decides, through a fair referendum, to withdraw from the Soviet Union, a certain agreed transition period will then be needed.' He asked for international sympathy and support in solving the problems faced by the Soviet Union and the world. Just afterwards he was also invited to the G7 summit in London. Gorbachev concluded by declaring that the prize was a vote of confidence in the policy that he had produced—his domestic policy as well.

Mikhail Gorbachev was a man with clear limitations. I met him three or four times and had the opportunity to interrogate him about various matters. Historians are divided and will in all likelihood continue to be so on the question of the extent to which Gorbachev had a clear plan for what he was going to do when he became party leader in the spring of 1985. I am relatively convinced that he had no plan. He clearly wanted reforms, but knew little of what the reforms would involve. In the book *Perestroika* he expresses an almost touching view on the relationship between the governor (himself) and the governed. He imagines that he need only abolish the extensive bureaucracy between him and the people in order to make use of the enormous creative power of the people.

Gorbachev's naïve notions of democracy also characterized his notions of economics. He believed firmly in communism in the form of Marxism–Leninism, and held for quite some time that no more democracy was needed within the party. He only reluctantly agreed to open things up to groups and parties outside of the Communist Party. During 1990 it became clear that he thought the reform policy had gone too far. He appointed a number of more conservative members of government. I once asked him why he did not hold a presidential election in 1988/89. That was when he was at his most popular and it is highly likely that he would have won. His policy undermined the monopoly power of the Communist Party. A new power basis needed to be established. This became increasingly clear to his main challenger, Boris Yeltsin. Yeltsin went up for election in an increasingly more independent Russia. Even many years later, Gorbachev had trouble understanding the question. During a dinner at the Grand Hotel he answered: 'I was General Secretary of the party. Why would I have held an election?'

Gorbachev's insight into the economy was even less developed. He realized the market had to play a greater role, but did not know how far this process should go and, least of all, how this could be done. It might be difficult to combine running the country and the market. Gorbachev's spokesman, Valery Gerasimov, was undoubtedly right when he, to defend his boss from all the criticism, said that the world would do well to remember that it was the Nobel Peace Prize Gorbachev had received, not the Nobel Memorial Prize in Economic Sciences.

Of course it is unrealistic to expect Gorbachev to have had a detailed plan when he took office in 1985. He would never have been elected General Secretary either if the other party leaders had had any idea what would actually happen. When the Politburo realized how dramatic the reforms Gorbachev had planned were, it was too late to react. The old system could not be restored. The failed coup in August 1991 was the final nail in its coffin.

Gorbachev had no comprehensive plan even in the area of foreign policy. He quickly realized the arms race cost too much. Gorbachev himself has said how surprised he was by the military costs when he finally obtained a vague understanding of what the realities were. He would rather have had balanced agreements with the USA and the West, but when this took time, he was prepared to take major unilateral action. Where Eastern Europe was concerned, it actually seems he believed the system could survive the major reforms he eventually realized were necessary. Just as he himself had managed to maintain control in the Soviet Union, the new reform politicians that he supported in Eastern Europe could stabilize the situation. He was wrong in this case. When the threat of Soviet intervention was gone, the power basis quickly crumbled. In a matter of months, everything collapsed. There was only bloodshed in Romania, which was the only country in which the regime had developed a basis independent of the Soviet Union.

Did Gorbachev deserve his Nobel Peace Prize? In my opinion few have been more deserving of the prize than Gorbachev. The Nobel Committee has awarded the Peace Prize to many people who tried to reform the East–West system. Their efforts have included everything from modest measures such as arms control and nuclear-free zones (Alva Myrdal and García Robles in 1982) to Willy Brandt and his *Ostpolitik* (1971). Gorbachev did more than anyone else to abolish the entire East–West system and to put an end to the Cold War. That has to be enough to be deserving of the Peace Prize. If Gorbachev does not deserve the Peace Prize, there is very little sense in awarding any peace prize at all.

There has been heated debate among historians about who is responsible for ending the Cold War. Many American historians give Ronald Reagan most of the credit. Apparently he had a long-term plan. By mustering forces, Reagan demonstrated that expansion was no longer an option for the Soviet Union. When the leaders in Moscow realized this, he was prepared to cooperate in a generous and non-gloating manner. Some American and most European historians have nevertheless given Gorbachev most of the credit, whether his actions were well planned or more improvised. Other players have also been mentioned: Pope John Paul II, Margaret Thatcher, Lech Wałęsa, the population of the Eastern European countries, etc.

It was undoubtedly Gorbachev who made major concessions, whether giving up Soviet control in Eastern Europe, unifying Germany, or disarmament and arms control. Many people encouraged him in this policy. Reagan was generous in his treatment of Gorbachev. Through his original firm policy, he facilitated a wider agreement in the West on the cooperation policy with the Soviet Union than anyone else.

History is full of examples of politicians who made dramatic choices entirely outside of the framework of conventional thinking. Hitler, Stalin, and Mao are obvious examples; Kim Il-sung, Fidel Castro, and Muammar Gaddafi slightly less obvious. Gorbachev had a choice. He could have carried on with the policy of the old regime, with the minor changes he initially intended to make. He could have used violence to bring the development under control, whether in the case of Eastern Europe, East Germany, or the Soviet Union.

Gorbachev could probably have threatened such a use of force, but he did not. Other great reformers in Russia/the Soviet Union, notably Alexander II and Khrushchev, had also realized that reforms were needed, major reforms, but when they saw what the reforms brought about, they changed their minds and backtracked. Gorbachev initiated a development that put an end to the Cold War. He was often tempted to change course when the development went far beyond what he had envisaged. But he did not. Perhaps Gorbachev's biggest contribution was what he did not do: he did not use violence and allowed events to unfold without intervention.

Aung San Suu Kyi (1991)

While the committee had felt much was clear in 1990, there was a lot of uncertainty the following year. There were no clear favourites. After Mikhail Gorbachev had received the prize, there was little interest in following this up with another big international name. There were also few suitable candidates, perhaps with the exception of Helmut Kohl and Vaclav Havel. I have already mentioned the perspective on Havel. Kohl had done much to unite Germany, and he was also a strong advocate for European integration. However, illegal financial contributions to his party, the CDU, put paid to any chance of him being a candidate. Of course, Nelson Mandela was big news, but he would have to demonstrate what he stood for through concrete action first.

Almost every year there are some more timeless candidates. In 1991 the Salvation Army in particular stood out as one such candidate. Many people have wondered why the Salvation Army has never received the Nobel Peace Prize. The organization has often been suggested; it has also been frequently discussed. During the committee's discussions I have never heard a bad word said about the Salvation Army. The fact that it has never received the prize must be due to something more than better candidates being nominated by the committee every year. I think there have been two issues: an uncertainty as to how peace-creating the Salvation Army's work has really been in Nobel's sense of the concept, and the fact that their activities have largely focused on wealthier countries.

One year several representative of the Salvation Army attended the announcement of the prize. This was no coincidence. Stein Kåre Kristiansen, a journalist and son of committee member Kåre Kristiansen, had hinted strongly that the Salvation Army would receive the prize. Many people, those in the Salvation Army included, thought that he must have heard this from his father. I wanted to go over to them and tell them they could just go home. They did not deserve to be humiliated in this manner. But of course, I said nothing.

It became increasingly clear to the committee that the laureate had to be Aung San Suu Kyi. As stated in the committee's announcement on 14 October 1991, she received the prize for 'her non-violent struggle for democracy and human rights' in Burma. This struggle was 'one of the most extraordinary examples of civil courage in Asia in recent decades'. She spearheaded an important struggle in Burma, and she was also a major symbol in the fight against oppression in general. Giving the prize to her would hopefully also serve to encourage the many people all over the world 'fighting for democracy, human rights and ethnic autonomy by peaceful means'.

Suu Kyi was born in 1945. She was the daughter of the great Aung San, who had led the struggle for the independence of Burma. He was murdered by conservative political opponents in 1947 before the struggle for independence was won. His wife, Suu Kyi's mother, later became the Burmese ambassador in New Delhi. Their daughter had received an excellent education in her home country, in India, and in Oxford. She then worked for a while at the UN in New York. In 1972 she married Michael Aris, who eventually became a professor and an authority on Tibetan Buddhism. They had two children, Alexander and Kim. Suu Kyi was a visiting researcher in Kyoto in Japan, and worked on her doctoral thesis in London.

Suu Kyi did not initially seem to show much interest in Burmese politics, but during her studies and through other activities she became increasingly interested in Burma's history, her father's struggle for independence, Buddhism, and Gandhi's policy of non-violence. In one of her many letters to her husband Michael, she wrote: 'I only ask one thing; that should my people need me, you would help me do my duty by them.' When she travelled back to Burma in 1988 to care for her sick mother, Michael had 'a premonition that our lives would change forever'.

I met Michael many times, even after 1991. We had several interesting conversations. He had been well aware of his wife's commitment to Burma, but I think he was surprised by the immense force of will it later transpired she had. She had lived a quiet life as a researcher and professor's wife, kept busy by her husband, children, and studies.

The fear Michael expressed when Suu Kyi travelled back to Burma would prove to be well founded. The military regime that had controlled Burma since 1962 was in crisis in 1988. The old dictator, Ne Win, was forced to step aside, even though he was still a strong man. Demonstrations broke out. Many people lost their lives when the military shot into the crowds. Soon Suu Kyi was in the middle of what was referred to as Burma's 'second struggle for independence'. She was Aung San's daughter, and by virtue of her skills as a speaker and leader she soon emerged as leader of the opposition. Her mother died, but Suu Kyi remained in Burma. The regime grew scared of her rapidly increasing popularity and placed her under house arrest.

The military had promised to hold free elections to form a national assembly. These were held in 1990. It is unclear why the military kept its promise. They probably overestimated their own popularity and expected to win the elections. To be on the safe side, they refused to hold political meetings and forbade Suu Kyi from standing as a candidate. A major campaign was launched against her. She had spent most of her life abroad; she was allegedly fond of communists and married to a foreigner, etc. The huge number of parties standing would also make it difficult for the opposition to square up to those in power.

The military were wrong. Suu Kyi's party, the National League for Democracy (NLD), won 392 of 485 seats in the national assembly. The NLD also won victories around the country. The party even won a majority in many of the military towns. This gave rise to a hope that they would be able to overcome the major ethnic tensions that had plagued the country since it had gained its independence in 1948. But the military just ignored the election results. They remained in power. Apart from shorter periods of relative freedom, Aung San Suu Kyi would remain under house arrest, or at least closely monitored.

The election of Suu Kyi was well received both in Norway and in the rest of the world. Many people had noticed her heroic struggle. As early as in 1990 she received the Rafto Prize, a Norwegian human rights prize, and in 1991 the European Parliament's Sakharov Prize. Several countries had condemned the military regime. The first international sanctions were already in place.

Suu Kyi did not attend the award ceremony on 10 December. She could probably have travelled out of the country, but she was afraid that the military regime would simply refuse to let her return. She did not want to risk this. The committee was well aware of this difficulty and did not pressure her at all. We were pleased when she said that Norway would be the first country she visited when she felt the time was ripe.

Committee chair Francis Sejersted spoke about the laureate during the ceremony, as was customary. He went over her history and struggle. Michael Aris had been able to get her book, *Freedom from Fear*, published, and through this Francis was able to let her voice be heard. He also expressed a hope that Suu Kyi's struggle would be crowned with victory, before concluding by encouraging people to 'show humility and show fearlessness—like Aung San Suu Kyi. The result may be a better world to live in.'

We had flown two Burmese musicians in from Los Angeles. They played Suu Kyi's favourite piece. The absolute highlight of the ceremony was nevertheless when her son, Alexander, gave a short speech on behalf of his mother, which he had written with help from his father, Michael. Alexander stressed that the prize was not first and foremost a prize to his mother, but to the many people fighting for democracy in Burma under the most difficult conditions. He expressed a hope that even within the military there might be forces that would allow democracy to prevail. 'I know that within the military government there are those to whom the present policies of fear and repression are abhorrent, violating as they do the most sacred principles of Burma's Buddhist heritage.' This was 'a conviction my mother reached in the course of her dealings with those in positions of authority'. He concluded by expressing a hope that the Nobel Prize for 1991 would 'be seen as a historic step towards the achievement of true peace in Burma'.

We were not fully prepared for how touchy a subject the name of the laureate's homeland was. Was it Myanmar or Burma? In the announcement of the prize we had written Myanmar with Burma in parentheses. It should probably have been the other way around, with Myanmar in parentheses. It was the military junta that had renamed Burma Myanmar in 1989. Michael and others made it clear that this was a political issue. They had a point. The words meant the same, but Burma referred to the largest ethnic group in the country, the Burmese.

We also celebrated the 90th anniversary of the Peace Prize in 1991. Sixteen previous laureates had come to an anniversary symposium we arranged. Most of them represented organizations that had received the prize, but well-known names such as the Dalai Lama, Desmond Tutu, Elie Wiesel, and Oscar Arias were also present. Unfortunately, Willy Brandt and Linus Pauling had to send their regrets at the last minute. A large number of prominent academics also attended the symposium on new dimensions in international politics.

All of these people were present at the award ceremony. The laureate was represented by a large picture on the stage. From the stage, where I sat together with the members of the Nobel Committee, I could see two mothers, Queen Sonja and Prime Minister Gro Harlem Brundtland. They were in tears when Alexander spoke on behalf of his mother. As were we all.

There was no lack of strange moments. Michael Aris had a twin brother. He was also present in Oslo. They were very alike. Francis Sejersted talks about how he spotted Michael in the middle of the hall when people were coming in for the ceremony. It would have been difficult to direct him up onto the stage where he was to sit while everyone was still coming in. He despaired until he realized Michael was already up on stage. It had been his twin brother he had seen in the hall.

The year 1991 saw the introduction of dancing to the Nobel banquet. That was one of my ideas. The banquet was a celebration, so why not have dancing? I cannot say that the committee was wholly enthused by the idea. I suggested calling Michael to find out what he thought. Michael was in no doubt. Of course it was a festive occasion. So there was dancing. Many Burmese people had come to Oslo from all over the world to celebrate the prize. Many of these were present during the ceremony, but it was hopelessly difficult to accommodate them at the banquet. Then I found out we could invite 80 to 100 Burmese people for coffee and dancing after the banquet itself was over. The Burmese people really appreciated this gesture. Many of them were on the dance floor until the small hours. The dancing would prove a popular part of the festivities in years to come.

Alexander told me that Suu Kyi was interested in football. She even had a favourite team. I myself am very interested in football. My favourite English team has always been Wolverhampton Wanderers. This is simply because they were perhaps the best team in the mid-1950s, when I first became seriously interested in British football. I had stuck by them through good years and bad. Eventually they were mainly the latter. Excited, I asked Alexander which team was his mother's favourite. I was overjoyed when he said Wolverhampton. Like me, Suu Kyi was born in 1945. I only know two other Norwegians whose favourite team is Wolverhampton. They were also born in 1945. In 2015, Suu Kyi nevertheless modified this image of herself as a Wolverhampton supporter. She was a fan, but she had lived in the Chelsea area of London for a while and had grown fond of Chelsea Football Club as well.

Both Suu Kyi herself and Michael were inclined to give Vaclav Havel a large part of the credit for her receiving the prize in 1991. This came as a surprise to us. Havel had indeed nominated Suu Kyi for the prize, but so had several others. In any case, it did not really matter who had submitted the nominations. There were well-known people behind many of the nominations. What was most important was the committee members' considerations of the proposed candidates, not who had nominated them.

Suu Kyi decided that the prize money she had received, six million Swedish kronor, would be used to establish a foundation to help the Burmese people, and students in particular, with healthcare and education. She was unable to bring the money into Burma, and so a foundation was established in the United Kingdom. There were complicated rules for how the foundation's money was to be used. On one occasion, I had to travel to London together with Deputy Executive Director of the Nobel Foundation Åke Altcus to negotiate these rules. It was Suu Kyi's money, when all was said and done, and we could not accept any arrangement that said otherwise.

The many previous laureates present at the ceremony in 1991 signed an appeal to the authorities in Burma imploring them to release Suu Kyi. They also sent a message to the world about learning from her courage and hope, and taking 'advantage of the strongest of all powers as intrinsic to us as our own hearts, the power of compassion'. In the years that followed, there would be many such appeals to the Burmese authorities, without these seeming to help in the slightest.

It is always difficult to point out any specific effects of a Peace Prize. Nevertheless, there is no doubt that the Peace Prize for 1991 contributed to Suu Kyi and her cause becoming better known around the world. Even now the fact that she is a laureate is very often mentioned when her cause is discussed in the media. Perhaps her life was somewhat better protected in Burma by virtue of the Peace Prize, but when we consider how difficult things have been for her, it is doubtful whether this was the case. The authorities would hardly have dared kill the daughter of the great Aung San, even without the Peace Prize.

The sanction policy against Burma was initiated before Suu Kyi received the Peace Prize. Many countries had strongly condemned the government's disregard of the elections in 1990 and agreed that the elected national assembly had to be allowed to convene. The aim was for power to be transferred to a government elected by the people. Amnesty International produced reports on the situation in Burma, most bilateral aid programmes were stopped, and arms supplies from Western countries ceased. The British government committed itself on many levels, including a purely humanitarian one. Michael Aris, Alexander, and Kim were sometimes able to visit their mother, but this was becoming more difficult. It was particularly tragic that they were unable to visit Suu Kyi when Michael developed cancer and subsequently died in 1999 at the age of 53. She could have visited her dying husband in the United Kingdom, but once again declined this offer since she was afraid she would not be allowed to return to Burma.

Nevertheless, it was striking to see how the Peace Prize in 1991 contributed to the UN finally adopting a resolution against the regime in Burma. The Peace Prize probably also reinforced the isolation of the regime. The USA had a clear policy—in many American states the opposition to the military junta was surprisingly high on the political agenda. The same could not quite be said for the EU, where the boycott of Burma was not what it could have been. Japan was even more wary.

Burma's neighbours in the Association of South East Asian Nations (ASEAN) had no faith in the isolation of the country. In 1997 Burma was even included as a member of ASEAN. The country's economy was poor, but the export of narcotics, among other things, helped keep the regime going. The country also had oil and gas that tempted French oil companies in particular. Some of the governments in ASEAN tried to establish a dialogue with the regime about Suu Kyi's situation, but there were no lasting results. China was Burma's main supporter from both a military and an economic perspective. It came as more of a surprise that India gradually established closer and closer ties with the military regime. In the end many people doubted whether the sanction policy was the right course of action. Nevertheless, it was not possible to achieve any uniform response to the regime, even among the Western countries. However, Aung San Suu Kyi was in no doubt. She wanted to isolate the regime to thereby try to achieve a transition to democracy. The generals still did not really know how to treat this tiny woman. They could not kill her, and they did not dare release her.

In November 2010 Aung San Suu Kyi was finally released after being under house arrest for fifteen of the preceding twenty-one years. The military was facing major problems. The economy was in crisis, and the decline extensive. The country was largely isolated and had become dependent on China. The military eventually realized that reforms and contact with the outside world, particularly the West, would only be possible if they released Suu Kyi. Extensive liberalization followed, particularly of the economy, but partly also of the political system. Many prisoners were released. The media was able to operate more freely. Armistices were entered into with several of the ethnic minorities. A major dam project with China was suspended, a clear signal of changes to the country's contact with the outside world. During the elections in April 2012, Suu Kyi's party won an overwhelming majority for the limited number of seats in contention in the national assembly. The regime was forced to acknowledge her. There was no way out of it.

Aung San Suu Kyi had promised that Norway would be the first country she visited when the conditions were right for it. She wanted to give her thanks for both the Rafto Prize and the Nobel Peace Prize. After a stopover in Switzerland, she arrived in Norway in June 2012. She was a very popular guest. Around 10,000 people attended an event for her.

Of course, the prize itself had already been awarded in 1991. Only her Nobel lecture remained to be held. Committee chair Thorbjørn Jagland started his presentation speech as follows: 'We have been waiting for you for a very long time. However, we are well aware that your wait has been infinitely more trying for you and of an entirely different nature than ours. But please know this: in your isolation, you have become a moral leader for the whole world.' Aung San Suu Kyi gave her thanks for the Peace Prize. The prize had meant that she had not felt forgotten in those many difficult years. The Peace Prize 'had made me real once again; it had drawn me back into the wider human community. And what was more important, the Nobel Prize had drawn the attention of the world to the struggle for democracy and human rights in Burma. We were not going to be forgotten.' Many people in the West were extremely optimistic about further development in Burma. Aung San Suu Kyi was more cautious: 'There have been changes in a positive direction; steps towards democratization have been taken. If I advocate cautious optimism it is not because I do not have faith in the future but because I do not want to encourage blind faith.'

There were several interesting moments during Aung San Suu Kyi's short visit to Norway. As usual, there was the dispute with the Ministry of Foreign Affairs over who her true host was. The Ministry had also invited her. On her arrival, the Ministry gave priority to the Nobel Committee, not least because it transpired that Minister of Foreign Affairs Støre could not be present to receive her. Conversely, only Jagland and I from the Nobel Committee were invited to the government's dinner for her. Many people wanted to meet her. Former Prime Minister Kjell Magne Bondevik was keen to spend as much time with her as possible, even though she was really more in need of rest. She had collapsed in Switzerland, but still made it to Oslo. Suu Kyi was quite anxious before her Nobel lecture. She only weighed 48 kilos, ate little, and clearly needed to rest. Suu Kyi was treated like a leading politician and received enquiries from all over the world, but she only had a small staff. It could be quite difficult to get in touch with her.

Aung San Suu Kyi would have given herself to politics, but the Constitution had not been changed for it to be possible for her to stand in a presidential election. Presidents are not allowed to have been married to foreigners or to have foreign children. In any case it is the Parliament and not the people that elect the President—the military maintains control there.

Suu Kyi said little about her private life. There was no doubt that her long struggle had required her to make major sacrifices as far as her personal life was concerned. What was most important to the committee was that Aung San Suu Kyi came to Oslo twenty-one years after she had been awarded the Nobel Peace Prize. The Chinese must have had their thoughts on that. No laureate is forgotten. Although Liu Xiaobo will not be able to come to Oslo, his cause will not be forgotten.

After the election, Aung San Suu Kyi became the dominant civilian politician in the country. She nevertheless had to rule with the cooperation of the military in all matters related to defence. This certainly included the expulsion of hundreds of thousands of Rohingya people from Burma to Bangladesh. Her lack of response to this tragedy led to her international position being strongly criticized in Norway and in the West in general.

Nelson Mandela and Frederik Willem de Klerk (1993)

The 1993 prize to Nelson Mandela and Frederik Willem de Klerk might seem to be among the more obvious peace prizes. The Norwegian Nobel Committee had been very committed to the struggle against apartheid in South Africa. The 1960 prize had gone to ANC president Albert Lutuli. This was a clear and early indication of the opposition to South Africa's policy and had garnered international attention. The prize had also strengthened anti-apartheid work in Norway. In 1984, Archbishop Desmond Tutu received the Peace Prize.

However, the choice of laureate was far from obvious. Mandela had been considered for the prize several times, particularly in 1984 when Desmond Tutu received it. The reason why Tutu was chosen over Mandela was obvious. Tutu had a clear policy of non-violence, whereas Mandela had been the leader of the ANC's armed branch from 1961 until he was arrested the following year. He was certainly no spokesman for non-violence. This was the same reason why Amnesty International had not adopted Mandela as a prisoner of conscience. De Klerk had been an important defender of the regime for a couple of decades. When he was elected leader of the National Party in 1989, few people expected major changes.

The committee was deeply unsure as to who should receive the prize. There were 108 candidates. The Oslo I Accord was entered into between Israel and the Palestine Liberation Organization (PLO) in September 1993. This was very promising. The problem here was that none of the relevant candidates had been nominated when the deadline passed on 31 January.

The committee had been following developments in South Africa particularly closely since de Klerk surprised everyone by lifting the ban on the ANC and other anti-apartheid organizations in 1991, releasing Mandela and other political prisoners, and announcing negotiations for a new South Africa 'in which every inhabitant will enjoy equal rights, treatment and opportunity in every sphere of endeavour—constitutional, social, and economic'. This was a revolution. Several of the committee members and I had met Mandela during the major Anatomy of Hate conference in August 1990. Mandela had made a significant impression. He had spoken of reconciliation.

The thing was, it took time to draw up a new constitution and to hold new elections. There was a lot of tension, partly between the ANC and the National Party, partly internally on both sides. Mandela was challenged by those who were impatient and by the communists in his own party, and by the black nationalists in the Pan-African Parliament. De Klerk was under pressure from influential groups within the police and the security forces that had more or less run campaigns by themselves for a long time. There was even more tension within the organizations that were simply pushed aside, particularly within the Zulus' Inkatha Freedom Party. During the autumn of 1991, Mandela and de Klerk withdrew from the broadly composed negotiations and signed an agreement on a transitional regime behind the other organizations' backs. When the committee announced the Peace Prize on 15 October, however, elections were still to be held and no new constitution had been drawn up yet. An estimated 10,000–12,000 people lost their lives in various clashes in the years following 1989. This was not much like peace.

It was clear that the committee would have preferred to wait a bit longer before awarding another Peace Prize to South Africa. After two previous prizes, another prize would hopefully be the last for the struggle against apartheid. We might then be relatively sure that the struggle had actually come to an end. Despite all the uncertainly over the situation in 1993, there were three conditions that eventually led to Mandela and de Klerk being awarded the prize. The Nobel Peace Prize had achieved such an international position that it was almost impossible to avoid awarding any prize. Awarding the prize to non-political organizations was in many ways like withdrawing from a political world developing rapidly in a positive direction in both South Africa and in the Middle East.

Secondly, Mandela's speech at the UN in September 1993 made a great impression. Mandela now claiming that the situation in the country was irreversible was an important signal. He agreed that the economic sanctions should be lifted. The military sanctions should nevertheless continue until a new government was formed.

In the end, committee member Odvar Norli suggested that I contact Tutu to find out what he thought of the situation. I did. His view was clear: the time had come to award Mandela and de Klerk a joint prize. Tutu had also thought this the preceding year, when he had nominated them both for the prize and not Rigoberta Menchú. But we all seemed to have forgotten this. The archbishop's words therefore carried a lot of weight. I quickly wrote another advisory statement that might ensure a greater degree of certainty considering the committee had been so unsure of what to do for so long.

There was nevertheless a clear sense that the 1993 prize was not a prize for a completed act. A lot had been achieved, but the prize would also serve as encouragement to finalize the process that had come so far. This was made clear in the statement that the committee released in October. This praised Lutuli and Tutu for the work they had done to put an end to racial discrimination in South Africa. Mandela and de Klerk had taken this process a step further. The Nobel Peace Prize for 1993 was 'awarded in recognition of their efforts and as a pledge of support for the forces of good, in the hope that the advance towards equality and democracy will reach its goal in the very near future'

In his presentation speech on 10 December, Francis Sejersted addressed the issue head-on: should the committee have waited to award a prize 'until the definitive breakthrough of the policy of reconciliation?' He openly admitted that there was still a danger of setbacks. South Africa was still characterized by violence and bitterness. Mandela and de Klerk had made major contributions. 'They have given peace a chance.' Somewhat soberly, Sejersted nevertheless noted that 'whether peace will prevail, time will have to show.' During the Nobel days in Oslo in December, both Mandela and de Klerk kept restating that the committee, through its decision to award them the prize, had put additional pressure on them to ensure the abolition of apartheid and the introduction of democracy in South Africa.

The reactions to the prizes to Mandela and de Klerk were positive both in Norway and abroad. *The New York Times* wrote that the prize was both 'useful' and 'deserved', and would contribute to focusing attention on the positive changes in South Africa. This was a popular opinion. Many people on the left and among those who had been most active in the struggle against apartheid nevertheless objected to de Klerk. Would the great hero Mandela really have to share the prize with someone with a past as shadowy as de Klerk's? Mandela should receive the prize alone, and he should have received it long ago. However, most people understood the point of the joint prize. To acknowledge the reconciliation and cooperation between black and white, you could not only award the prize to Mandela alone.

Mandela and de Klerk agreed on the need to bring South Africa out of one era and into another. They had to cooperate to achieve this. But it was clear that their personal relationship varied. As the Nobel Committee stressed in its grounds for the prize, the two laureates had very different points of departure. In Oslo, their relationship was strained. They did not want to give a joint press conference, instead each holding their own. They were photographed together during a photo shoot at the Grand Hotel, but this was entirely without ceremony.

There was some discussion of how they should be treated in relation to each other. De Klerk was President. Of course, Mandela was president of the ANC, but where protocol was concerned, he was to be considered a private individual. We cooperated closely with the Ministry of Foreign Affairs' protocol department during the Nobel days. It is nice to have help placing the many people who are very interested in where they will sit. Even so, sometimes there had to be deviations from national protocol and the protocol that we on the Nobel side of things followed. This was such an example. It was no coincidence that Mandela was named first in the committee's grounds for the prize. This meant that he would receive the prize first, speak first, etc. This was met with some resistance from governmental quarters, but it was our event, so we would be the ones making such decisions. We nevertheless let de Klerk speak first at the banquet. When they both travelled to Stockholm after the visit to Oslo, the Swedes placed de Klerk in the government guesthouse and Mandela in a hotel. We received reports that Mandela had really not liked this. The following year, Mandela became President. In his memoirs, de Klerk also wrote that Stockholm had 'a much more sophisticated city atmosphere' than Oslo.

We were all filled with admiration for Mandela. It is just amazing that a person can spend twenty-seven years in prison and then, when he is released, decide to focus exclusively on the future. The country needed building. The oppressors and the oppressed, all races had to cooperate for the common good. That was just how it had to be. In private conversations I tried several times to challenge Mandela. It was almost superhuman for a person to behave in such a way. He was entirely consistent. It was incredibly impressive. There are not many people in the world who have behaved so constructively after such a life. That is also why Mandela has achieved the wholly unique status he has.

His years in prison had of course taken their toll. Mandela was 75 in 1993. He had some trouble walking and did not hear very well either. He suffered from back pain and received physiotherapy during his stay in Oslo. His staff tried to limit the official programme, and Mandela always withdrew as soon as he could. It was also clear that he did not like the Norwegian winter.

He needed warmth and looked forward to his trip to West India after his visit in Scandinavia was over. Some of his employees had a particularly strained relationship with snow. They had never seen the like before. Was it dangerous for it to land on you? A couple of them did their utmost to prevent any snowflakes from landing on Mandela. They did not quite succeed.

Mandela was not particularly keen on prizes either. As he wrote in his memoirs: 'A man does not become a freedom fighter in the hope of winning awards.' He was nevertheless happy and excited to be receiving the Nobel Peace Prize. He probably had his doubts about de Klerk's qualifications, but realized the point of them receiving the prize together. In his characteristic style, he wrote: 'If you want to make peace with your enemy, you have to work with your enemy. Then he becomes your partner.' He respected the Peace Prize because the prizes to Lutuli and Tutu clearly demonstrated what side the Norwegian Nobel Committee were on in the struggle against apartheid. He also appreciated Norway and Sweden's political and eco-nomic contributions to the fight for freedom. Still, as mentioned, he never developed quite the same close relationship with Norway that Tutu did.

I was tasked with ensuring that the Nobel Committee received the best possible information about the candidates for the Peace Prize. This could also include information on their personalities. There is one laureate I was really wrong about, not in terms of my political analysis, but in my comments on their personality. That was de Klerk. I learned that there is an expression in Afrikaans, verkrampfet, which means locked, rigid. I was convinced that de Klerk would be like this. This proved to be incorrect, at least during his days in Oslo. The man was very open, particularly in more private contexts. He laughed and he cried. He was easy to relate to.

But through this openness, de Klerk also revealed that he had simply failed to unite the old and the new in his analysis of South Africa. Through his actions, de Klerk abolished apartheid, but he had great difficulty distancing himself morally from this past. He did not like to be confronted with his personal and his family's long-term support for apartheid.

Mandela was joined by his daughter, Zindzi, and de Klerk by his wife, Marike, at the more intimate dinner on the evening of 9 December. While Mandela could be quite reserved, de Klerk chatted away. Perhaps it is partly because he spoke so much that Mandela was so quiet. It was de Klerk who answered many questions on various conditions in the South African society. Mandela let him. De Klerk wrote that the dinner 'was lovely and our hosts were polite and considerate'. It was a nice testimonial to receive, but he added that 'the atmosphere was very stiff—particularly for Mandela's part'.

Mandela and de Klerk's speeches during the award ceremony itself were relatively brief. Mandela called the prize 'a great step forward in history' that 'must be measured by the happiness and welfare of the children, [...] the greatest of our treasures'. He was generous where de Klerk was concerned: 'He had the courage to admit that a terrible wrong had been done to our country and people through the imposition of the system of apartheid.' He praised the prizes to Lutuli and Tutu. Somewhat surprisingly, he also praised the prize to Martin Luther King and strongly appealed to the Burmese authorities to release Aung San Suu Kyi.

De Klerk mentioned Mandela several times, but most often in contexts where it was 'Mandela and I' having done this or that, or should do this or that. He was not prepared to give Mandela any real precedence. To de Klerk they were entirely on a level. In his speech, Francis Sejersted had openly asked to which degree the abolition of apartheid was due to 'a strategic adjustment to a situation characterized by internal dissolution or the fruits of moral reflection'. This was a question that only those individuals could answer. De Klerk came closest to answering it in his speech when he said that this was the result of 'a fundamental change of heart', not something sudden, but a product of a process of 'introspection, of soul searching; of repentance; of realization of the futility of ongoing conflict, of acknowledgement of failed policies and the injustice it brought with it'. He also read a poem in Afrikaans to his voters in South Africa about how the country should be lifted into a future of 'real and lasting peace'.

The visit to Oslo had its major ups and downs for de Klerk. He cried openly after the ceremony. This had been a big deal for him. You could tell straight away by looking at his face. And if you were in any doubt, he expressed his immediate reactions to this and that. The Peace Prize brought him international acceptance. Now he could travel wherever he wanted in the world. 'The world's most prestigious prize' opened all doors. On his way to Oslo he met Queen Elizabeth. He writes in his memoirs that this was 'the ultimate recognition that my party and my people, the Afrikaners, are now finally part of the solution to our country's complex problem after so many years of isolation'.

De Klerk did not understand the extent to which his past limited the enthusiasm with which he was received. Both he and his employees were upset about Francis Sejersted's Nobel speech. It had been too biased in favour of Mandela. Sejersted had talked about their different points of departure. One represented the oppressed, the other the oppressors. In his memoirs, de Klerk writes that Sejersted was 'overwhelming in his praise of Nelson Mandela, but cautious when he referred to me'. De Klerk did not realize that most people in Norway had considered the apartheid regime one of the most abominable things on Earth. De Klerk had represented this regime for ten years. His repentance was still quite recent. Many people were waiting for him to apologize unreservedly for his involvement. He never did.

Things were even worse during the traditional torchlight procession in honour of the laureates before the Nobel banquet on 10 December. De Klerk was in an exuberant mood. Most of the people in the torchlight procession were of course admirers of Mandela, and many of them had no admiration whatsoever left over for de Klerk. However, the President was so excited that before I knew it he was standing on the balcony, alone, to receive the people's tribute. He was met by fury and protest. Then when Mandela came out, the crowd applauded. ANC slogans were shouted, fists were clenched in the spirit of the ANC. Some people even shouted 'De Klerk go home' and 'Kill the farmer, kill the Boer.' De Klerk was crushed. It took him a long time to recover from that.

In his memoirs, de Klerk writes that 'our Norwegian hosts were charming, but clearly in favour of the ANC.' Both Sejersted and I had tried to prepare de Klerk for the way in which he would be received. A few months previously it would quite simply have been impossible for de Klerk to visit Norway. Now he would receive the Peace Prize. However, this did not erase his past. De Klerk thought that abolishing apartheid would mean everyone forgot his past.

The timing of the prize would nevertheless turn out to be excellent. The committee quickly realized, to its great delight, that it had struck gold. Mandela and de Klerk were close to achieving their goal, but not quite there yet. Therefore, the prize might give the impression that we knew something others did not yet. Most people know what happened next. In 1994, general elections were held in South Africa. During the elections for the constituent assembly, the ANC received 62 per cent of the votes, the National Party 20 per cent, and the Zulus' Inkatha Freedom Party 10 per cent. Mandela was elected President. He quickly became the national patriarch able to unite almost everyone.

When the committee met early the following year, it congratulated itself that everything had gone so well the year before. However, 1994 would not be as easy.

Yasser Arafat, Shimon Peres, and Yitzhak Rabin (1994)

It was with clear reluctance that the committee looked once again to the Middle East. In 1978, the Peace Prize had been awarded to Anwar Sadat and Menachem Begin. Sadat did not attend the award ceremony. This was a shame, since he was the one who had sped up the peace process through his trip to Jerusalem in November 1977. Begin came, but it was a little strange having him standing there alone like the prince of peace. Jimmy Carter, who was largely responsible for the Camp David Accords, was not included among the laureates. The ceremony was held at Akershus Fortress due to strict security measures.

The Camp David Accords had indeed resulted in peace between Israel and Egypt. This was quite an achievement. But it had not resolved the conflict with the Palestinians. It gradually became clear that this was at the heart of the difficulties between Israel and its neighbours. War and conflict were still an everyday reality in the Middle East. But on 20 August 1993 a temporary agreement was signed between Israel and the PLO in Oslo. On 13 September it was formally entered into on the lawn in front of the White House in Washington, DC. The Oslo I Accord, as it was called, was to secure mutual recognition between the two parties. It also paved the way for a peace treaty between Israel and Jordan. The accord gave the Palestinians limited autonomy. Initially restricted to the Gaza Strip and Jericho on the West Bank, this autonomy would later be expanded to include the West Bank. The Israeli settlements would still be under Israeli control. Jerusalem's status, and many other issues, would be determined in a future peace treaty. Mutual recognition aside, the Oslo I Accord was primarily a framework for further negotiations.

The restrictions in the accord would become increasingly clear, but, as the Nobel Committee said in its statement in October: 'By concluding the Oslo Accords, and subsequently following them up, Arafat, Peres and Rabin have made substantial contributions to a historic process through which peace and cooperation can replace war and hate.'

But it was not at all clear which of the many people who had been involved in the Oslo I Accord would receive the prize. There were two main options: awarding it to either the experts who had actually negotiated the accord or to the politicians who had of course made the key decisions that had led to the accord. The former were first and foremost director-general Uri Savir on the Israeli side, chief negotiator Abu Alaa on the Palestinian side, and director and subsequent ambassador Terje Rød-Larsen on the Norwegian side. A significant objection to this option was that the person who was perhaps most important of all, Yossi Beilin, had not been nominated and was therefore excluded.

There were also arguments both for and against including a Norwegian. Even though Rød-Larsen had never presented specific proposals during the process, he had passionately encouraged the parties to never give up. The entire process was of course politically controlled from Norwegian, Israeli, and Palestinian quarters. Even Rød-Larsen received his mandate from Minister of Foreign Affairs Thorvald Stoltenberg.

After long discussions, the committee decided to award the prize to the key politicians. These were the people who had taken the majority of the personal and political risk inherent in any peace treaty in the Middle East. The experts had done a great job, but there was less personal or political risk associated with their work. Without the politicians there would not have been any process or accord. You might never know who did the groundwork, but there is no doubting who the politicians were. On the other hand, a prize to the experts could have unified the committee. Nevertheless, they eventually settled on the politicians. This was the result for which I personally had hoped.

Nobel's will states that the prize should be awarded to the person who had worked hardest to achieve peace 'during the preceding year'. This was a point that the committees over the years had had trouble taking literally. It is inevitable that they will look back further than just the preceding year. But in 1994 only considering the preceding year worked well. The prize was primarily awarded for work performed in 1993 and thereafter. If you looked further back in time, the careers of all three laureates had clearly doubtful aspects. Arafat had long been linked to terrorism, although it was unclear what his specific role had been. Rabin had fought to oust the British and could therefore be said to have a past with certain links to terrorism. He had been commander of the Israeli forces during the Six-Day War in 1967. In that instance Israel had been the attacker, at least formally. Peres, seemingly the most 'peaceful' of the three, was known as 'the father of the Israeli Bomb'. But they would not be receiving the prize for their pasts. They would be receiving it because they had been in a position to exceed their pasts. Such considerations are always difficult.

Despite reports in the newspaper *Aftenposten* that the committee had originally settled on Rabin and Arafat, and that Peres had been added at the last minute, it was always agreed that both Rabin and Peres should be included on the Israeli side. Peres was deemed the visionary, the person who most desired peace with the Palestinians. He needed to be included. But if he had not had support from Rabin, there would not have been any accord. It was Rabin who had the necessary political influence. In his memoirs, Peres writes that 'together we drew up the directives for the Israeli delegation' in Oslo.

Of course, Arafat had to be included on the Palestinian side. Nothing happened in the PLO without his involvement. The committee had probably intended to include an additional Palestinian initially. This would have been Abu Mazen, second-in-command in the PLO. However, two conditions contributed to it only being Arafat. The statutes make it clear that there can be no more than three laureates. The Nobel Foundation in Stockholm stressed that this provision should be taken literally. Secondly, the committee thought that the political realities of the Palestinian side were such that they could justify only choosing Arafat. To make up for this, Arafat was mentioned first in the grounds for the award, though luckily he also came first alphabetically. Would Arafat receive half of the prize and the other two share the other half? This was not a popular idea. The prize ended up being split equally between all three laureates.

Should we have waited before awarding a prize for actions in the Middle East considering how fragile the peace was? In light of what happened afterwards, this argument is obviously strong. Nevertheless, the Oslo I Accord was an important agreement in itself. Of course, the candidates already had to have achieved something to be able to receive the Peace Prize. Arafat, Peres, and Rabin had achieved the Oslo I Accord. In this area, peace was not something that one established once and for all. It had to be re-established again and again. If we were to wait until the problems were 'finally' solved, there would most likely never be any Peace Prize for treaties in the Middle East.

The fact that the Oslo I Accord was entered into in Oslo with Norwegian aides was certainly also something that pushed the committee in a positive direction. When it came to such a high-profile prize, the party leaders were undoubtedly consulted. As I have already mentioned, it is the Norwegian Parliament that appoints the committee members. Most of them are ex-politicians, who do not violate their political ties even if they become members of the committee. Some of the members have probably spoken to political allies whom they trust on occasion. This happened in 1994. The committee also had support from international consultants. The leading expert, William B. Quandt, concluded that the chance of a lasting solution to the problem of the relationship between the Israelis and the Palestinians was only 60 per cent.

The prize announcement was coloured by Kåre Kristiansen disagreeing with the decision to award the Peace Prize to these three people. Kristiansen was Likud's leading spokesman in Norway, so his position was not surprising. He was entirely against awarding the prize to Arafat. He was actually sceptical of Rabin and Peres as well, but downplayed this. Kristiansen had thought that all the committee members had to support a decision and therefore that he had power of veto. The four other members agreed in principle that consensus was desirable, but did not think that this meant each individual member had the power to veto the decision. This would have quickly rendered the prize spineless. Members had withdrawn from the committee before as well, in connection with the prizes in 1935 and 1973.

Kåre Kristiansen was having issues in 1994. He sometimes forgot committee meetings. Sometimes he was also somewhat absent even when physically present. He might suddenly start reading newspapers. He complained constantly that statements of support for 'his' candidates were not being submitted to the committee. If statements of support were to be submitted, this had to be for all candidates, not only those he supported. He never accepted this reasoning, but it has to be said that he handled all the attention over his own departure impressively.

The interest from the media was enormous, even greater than I had anticipated. Although everyone knew he would leave the committee if the three politicians were chosen, not everyone was prepared for Kristiansen to receive so much of the attention. The media loved disagreement within the committee. Kristiansen had spoken warmly about Israel, and against Arafat, for several decades. Now all he had to do was restate all his old opinions. He enjoyed all the attention from the right wing in Israel. I asked him several times whether he had any scruples about being groomed by such irreconcilable powers. He saw no problem with this. After Kristiansen's departure, it was not as easy to invite him to the annual Nobel events. But after a couple years of quarantine I decided that he should once again be invited, as other former committee members were. This decision was difficult, particularly for Hanna Kvanmo, but he was invited.

Kåre Kristiansen was probably behind a tip-off to Harald Stanghelle at *Aftenposten* that Arafat and Rabin would receive the Peace Prize. He was the only one who did not think that Peres would be included. I never figured out how he had come to that conclusion—it had no basis in the committee meetings. Throughout the entire process all three of them were given equal consideration, and Peres was definitely not only included after Kristiansen left the decisive committee meeting. Getting it two-thirds right was nevertheless considered a major accomplishment in press circles. Many years later, in connection with Terje Rød-Larsen receiving a prize from the Peres Foundation, Carl I. Hagen of the Progress Party publicly claimed that this was a reward for Rød-Larsen ensuring that Peres was included in 1994. That was when I called in Inger-Marie Ytterhorn from the Progress Party, who joined the committee in 2000, and showed her the documents from 1994. They showed clearly that Peres had always been included, and on equal footing with the others.

The reactions to the prize to Arafat, Peres, and Rabin were largely positive, not just among the Norwegian public, whose reaction was very important to many of the committee members, but also around the world. Not just the Norwegian Nobel Committee but also large parts of the world hoped the Oslo I Accord would put an end to the conflicts between the Israelis and the Palestinians.

However, the problems started as soon as the prize was announced. An Israeli soldier, Nachshon Wachsman, had just been kidnapped by Hamas. They demanded that around 200 Arab prisoners be released. Israeli forces found out where Wachsman was being held, and the Israelis stormed the hideaway. The hostage-takers were killed, but so was Wachsman and another Israeli soldier. We received enquiries from the Israelis demanding that the committee express unease over what had happened when making its announcement. Otherwise the announcement would be overshadowed by the sad event. Committee chair Sejersted said a few words after the announcement itself was made. This was awkward, both because of what had happened, but also because of the pressure on the committee.

I have many strong memories from the Nobel events in 1994. The ceremony, which is normally held at 1 p.m., had to be put off until 5 p.m. since it was the Sabbath. The security arrangements were extensive, with hundreds of police officers on the ground and on rooftops, with helicopters hovering in the air. When I walked together with Rabin and Peres up main street Karl Johans Gate to the audience at the palace, I encouraged them to make a small detour to greet some of the many people lining the way. They both had to abstain from using cars on the Sabbath. I should not have done this. When the police saw movement behind the crowds, they suddenly formed an iron ring around them both.

There were also several unpleasant episodes. An irreconcilable rabbi insisted on handing me a casket of bombs made from black balloons. I took it and said it would be displayed as a symbol of implacability in connection with prizes being awarded at the planned Peace Centre. However, nothing ever came of this.

Yitzhak Rabin was undoubtedly the one of the three who made the strongest impression. He dominated the small dinner. He was in an outstandingly good mood, talked a lot, and was humorous and concise. It was clear who ran the show on the Israeli side. Peres played second fiddle, even though their relationship was good. Israeli journalists told me it had been a long time since they had got along so well. In his memoirs, Rabin described Peres as an 'incorrigible intrigant'. The only person able to rein Rabin in a bit was his wife, Leah. When he became too rambunctious, she would interject with a comment that subdued him. Arafat did not say much. Even though this might have been due to his lack of good English, it worried me. However, those who knew Arafat and who were present at the Grand Hotel reassured me. He did not usually say much when he was not the centre of attention.

Rabin also gave the most impressive Nobel speech. He talked about the two great silences. The first came after a decision on war was made: 'the hush as senior officers or cabinet ministers slowly rise from their seats; the sight of their receding backs; the sound of the closing door; and then the silence in which I remain alone.' The second is the silence immediately before an attack is made: 'the hush when the hands of the clock seem to be spinning forward, when time is running out and in another hour, another minute, the inferno will erupt.'

I have never witnessed mood swings like Rabin's. At that intimate dinner he was in an incredibly good mood. The next day, at the Nobel banquet in the evening, he had had enough. There had been far too much talk of peace. He gave an almost warlike speech at the table. Many of us had to intervene to stop Arafat giving an equally warlike speech in return. We managed.

One moment Rabin would be gushing at you, then suddenly he would completely ignore you.

Chaos seemed to hound Rabin. While receiving his diploma and medal at the ceremony, his medal fell out of its case. Rabin was pictured running after the rolling medal in many newspapers. This led to the introduction of double-sided tape at the Nobel ceremony. During the Nobel Concert he was not aware that he needed to be on the stage, and then he was hit on the head by the curtain when it was all over. Nevertheless, the overall impression must have been positive. Leah Rabin writes in her memoirs that: 'the programme was brilliantly executed by the Norwegians from start to finish.' Rabin is also the only laureate to have requested a new copy of his diploma. He hung his diploma in his office, where a particularly thorough cleaning lady used a wet cloth to wipe the inside of the diploma. This made the ink run. The artist, Anne Lise Knoff, had to make a new one.

The menu was also quite special during the Nobel days that year. We asked the vanguard what the three men could eat. What one of them could eat proved unsuitable for another. We decided to serve fish for all the meals, and we tried to make sure that it was deboned in advance. When the government arranged a lunch for the laureates at Akershus, they left it to the dinner guests to debone their own salmon, despite our advice. Many of the main courses were barely touched.

What struck me during the Nobel days was how easy the conversation was between the three laureates when they were in the right mood. I had thought a lot about what we would do if the atmosphere was strained. I need not have worried. They had a lot to talk about, even conducting negotiations between themselves during the days in Oslo in order to forward the peace process.

The easiest to relate to was undoubtedly Shimon Peres. He was very pleased to be receiving the Peace Prize. I asked Peres why there had been a shift from Swedish to Norwegian mediators in the run-up to the Oslo process. His clear answer was that Sweden was too pro-Palestine to play the role that Norway later did. Israel had more confidence in Norway than it did in Sweden. Peres was always pleasant, even when I met him later on, most recently at an event at the Nobel Institute in 2014.

It was not easy to get a handle on Arafat. He did not say much, and when he did, he often repeated himself. I cannot say how often he referred to 'the peace of the brave'. He nevertheless had answers prepared for direct questions. When he was asked how having a son would affect his political work, he said he knew many politicians who had become fathers without this affecting their work that much. Arafat followed what was going on carefully. During the rehearsal the day before the actual ceremony, I instructed the laureates carefully on where they should sit and stand at any given time. Arafat grasped all the details. Committee member and former Prime Minister Odvar Nordli always told me that Arafat was my best student.

In his Nobel speech, Arafat was aware that they had not received the prize 'to crown an achievement'. Something had been achieved, but the prize was first and foremost 'an encouragement to pursue a route with greater steps and deeper awareness, with truer intentions so that we may transform the peace option, the peace of the brave, from words into practice and reality'.

When I came to his suite at the Grand Hotel to collect him for the Nobel banquet, Arafat and a large part of the leadership of the PLO were sitting watching a Tom and Jerry cartoon. It was made clear that they wanted to watch it to the end. It was something of a situation. The cartoon went on and on. Then his wife, Suha, made it clear to me that the only way to get them moving was to state clearly that we simply had to leave to make the banquet in time. That helped.

Suha was an interesting woman. She was a lot younger than Arafat and mostly lived in Paris. It was clear that she had lavish habits. She mostly kept to herself, but spoke well when she had the occasion to. When the laureates visit the committee room at the Nobel Institute, I always ask whether they like their portraits that hang on the wall in there. The answer is usually yes, since it is usually chosen by them or one of their secretaries. Arafat said nothing, but Suha was not keen. She wanted a picture in which her husband was smiling and said she would send us another. She did. That is why Arafat is smiling in the picture that now hangs on the wall.

The day after the ceremony, Arafat suddenly found out that he needed to travel on to Helsinki. A plane had to be found at short notice to make this possible. Arafat left all such arrangements to others. This meant that he did not attend the Nobel Concert. Suha took his place next to Rabin and Peres. After the concert some of us ate dinner with Suha. During this she really opened up, telling us stories and handing out gifts.

The opposition to the Oslo I Accord had been significant on both sides from the start, and it gradually increased as more and more violent episodes took place and no political progress was made. The assassination of Rabin in November 1995 was fatal to this process. Rabin had been guarantor for

Israel's security during the peace process. Now he had been killed by a Jewish extremist. The opposition to a compromise was increasing; the two remaining laureates, Arafat and Peres, distanced themselves from each other. The situation went from bad to worse.

The many critics of the prize in 1994 deemed this proof of our missing the mark. Requests that we take back the prize from one or the other came in from several quarters. At times the pressure to revoke Arafat's prize in particular has been great. The formal response is easy. A prize cannot be revoked. Luckily. That is how it should be. The committee needs to stand by its decision. It would be difficult if all the laureates were to be continuously assessed even after receiving the prize.

It is not difficult to understand the criticism. It would undoubtedly have been best if the Oslo I Accord had developed into a successful peace process. This proved impossible. I am nevertheless prepared to defend the award in 1994 at all times. The three laureates risked their personal lives and political careers for a compromise in the most difficult of all international issues, the relationship between the Israelis and the Palestinians, two peoples who both have major demands on the same territory. Rabin paid for it with his life. The opposition to further concessions was so great that the peace process came to a standstill. But there is no military solution to the problems. Sooner or later a political compromise will have to be made. This will not be easy. Many people will lose if a compromise is made, but there is no other solution. Arafat, Peres, and Rabin tried. That in itself was a heroic deed. It would have been best if they had succeeded. But the opposition to the award also served to emphasize how heroic their attempt to create peace really was.

Kim Dae-jung (2000)

Of the many people who received the Nobel Peace Prize in the years 1900 to 2014, Kim Dae-jung was probably the most delighted, though Jimmy Carter and Muhammad Yunus were close on his heels in this regard. I am told that Elie Wiesel was also very happy to receive the prize.

Kim Dae-jung worked hard for many years in the hope of receiving the prize. When he was finally awarded it in 2000, it was a dream come true for him. Despite usually being quite restrained, when he heard the news he smiled almost from ear to ear. When the Peace Prize celebrated its centenary in 2001, it was with great pleasure that he returned to Oslo. We were told that he had arranged a couple of state visits in Europe to conceal the real reason for his trip to Oslo: to celebrate the prize's centenary. He also returned to Norway later. He liked it there.

The road to the prize in 2000 had been long and difficult. Kim was born in 1925 to a Korean middle-class family. He studied economics at upper secondary school and at university, and earned good money in the business sector. During the Korean War he was captured by the North Koreans, but escaped. After two unsuccessful attempts, he was elected to the National Assembly in 1961. Three days after the elections, there was a military coup. The National Assembly was dissolved and General Park Chung-hee took power. And on and on it went. Time and time again he stood for election, but he was always impeded by the military. In 1971, he ran for President. He received 46 per cent of the votes, but lost to General Park, who had changed the Constitution so that he could serve a third term. At least five attempts were made on Kim's life. During one of them, a lorry drove into his car. Kim was seriously injured, as were his two aides. He survived, but had trouble walking for the rest of his life.

Park decided he should be able to serve for as long as he liked. Kim Dae-jung was his main opponent. In 1973, Kim was kidnapped from a hotel in Tokyo by agents from the Korean intelligence agency. He was taken out to sea, where concrete blocks were tied to his body and he was about to be thrown overboard. Kim is happy to tell people that this is when he beheld God in a flash of light. God intervened and saved his life, but God was undoubtedly assisted by the CIA, which had been informed of what was happening. The Koreans gave up. Kim was put under house arrest and subsequently imprisoned. After Park was assassinated in October 1979, Kim was released, but a new military regime followed. He was initially sentenced to death before the judgment was commuted to life imprisonment and then to twenty years in prison. However, he was granted permission to travel to the USA in 1982. He spent much of his time there at the Center of International Affairs at Harvard, where he was a fellow. I was also there during the spring semester of 1983. We all knew about his struggle for democracy and human rights, but it was not easy to communicate with Kim. His English was not very good.

Kim returned to Korea in 1985. In 1987, all charges against him were dropped. He ran for President during the elections in 1987 and 1992, but lost both times. In 1992, he announced he was done with politics. He with-drew 'to continue the study of moral and political principles', as he put it, but changed his mind, and in December 1997 he was finally elected President of South Korea. He only received 40.3 per cent of the votes, but won because his opposition was divided. This was the first time that a South Korean President had come from Jeolla, the south-western part of the country. There is a prominent regional divide in the country, and Kim came under fire more or less from day one of his presidency. The political climate was toxic. In 1997, the country suffered a severe financial crisis, as did most East Asian countries, which of course also had an impact on the new President.

Kim started focusing on the Nobel Peace Prize as early as during the 1980s. His struggle for democracy and human rights was in many ways very impressive. He definitely suffered for his conviction. When he was elected President in 1997, this was South Korea's definitive breakthrough as a democracy after a period of liberalization in the 1990s. The opposition and the military accepted each other, even though the climate was still poor. This was a signal that the rapid economic growth that had taken place under General Park would sooner or later lead to democracy. In 1960 South Korea had a standard of living on a par with Ghana's. At the turn of the century, the country had finally achieved a standard of living on a par with many countries in Southern Europe. After Kim Dae-jung was elected, democracy was consolidated in the country, although the political and regional polar-ization is still dramatic.

Many people have referred to Kim Dae-jung as 'Asia's Mandela'. He publicly pardoned President Park, the man who had kept him locked up and who had even tried to kill him. Kim demonstrated a significant com-mitment to democracy outside of South Korea as well. He rejected the theory of 'Asian values' that was popular in some circles and that was apparently at odds with human rights in the West. For a long time, Singapore's Lee Kuan Yew was the foremost spokesman for this perspective. Instead, Kim Dae-jung emphasized the democratic foundation found in many Asian cultures. He often quoted Mencius, a disciple of Confucius: 'The king is son of heaven. Heaven sent him to serve the people with just rule. If he fails and oppresses the people, the people have the right, on behalf of heaven, to dispose of him.' Similar ideas existed in both Buddhism and Hinduism for centuries or even millennia before Western notions of democracy started to gain ground. Kim considered the notion of 'Asian values' an attempt by more or less authoritarian rulers to undermine elections and other mechanisms that might threaten their own position.

Kim Dae-jung also supported the criticism of the regime in Burma and the fight for independence in East Timor. Considering the Peace Prize had been awarded to laureates from both of these countries, in 1991 and in 1996, this of course made an impression on the Nobel Committee. However, his democratic record was not entirely flawless. There were still political prisoners in South Korea while he was President, and workers' rights were inadequate. These were points that committee chair Gunnar Berge also mentioned in his presentation of Kim Dae-jung. Several Norwegian trade unions contacted the committee to point out the inadequate rights of workers in South Korea.

There were two main reasons why Kim Dae-jung received the Peace Prize: his long and persistent commitment to democracy and human rights, and his 'Sunshine Policy' as regards North Korea. It was the latter that bumped Kim up from being one among many good candidates to being *the* candidate. He wanted to forge a closer relationship with North Korea, a relationship that might contribute to unifying the Korean peninsula in the long term. After becoming President in 1998, he quickly set to work on this. His policy was most reminiscent of Willy Brandt's *Ostpolitik*, though the South Koreans feared the enormous cost that any unification might involve. In 1998, Kim said: 'We are all aware of the political, economic and psychological problems that both the West German and the East German people faced after West Germany absorbed the DDR. I cannot even imagine what difficulties we might encounter if we tried to undermine and annex North Korea.'

The unification had to take place gradually and willingly. North Korea was hesitant. Was this a refined attempt to undermine the regime? Then they relented. The highlight was the summit in Pyongyang in June 2000 with North Korean leader Kim Jong-il. The summit was a triumph for Kim Dae-jung. He had been a candidate for the Peace Prize for many years. It was no coincidence that he received the Peace Prize the year the summit took place.

However, the summit was not well organized. No one expected a peace treaty between the two countries. There was no proper agenda in terms of what would be discussed. Nevertheless, it would seem the summit was a success. Kim Jong-il spoke of a 'dialogue without reservations', while Kim Dae-jung declared that he had come to Pyongyang in the hope that this would help release 70 million people from fear of war. The fact that the two leaders met at all after decades of complete isolation was sensational in itself.

They agreed on an exchange programme for family members who had had absolute minimum contact since the Korean War. Trade and investments were also to be stepped up. North Korea did not have much to export, so this mostly related to goods and investments from South Korea to North Korea. Communication was to be strengthened. It was decided that Kim Jong-il would visit Seoul, even though no date was set. The summit promoted better Western contact with North Korea. As a result of this, US Foreign Secretary Madeleine Albright visited the country in October 2000. Bill Clinton also wanted to visit.

Kim Jong-il never visited Seoul. Clinton never visited North Korea. Railway stations were built, but no trains ran between the North and South. The investments were more modest than expected and carefully regulated by North Korea. Several rounds of family reunions took place, but the participants from the North were politically handpicked, and every measure was taken to prevent defection. Extensive humanitarian aid was sent from the South to the North.

Of course, there was never any discussion of the dictatorship in the North receiving any Peace Prize. It was and is brutal and impoverishing. Hundreds of thousands have died due to a flawed economic policy. Kim Jong-il blamed 'bureaucrats' for how wrong it has all gone. The regime in the North had to content itself with a brief mention in the announcement from the Nobel Committee that it wished 'to express its recognition of the contributions made by North Korea's and other countries' leaders to advance reconciliation and possible reunification on the Korean peninsula'.

Everyone was aware that the relationship between the two countries still left much to be desired. They had still not even made peace following the Korean War. Kim Dae-jung's formula was 'one people, two systems, two independent governments' in a kind of federation. North Korea even suggested a 'loose form of federation'. The Nobel Committee nevertheless cautiously noted that 'there may now be hope that the Cold War will also come to an end in Korea.' Committee chair Berge noted 'nothing ventured, nothing gained'. Unification might take time, but: 'The world may see the sunshine policy thawing the last remnants of the Cold War on the Korean peninsula.'

The Sunshine Policy was popular for a long time in South Korea. It provided relief and hope for better results later. Kim Dae-jung was considered a hero in many countries. However, his popularity was on the wane in South Korea itself. The recession had a negative effect even though the country recovered quickly after the Asian financial crisis. Regional polarization remained troublesome. There were many allegations that Kim favoured his own home province, even though these later proved to be exaggerated. The amount of travelling he did was unpopular. A majority were actually against him travelling to Oslo to receive the Peace Prize.

Kim came to Oslo in a jumbo jet full of friends, colleagues, and members of the press. We had heard a lot about how unsteady he was on his feet and wondered how he would get down the steps from the plane. He managed it surprisingly well. He descended without much need for help. That solved the biggest practical challenge of his visit. He could walk the few steps required at the various events. He was more interested in making sure it was warm enough in the rooms in which he was staying; 27 degrees was a kind of minimum for him. Someone always checked in advance that the temperature was right. It was one of the warmest Nobel parties I have ever attended. The temperature often exceeded 30 degrees. His lovely wife, Madame Lee, who spoke passable English, told me she really did not like it to be warmer than 20 degrees. I told her we have the same problem at home. I like 20 degrees, and my wife prefers it to be over 25. Madame Lee laughed when I suggested a wife swap so that those who liked to keep warm could do so together.

Korean soprano Sumi Jo singing the Korean national anthem *Arirang* at the Nobel Concert was a real highlight. It was a big moment for Kim. The most peculiar episode during his visit to Oslo was undoubtedly when Kim, Madame Lee, myself, and a security agent became trapped in the lift at the Nobel Institute. Our lift was not in the best condition. That was why we had hired a lift engineer in advance of the visit. Then the South Koreans kept testing it. By the time the President had finally arrived it already needed servicing again. We got in and it only moved a little before it became stuck for around twenty minutes. I tried to keep everyone's spirits up while we were trapped. The President later said I must have experienced this many times before to remain so calm.

The big surprise for Kim Dae-jung was the visit to Washington, DC in March 2001, after George W. Bush had taken over in the White House. Clinton was a fan of Kim Dae-jung and his Sunshine Policy. Bush wanted a 'regime change', a new regime in the north, despite the fact that Secretary of State Colin Powell would rather have continued with the existing policy. I was on a research trip to Washington during the days Kim was there. The shift in view was quite obvious. The focus on a 'regime change' was clearly a major blow to Kim, who despite his commitment to the Sunshine Policy maintained there should still be a significant number of American troops in South Korea. He claimed that Kim Jong-il had expressed his agreement on this point during the summit. In his State of the Union speech in January 2002, Bush designated the three members of the Axis of Evil: Iraq, Iran, and North Korea. The regime in the north was one of the worst dictatorships in the world, and the country also had plans to obtain nuclear weapons. However, it was easier said than done to overthrow the government in the north. Nothing happened.

There were soon persistent rumours that Kim Dae-jung had actually bought his Nobel Peace Prize. It emerged that South Korean companies had paid several hundred million dollars to North Korea in connection with the summit in 2000 to ensure the right conditions for a successful summit and for future economic contacts. Donald Kirk, who has written a critical book about Kim Dae-jung, *Korea Betrayed: Kim Dae Jung and Sunshine*, summed all this up in statements such as 'the corruption inherent in the quest for an inter-Korean summit and Nobel Peace Prize'.

I visited South Korea three times. In 1997, it was apparent that Kim wanted to meet with me during my week-long visit to the country. I made it clear that although I was keen to learn as much as I could about the country, I did not intend to meet any known candidates for the Nobel Peace Prize. There were a couple of others in addition to Kim. During my two visits to South Korea after Kim received the prize, much was made of the bribery accusations. I was interviewed by one of the major TV stations for forty-five minutes. Almost all of the questions were about the alleged corruption and the Nobel Committee's implication in this. Of course, the committee had not received any money from Kim. However, my obstinate denial was received with great scepticism. Nothing helped.

The years following this zenith in 2000 were something of a comedown for Kim Dae-jung. South Korean presidents often only serve one term. He would not have been re-elected anyway. When he departed office in 2003, his health had really started to deteriorate. He attended the Point of Peace Summit in Stavanger in 2008, but he was very weak. That was the last time I saw him. He was clearly happy to be in Norway again, and was once again celebrated as a laureate. The North Korean bribery accusations resurfaced, though the sums of money involved varied from 450 million to 8 billion dollars. It has subsequently emerged that Hyundai were forced to pay North Korea 450 million dollars shortly before the summit took place in 2000.

The Sunshine Policy did not bring the results for which we had hoped. North Korea is still one of the worst dictatorships in the world. Although some economic reforms were implemented, its economy is still terrible. The nuclear programme continued even though agreements were entered into on restrictions. North Korea was not at all integrated with an international community that would bring reform on many levels. But Kim Dae-jung remained wrapped up in his Sunshine Policy. He seemed unable to criticize the conditions in North Korea. Any criticism was quickly deemed 'slander'. Kim Dae-jung died on 18 August 2009. One of his greatest joys was receiving the Nobel Peace Prize.

The UN and Kofi Annan (2001)

When the Norwegian Nobel Committee celebrated the centenary of the Nobel Peace Prize in 2001, there were, as always, many candidates and many different opinions among the committee members. Nevertheless, it was almost inevitable that the prize would be awarded to the UN. The strongest and longest recurring theme in the history of the Peace Prize is the recognition of the work for a better organized world. For a small and, internationally speaking, progressive country such as Norway, the work for international cooperation is almost a matter of course. It satisfies an idealistic need and contributes to reducing the significance of physical power, something of which small nations have little. In his presentation speech for the prize, committee chair Gunnar Berge said that for the centenary the committee felt the need to emphasize the recurrent theme of the prize's history: 'the hope for a better organized and more peaceful world. Nothing symbolizes that hope, or represents that reality, better than the United Nations.'

During the years before the First World War, most of the prizes were awarded to representatives of organized peace movements, either on a parliamentary level through the Inter-Parliamentary Union or on a popular level through the International Peace Bureau. These were the first attempts to strengthen work towards fraternity and cooperation between nations and people in the world.

When the First World War broke out in 1914, the masses did not rise up in opposition to it. Instead they largely supported it, though they had thought it would be short-lived and that they would emerge victorious. In the end it came to last more than four years, and the losses were devastating.

After the First World War, the League of Nations was established in an attempt to prevent future war and to bolster peace and cooperation between nations and people. The main inspiration for the League of Nations, US President Woodrow Wilson, proclaimed that the First World War would 'be the war to end all wars' and that would make the world 'safe for democracy'. The League of Nations was nevertheless contested in Norwegian politics. The Labour Party and the left wing looked on the League as the victors' organization, while Hambro and parts of the right wing looked on it as an attack on Norwegian sovereignty. However, the League of Nations was popular among the Liberal Party, which at that time dominated the Nobel Committee, even though its endorsement of the sanction system against nations violating peace was half-hearted.

As we have seen, at least ten of the interwar laureates were affiliated with the League of Nations, from Woodrow Wilson (1919) to Robert Cecil (1937). No politician was more closely linked to the League of Nations from start to end than Cecil. Several other laureates also had looser connections to the League, such as foreign ministers Aristide Briand and Gustav Stresemann (1926). Only committee member Halvdan Koht's opposition to a prize directly to the League of Nations prevented such an award.

The League of Nations was unable to prevent the outbreak of the Second World War. However, the experiences of the war led to a lot more support for the United Nations. This time all the superpowers participated from the very start. In Norway, support for the new organization was almost unanimous. Of the prizes from 1945 to 2000, at least thirteen had a clear link to the UN, from Cordell Hull (1945) to Kofi Annan and the UN itself (2001). A number of other winners also had a greater or lesser connection with the UN's many different activities.

The Cold War had prevented the high expectations of the UN in 1945/46 from being realized. The conflict between the East and the West meant that, in practice, the UN stood on the sidelines in many of the most significant international issues. The most spectacular exception was the Korean War, where the UN actually directly supported the USA and the West. This was possible because the Soviet Union stayed away from the meeting of the Security Council in protest against Communist China not being able to take the country's place in the UN.

This did not mean that the UN's activities were insignificant during the Cold War. The UN made itself useful in other ways. Peacekeeping operations were able to take place where the superpowers were not facing off directly.

There were several such involvements in the Middle East from 1948, on the border between India and Pakistan from 1948, and in Cyprus from 1964. Several of these operations are still ongoing today. The UN was also able to do important work to improve human rights, such as by drafting the Universal Declaration of Human Rights from 1948. As decolonization increased and new countries joined the UN, it was inevitable that the continued struggle for independence for the colonies in Asia and Africa would remain high up on the international agenda. From the end of the 1940s, aid from wealthy to poor countries became gradually more important, especially in a UN context. There was constant pressure on the wealthy countries to do more. For a long time the Eastern bloc played little part in this context.

After the end of the Cold War, the UN's role became significantly more central. By virtue of Mikhail Gorbachev's new attitude, the UN was able to play a direct role in the Gulf War in 1991. The UN was involved in Soviet withdrawals from Angola, Namibia, and Afghanistan. The number of peacekeeping operations increased rapidly. Previously, fewer than 10,000 soldiers had been involved. Now this number increased to 70,000–80,000. UN observers participated in more and more decisions around the world.

Kofi Annan was appointed the UN's seventh Secretary-General in 1996 and served two terms, from 1997 until 2006. He had spent almost all of his adult life within the global organization's various divisions and was the first Secretary General to have such a background. Annan received much of his education in the USA, and it was primarily Americans who had opposed the re-election of Boutros Boutros-Ghali and—along with the sub-Saharan African countries—favoured the election of Annan.

Annan was an activist. Among other things, he tried to resolve the difficult situation regarding the entry of international weapons inspectors into Iraq to check whether it had weapons of mass destruction. Initially his work was successful, though he was unable to prevent the Iraq War in 2003. He had clear sympathy for the cause of the Western powers in Kosovo, but Russia and China limited his formal role here. Annan was a key figure in the introduction of democracy to Nigeria. He was involved in the process that led to East Timor gaining its independence. He was extremely active in Lebanon and in the Middle East more generally. After the terrorist attacks in New York and Washington on 11 September 2001, it was also inevitable that the UN would be involved in the fight against international terrorism. Annan initiated extensive reform work within the UN. The UN peacekeeping operations system was significantly strengthened, with a proper command centre. Human rights would be strengthened though a dedicated Human Rights Council. The Millennium Development Goals were set and eventually very successful. The fight again AIDS was brought into the spotlight through the foundation of the Global Fund to Fight AIDS, Tuberculosis and Malaria. Initiatives were also taken to more actively involve the business community in facing the world's many challenges.

In his meticulous manner, Annan spoke about the new role he envisioned for the UN using some dramatic turns of phrase. Article 2.7 of the UN Charter had protected nations' sovereignty when it came to domestic issues. However, even in his Nobel lecture Annan said that: 'The sovereignty of States must no longer be used as a shield for gross violations of human rights.' Informally this was referred to as the 'Kofi Doctrine'. Intervention had been a difficult word in a UN context. Annan tried to make it positive. The police intervene to prevent violence; doctors intervene to cure patients. The UN should intervene to resolve conflicts. This led to the unveiling of a grander plan in *Responsibility to Protect*. According to this plan, conflicts ought to be resolved as quickly as possible at the lowest possible level, but ultimately the global community has a duty to prevent major catastrophes such as the massacres in Rwanda, in Cambodia, and in Bosnia.

Responsibility to Protect was likely the result of two matters for which Annan received significant criticism in his previous UN positions. Annan, as Deputy Secretary-General for peacekeeping operations, failed miserably in terms of the UN's passive role in Rwanda in 1994. He personally had limited the UN's intervention. He had expressed a lot of regret over this, albeit rather late and only after various commissions and investigations had resulted in significant criticism, even of Annan personally. In Bosnian Srebrenica in 1995, the UN once again looked on as almost 8000 Muslims were massacred by Serbian troops. The UN had actually had forces in the area in both cases, and it was clear early on, particularly in Rwanda, what was happening.

Annan was undoubtedly the most active Secretary-General that the UN had had. The expectations of the UN had also increased dramatically during the 1990s. The organization was now able to do so much more. Annan said in jest: 'I find that I am expected to issue official statements on almost everything that happens in the world today, from royal weddings to the possibility of human cloning.'

The announcement that the 2001 prize would be awarded to the UN and Kofi Annan led to discussions within the organization about what the UN really was and who would represent the UN in Oslo considering Annan himself was also a laureate. The outcome was that Han Seung-soo, South Korea's Minister of Foreign Affairs and that year's President of the UN General Assembly, would receive the prize on behalf of the UN. This was a major victory for South Korea, whose President had received the Peace Prize the year before. There were many discussions about whether two Nobel lectures would be held since there were two laureates. In the end, only Annan gave a lecture—a clear victory for the Secretary-General of the UN.

Since 2001 marked the centenary of the first Peace Prize, a centennial symposium was held with broad participation. All of the laureates still living were invited to the symposium, and to other events in Oslo. Around thirty laureates came, including representatives of the many organizations that had received the prize since 1901. Mandela was the only person to decline the committee's invitation. He did so for health reasons. A number of other important names also sent their regrets at the last minute: Peres and Arafat did not come due to the situation in the Middle East, Gorbachev fell ill, de Klerk's first wife was killed the day he was due to travel, and Bishop Belo experienced difficulties during his trip and did not make it to Oslo.

I thought we should also invite a number of the world's leading intellectuals to the centennial symposium. Leading historians and social scientists attended: Amartya Sen, who was also a recipient of the Nobel Prize in Economics, Eric Hobsbawm, Joseph S. Nye, Michael W. Doyle, Akira Iriye, Mary Kaldor, and others. It was an interesting experience to see these two groups interact. They behaved respectfully towards each other, but it was clear that the laureates thought the academics were too theoretical in their approach, whereas the academics considered the laureates' analyses of various global issues to be somewhat inadequate. It was also impossible to obtain any suitable papers from the laureates, Kim Dae-jung aside. In a book that head of research Olav Njølstad and I edited from the symposium, *War and Peace in the 20th Century and Beyond*, Kim Dae-jung was the only person to represent the laureates. The academics delivered as expected.

Jody Williams, Mairead Corrigan, and some others thought that the symposium should issue a statement on the laureates' impression of the global situation. The academics would not participate in this. It was clear that the laureates intended to target George W. Bush and his foreign policy.

I made it clear to Jody and company early on that I did not have a lot of faith in this project. Such a statement, if it were to be issued at all, ought to be approved by all of the laureates present. A statement that was only approved by twenty-five out of thirty laureates would only serve to indicate dissent within the group. It was clear that the more conservative laureates such as Elie Wiesel, David Trimble, and Lech Wałęsa would not be in favour of the text the more radical laureates wanted. The press asked at regular intervals how things were going with the statement. I tried my best to curb expectations. It went as expected: after lengthy discussions, the laureates stuck to paying tribute to the laureates for the year, the UN and Kofi Annan.

Committee chair Gunnar Berge, assisted by me, chaired the symposium. We had trouble keeping things sedate in the corner of the room where the Dalai Lama and Desmond Tutu were sitting. With their senses of humour and animated repartee, it was as if they were holding their own little conference, and this attracted much attention in the media. John Hume felt unwell during the gathering so Morten Rostrup, representing Doctors Without Borders, took him to Ullevål Hospital, where he was admitted with suspected heart trouble. We were all quite anxious—all of us apart from John's wife, Pat, who was quite calm about the whole thing. John's health was not the best, and she had experienced this several times before. And she was right—after a couple of hours John and Morten were back. During the Nobel banquet on 10 December, John Hume was in such good form that during the dance he performed both *Danny Boy* and *We Shall Overcome*. This is the only time in my twenty-five years as Director that I remember a laureate contributing musical numbers.

Kofi Annan was very pleased with the prize on both his own and the UN's behalf. Kofi's wife, Nane, was however almost ecstatic on her husband's behalf and very expressive of her feelings. Annan also had a busy Nobel schedule. I accompanied him to his meetings with Prime Minister Kjell Magne Bondevik, Minister of Foreign Affairs Jan Petersen, the Norwegian Parliament and the Standing Committee on Foreign Affairs, the press, and others. My admiration for Annan, which was not insignificant to begin with, increased during these meetings. He was asked the same questions again and again. It all became very predictable, but not only did Annan retain his good mood, he answered the questions as if they expressed a deeper insight he was particularly pleased to encounter. There are few who could be compared to Annan when it came to dealing with people. It was easy for us to forget that he, in the midst of everything, had to keep an eye on what was happening in the UN. Just before he and I headed to concert arena Spektrum to enjoy the Nobel Concert, he had to take a call from his close adviser Lakhdar Brahimi about the situation in Afghanistan. We only just made it in time for him to make his entrance into the arena.

When Annan left, I expressed my admiration at how he had handled it all. He took this calmly and, as expected, did not expound on this. In my many years in the Nobel system, I only met one person who rivalled Annan when it came to dealing with people. This was Bill Clinton, who was not a laureate. No one else came close to him in this respect.

Jimmy Carter (2002)

On 11 October 2002, when the Norwegian Nobel Committee was ready to announce that the Peace Prize would be awarded to Jimmy Carter, we encountered a minor problem. The committee wanted to announce this joyous news to the laureate himself first. But how were we to get in touch with Carter when it was the middle of the night in Georgia? Former presidents are also protected by the Secret Service. The security service at the US Embassy in Oslo quickly put us in touch with Carter's Secret Service agents and then in touch with Carter himself. This went well. We were promised that Carter would call Gunnar Berge and me soon. He did. The only thing was, when Carter called, Berge asked him to call back in five minutes. It came as a shock to me that he could do this, and Carter must have wondered whether yet another obstacle had arisen on his unbelievably long road to the Nobel Peace Prize. Was someone trying to play a prank on the former President? Perhaps Berge needed a minute to gather his wits before he spoke to Carter. When Carter called back, he finally received the message for which he had hoped for so many years.

Jimmy Carter should have received the Peace Prize in 1978 when the prize went to Begin and Sadat. The Camp David Accords between Israel and Egypt were entered into in September the same year, so in this case the prize really was awarded for actions that had just taken place. Carter had played a key role during the thirteen days of negotiations at Camp David. There would quite certainly not have been any accords without Carter's tenacious assistance. The only problem was that Carter had not been nominated for the Peace Prize when the nomination deadline passed on 1 February. Begin and Sadat had been nominated, obviously for entirely different reasons than their involvement at Camp David. The committee had not had Carter's name on the list during the first committee meeting either, as the rules indicated they should have. The matter was taken up with the Nobel Foundation in Stockholm. Could the committee legally add a completely new name at this late juncture? The response from Stockholm was clear and obviously in accordance with the statutes: the committee could not. Carter did not therefore receive his well-deserved prize in 1978. The story of Carter's omission became known in 1994 through the memoirs of Nobel Director Stig Ramel.

When Carter finally came to Oslo to receive the prize in 2002, he told us how he had hoped that he would perhaps receive the prize in 1979. This did not happen. It would have been unthinkable to consider the same event two years in a row. He also said that he had kept close track of the announcements of laureates in the years that followed, which of course took place at four in the morning in Georgia. In the end he had given up hope. The outside world was constantly reminding him of the prize. Every year he was asked whether he was disappointed that someone else had received the prize. Every year he praised the person who had received the prize. Out of sympathy for Carter, I told the media what the situation in 1978 had actually been at regular intervals.

In an open interview in the mid-1990s, Jimmy Carter answered a question on whether the Nobel Peace Prize had actually been the motivation for all his peace work. 'But then what if it never happened? And it probably won't. There are several hundred people with the same aims that I have, all working just as hard as I am, and some of them probably much harder. What if this was what meant the most to me and then it never happened? What kind of dried-up, disappointed and frustrated old husk of a man would I be then?' Poor Jimmy Carter. In the same interview, Carter also said 'I would be delighted, not to mention surprised, if it were ever the case that no one suggested my main aim through all these years, my secret agenda, was to win the Nobel Peace Prize.' Really, these comments said everything about what the prize meant to him. Carter often visited Oslo, mostly to ask for money for the Carter Center that he had built, but probably also to remind the committee that he existed. However, he never engaged in any direct lobbying. Carter received money from many sources, including the Japanese Sasakawa Foundation, which had a slightly dubious reputation. Carter responded by nominating the Sasakawa Foundation for the Nobel Peace Prize.

The Peace Prize was sometimes awarded for achievements 'during the preceding year'. The prize for 1978 to Sadat and Begin was a striking example of this. But more often than not, the prize was awarded for achievements over a longer period, perhaps even over a whole lifetime. This was very much the case for Jimmy Carter. He was nominated many times and made it onto the shortlist several times without winning.

The arguments in favour of Carter were really quite strong. During his time as President, he did much more than help to negotiate the Camp David Accords, which made a lasting peace treaty between Egypt and Israel possible, a treaty that has remained in force to this day despite the constant trials in the Middle East. He also gave the Panama Canal to Panama, thus resolving an issue that had tested not only the USA's relationship with Panama, but also its relationship with all of Latin America. He had negotiated a SALT II treaty with the Soviet Union and established diplomatic connections with the People's Republic of China. These were significant achievements that were somewhat overshadowed by the dominating fact that he was not re-elected in 1980. He was a loser, which was something of a sin, particularly in the USA. Even Gunnar Berge's presentation of the laureate partly reflected this sin. He said: 'Jimmy Carter will probably not go down in American history as the most effective President. But he is certainly the best ex-President the country ever had.' This utterance was in many ways correct, and perhaps even self-evident, but it caused negative reactions in Carter's large delegation during the award ceremony in Oslo. They were probably not prepared for that kind of open assessment in a Nobel speech. Although the speech was of course Berge's, I have to admit I was the one who came up with that particular phrasing.

Carter's work as a former President really was remarkable. If you do not think he should have been President, you will find that many people think much the same. While former presidents have an unclear role and many are happy enough to make easy money through memoirs and speeches, Carter has stood up for his ideals year after year. And not only that: he also had time to write a large number of books about everything from politics and religion to fly fishing. No former President's level of activity is comparable to Carter's. His only serious competitor was Herbert Hoover (President from 1929 until 1933), but he was all but forgotten, overshadowed by a combination of the Great Depression and Franklin D. Roosevelt.

The grounds for the award stated that Carter received the prize 'for his decades of untiring effort to find peaceful solutions to international conflicts, to advance democracy and human rights, and to promote economic and social development'. This was no exaggeration. The Carter Center, which the former President had founded, celebrated its twentieth anniversary in 2002. The centre's slogan was: 'Waging peace. Fighting disease. Building hope.'

Carter's peace work was what garnered the most attention. There were barely any conflicts in which Carter had not been active. His most successful interventions were in Haiti, and in North Korea in 1994. In North Korea, Carter actually managed to persuade Kim Il-sung to stop the country's nuclear programme in exchange for nuclear reactors that could not be used to develop weapons, oil supplies that the country desperately needed, the abolition of the American economic embargo, and a gradual normalization of diplomatic relations. Carter was also promised that a summit between North Korea and South Korea would take place for the first time since the formation of the nations. He even said he had found Kim Il-sung to be in good health. President of South Korea Kim Young-sam commented that 'Carter is a smart man, but he does not know much about old people.' This was true. Three weeks after Carter left North Korea, the 'great leader' died from a massive stroke. Thus nothing ever came of the planned summit. In the end the nuclear agreement also broke down. All that could be done then was for others to start new negotiations. North Korea's negotiating position was very weak. All they had to offer were restrictions on their nuclear programme. The same horse was flogged again and again. The problem has still not been solved despite persistent efforts.

In Haiti, in cooperation with Senator Sam Nunn and General Colin Powell, Carter managed to get the military junta to accept an amnesty and to put an end to American and international sanctions. Democratic elections would be held for its Parliament, and the democratically elected but displaced President Jean-Bertrand Aristide would return to the island. All of this happened under severe threat of large-scale American military intervention. When Carter left the island, several hours after the deadline he had promised the Clinton administration, the first American troops had already left the USA for Haiti. The agreement was initially received with great enthusiasm in Haiti.

Carter was also active in the Middle East, where he supported the Arab Peace Initiative of 2002 and became more and more critical of Israel. In Bosnia he negotiated an armistice which proved to be very short-lived. He was also active in Sudan and in Uganda, where wars had been raging for a long time.

Douglas Brinkley, one of Carter's biographers, has written that Carter's peace work was 'the Christian engineer's approach to problem-solving, a high-octane mixture of astonishing optimism, endless determination and pragmatic precision'. The Clinton administration gave Carter very half-hearted support. Many people considered the former President a loose cannon, someone who carried out his assignments more or less on his own. At times, Carter was almost persona non grata at the White House. Carter sometimes publicly criticized aspects of the administration's policy. Various attempts to dispel this tension were only partly successful.

Although high-level political matters garnered the most attention, Carter actually spent most of his time on less controversial things. Until the prize in 2002, Carter himself and the staff at the Carter Center had served as election monitors for more than three dozen elections in twenty countries. The centre developed procedures that influenced such activities in many other countries as well. In China, Carter had even set up a programme for establishing elections at a local level; 50,000 copies of a handbook were distributed to local authorities; and various conferences were held with the blessing of the Chinese authorities.

The Carter Center also developed an extensive humanitarian programme. From 1986, the centre contributed to ridding Asia of Guinea-worm disease, which caused severe infections, which meant it only remained a problem in a few countries in Africa. Sudan, where the civil war limited opportunities to fight the disease, was worst affected. River blindness was another major challenge. The disease, caused by small black flies that bred in drainage basins, was a primary cause of blindness. In 2001, the Carter Center contributed to treating more than 7 million people in eleven countries.

It is a mystery how Carter had time for all this. He was not a man to delegate most things to his subordinates. On the contrary, he was often criticized for getting too involved in various details. We also noticed this when making preparations for the award ceremony. I had to keep his secretary, Nancy Koningsberg, apprised of everything—and I mean everything. No detail was too small. It was likely Carter who wanted it this way.

Carter had meetings with all sorts of people. Religion meant a lot to him. He regularly taught at Sunday school, even when he was President. In his farewell mass as President, he asked what made a man great. The answer was clear: Jesus had shown that doing good for one's fellow man was the very foundation for greatness. One week a year, he and his wife, Rosalynn, helped to build houses for the poor through Habitat for Humanity. Carter's hobbies included fly fishing, hunting, whittling, cycling, tennis, and skiing. He has also written at least twenty-seven books, and he paints. He has learnt Spanish. He keeps up all of these activities, albeit to varying degrees. He almost looks on fly fishing as a religion. Even now, at the age of 94 and after a brain tumour, he maintains an astonishing pace. He is always looking to the next thing. During the years the Nobel Institute cooperated with various American institutions on what was known as the Carter–Brezhnev Project, we never got Carter himself to participate. He was not interested in the past. He always looked to the future.

Almost everything he did, he did with Rosalynn. They both came from Plains, Georgia. Carter had grown up in Archery, a few kilometres west of Plains, where two or three white families and around twenty-five black families lived. That was all. Racial segregation was an utterly foreign concept to the Carters. There were some people who thought Carter and his wife should receive the Peace Prize jointly, but it was clear that it was Jimmy's impetus that drove their achievements. Any small gesture for Rosalynn was greatly appreciated by Jimmy. After I travelled with her into Oslo after they arrived in December 2002, he made a point of coming over to me to say how useful and entertaining Rosalynn had found the drive. Few presidential couples in American history have cooperated more closely than Jimmy and Rosalynn. Carter himself stressed that 'when *we* decided to go into politics, Rosalynn helped me in every way. We have always been equal partners in every important decision since we were married.'

Jimmy Carter undoubtedly deserved the Peace Prize he was finally awarded. His supporters had started to say that his lack of a prize was becoming one of the Nobel Committee's sins of omission. Nothing much happened in 2002 to prompt the prize to be awarded to him that specific year, but committee chair Gunnar Berge managed to generate an extra buzz around the prize when he said that the reason why Carter was finally being recognized was because he represented a counterpart to the ongoing policy of the Bush administration. Berge confirmed that the prize to Carter 'should be interpreted as a criticism of the line that the current administration has taken'. Something similar had happened in 1987 in connection with the prize to Oscar Arias, when committee chair Egil Aarvik said in an interview that Reagan's policy in Central America had led to 'chaos' in the region. However, Berge took things even further when he confirmed that the prize to Carter should be considered 'et spark på leggen' where Bush was concerned, often translated as 'a slap in the face'. A 'kick in the shin' would be more accurate.

This comment caused uproar. Particularly in the international press the prize was quite clearly presented as an attack on Bush. *The Times*, at that point no great admirer of the Peace Prize, went as far as to write that Berge's comments 'diminish Carter's achievements, damage the prize's prestige and influence, and bring shame on the other committee members'. Two of the committee members, Hanna Kvanmo and Inger-Marie Ytterhorn, took the unusual measure of publicly distancing themselves from Berge's comments. Kvanmo said that Berge's initiative had not been discussed by the committee, and Ytterhorn claimed that she would not have agreed to the final section of the committee's announcement if she had known that it would lead to such a direct attack on the Bush administration.

The final section of Berge's statement said that 'in a situation currently marked by threats of the use of power, Carter has stood by the principles that conflicts must as far as possible be resolved through mediation and international cooperation based on international law, respect for human rights, and economic development.' You would have been hard pressed not to realize that this was an indirect reference to the Bush administration's preparations to intervene in Iraq. Berge and I had talked about this before the announcement, but I too was surprised by how it sounded when presented in Berge's very forthright manner. I realized that it was unfortunate and told Berge this immediately after the press conference. For Berge the comment was probably also intended to be a means of placating those in Labour quarters who were perhaps not pleased that the prize was being awarded to a US president, even one of Carter's ilk. In his memoirs, *Til Kongen med fagbrev* ('*To the King with Guilds Certificates*), Gunnar Berge himself writes that 'it should be no secret that I was very sceptical of awarding the prize to Carter. In my opinion, he should have received it in 1978, but not in 2002. To be quite honest, in this instance I was overruled by the other committee members.'

Carter's Nobel lecture was not particularly inspiring. It was too much of a litany of what various other laureates, particularly American laureates, had said and thought. He also condemned 'preventive war'. However, the Nobel Concert was inspiring. The highlight was when opera star Jessye Norman sang *He's Got the Whole World in His Hands* and Carter blew her a kiss. Several of Carter's friends and admirers, such as Norman, Willie Nelson, and Santana performed. We did not often achieve such a synergy between laureate and artists. They enjoyed performing for Carter, and Carter thanked them with his broadest smile. No one could top Carter when it came to smiling broadly in pictures. He was a nice man with whom it was relatively easy to get along. Many of his employees from his time as President were present in Oslo during the Nobel days, even though the most famous among them, such as Zbigniew Brzezinski and Cyrus Vance, were not. Most of those who were in attendance came from Georgia and had known Carter for many decades.

Thus the Nobel Committee had finally squared things with Jimmy Carter, a candidate who to a greater or lesser degree had been on the committee's table since 1978. The story had had a happy ending for the laureate, but perhaps not as much for the committee.

Barack H. Obama (2009)

No Peace Prize has garnered as much attention as the prize awarded to Barack Obama in 2009. Whispering rippled through the Grand Hall at the Nobel Institute when committee chair Thorbjørn Jagland announced his name. A huge media storm followed across large parts of the world. Websites affiliated with the Nobel prizes have never seen as much traffic for any other prize. All records were broken, and no one has come close to beating them since.

Many of the reactions were negative, even very negative, particularly in the USA. One analysis in *The New York Times* concluded that 'it is striking how so many people seemed to greet the Nobel news with shock followed by laughter.' Some people thought the award was so ridiculous that Obama should refuse the prize. In a Gallup survey in the USA the week after the announcement, 61 per cent responded that Obama did not deserve the Peace Prize, while 34 per cent responded that he did deserve it. Conservatives were very against the prize, but not that surprised: 'What else can you expect from a group of Scandinavian lefties who have already awarded the prize to Gore, Carter, ElBaradei and Annan?'

Of course there were some who defended the prize. *The New York Times* remained fixated on the connection to George Bush: the prize was 'a poorly concealed indirect condemnation of Mr Bush's time in office. But opposing the criticism Mr Bush met around the world is one of Obama's major achievements in his nine months as President. Mr Obama's will to respect and work together with other nations is another.' John McCain, who had lost the election to Obama in 2008, said: 'As Americans we are proud when our President receives such a prestigious prize.' Conversely, many of Obama's own supporters did not think that he deserved the prize. A famous columnist for *The Washington Post* wrote: 'This is ridiculous—embarrassing, even. I admire President Obama. I like President Obama. I voted for President Obama. But the Peace Prize? This is supposed to be for doing, not being— and it's no disrespect to the President to suggest he hasn't done much yet. Certainly not enough to justify this prize.'

The reactions were more positive in most other parts of the world than they were in the USA. The UN Secretary-General praised the award, as did many of the previous laureates. Desmond Tutu put it best when he said that the prize to Obama 'anticipates an even greater contribution towards making our world a safer place for all'. Of course, allied heads of state in Europe congratulated Obama on his prize. In Norway, opinion polls showed that 43 per cent agreed with the prize, while 38 per cent did not. Prime Minister of Russia Dmitry Medvedev said that the prize would contribute to a better relationship between the USA and Russia. He hoped that the prize 'would serve as an additional incentive' for an improved 'climate in international politics'. Many people in Africa were very proud that an African-American had received the prize. In the Middle East, most people were either critical or reserved judgment. A lot of people had strong opinions on this prize.

In the Nobel Committee, there will always be differences of opinion during the selection process. It is not uncommon for committee members to switch favourites two or three times as new information comes to light or the discussion shows little support for their original favourite. The only thing that really counts is the situation in the final meeting. In that sense, 2009 was easier than some other years. Everyone agreed with the decision in Obama's favour, even though the enthusiasm varied from member to member. Everyone was along for the ride.

Of course, the committee members were aware that a prize to Obama would garner a lot of attention, but nevertheless thought the arguments for such a decision were strong. These were summarized in the final section of the grounds for the award: 'For 108 years, the Norwegian Nobel Committee has sought to stimulate precisely that international policy and those attitudes for which Obama is now the world's leading spokesman.' Obama represented all the ideals for which the Nobel Committee had worked hard for many decades: a better organized world with a focus on the UN and multilateral diplomacy; dialogue and negotiations in almost all situations; the vision of a world free from nuclear weapons; strengthening of democracy and human rights; a new climate policy. Naturally, the committee was aware that it would take time for Obama to be able to realize these ambitious ideals. However, he needed all the support he could get. The final sentence in the grounds for the award was actually written in English: 'The Committee endorses Obama's appeal that "Now is the time for all of us to take our share of responsibility for a global response to global challenges".'

There was an important additional point. Most people had forgotten the point in Nobel's will about the prize being awarded on the basis of achievements in 'the preceding year'. The Nobel Committee has been in no way consistent in its observance of this. Many prizes were awarded for achievements over a lifetime. Nevertheless, Nobel's original stipulation was the person who had done the most to promote peace since the previous award, in this case on 10 December 2008. The prizes to Begin and Sadat in 1978 and to Oscar Arias in 1987 were prizes determined by recent developments. It was irrelevant how much the candidate had done when the nomination deadline passed on 1 February. What mattered was what the person in question had done when the committee held its final meeting before the announcement of the prize in October.

Committee chair Thorbjørn Jagland almost always justified the prize to Obama by primarily making reference to the arms control agreement between the USA and Russia which was entered into in April 2010. The number of strategic nuclear weapons was to be reduced by half, and the number of warheads even more. Even though the agreement was entered into several months after the Peace Prize was awarded, the negotiations gave reasons to be optimistic early on. Jagland usually added that it was in this way that the treaty on anti-ballistic missiles was saved. Since the ABM treaty had already been terminated by George Bush, there was no treaty to save. I informed Jagland of this sad fact, but he continued on with the same argument. Not one single journalist pointed out this obvious contradiction.

Everyone could tell how surprised Obama was by the award. The committee had not called him in advance. It did not want to wake the President in the middle of the night and assumed he would manage to handle the situation as best possible. Later, in this age of wiretapping, it struck me that the Nobel Institute actually had indirect proof that we had not been bugged by the US Embassy on the other side of the street. If we had been bugged, the advisers would surely have made sure that the President was better prepared for what followed.

Obama openly confessed that: 'Well, this is not how I expected to wake up this morning. [...] I am both surprised and deeply humbled by the decision of the Nobel Committee. [...] To be honest, I do not feel that I deserve to be in the company of so many of the transformative figures who've been honoured by this prize.' David Axelrod, Obama's political guru, was even more open, greeting the news of the Peace Prize 'as more of a surreal challenge than a cause for celebration'.

Yes, Obama was undoubtedly surprised. As he said at the Nobel banquet after Jagland's presentation speech: 'I told him afterwards that I thought it was an excellent speech and that I was almost convinced that I deserved it.' We were told that when Obama gave his comments the morning the prize was announced, his staff had already investigated whether anyone had failed to travel to Oslo to receive their prize. This had happened, as in the case of Lech Wałęsa in 1983 or Aung San Suu Kyi in 1991, but generally the answer was no. Those in the White House realized quite quickly that they would have to prepare to travel to Oslo.

Obama was undoubtedly pleased with the prize. He had received the same prize as several of his heroes, particularly Martin Luther King and Nelson Mandela. He wrote the following in the Nobel Institute's guest book: 'I am deeply honoured to receive this esteemed prize, and grateful for the extraordinary work that the committee has done over the years to promote a global peace, liberate the oppressed and give voice to the voiceless.' To be on the safe side, Michelle added, somewhat more ambivalently: 'On behalf of the Obama family we are so moved and touched by this great honour. We will work hard to live up to it.'

I myself had written the main consultant statements on Obama in 2009. Since I spent many years of my life studying American politics, the committee felt this was acceptable. However, I personally greatly doubted their decision, to the extent a consultant was in any position to do so. It would be difficult, even impossible, for Obama to live up to the enormous expectations that so many people had of him. If he were unsuccessful, many people would ask why the Nobel Committee had awarded him the Peace Prize. On the other hand, several times during the selection process I alone could probably have stopped any further assessment of Obama. I did not. He represented the ideals that the committee had pursued for so many years, and he needed help to achieve his goals.

In retrospect it must be said this argument for giving Obama help was only partly right. His position was probably strengthened in some countries and regions, where he received extra prestige as a laureate. But in the USA, the prize remained the subject of criticism and amazement. Obama himself never made a big deal of the Peace Prize. He made it clear on several occasions that he was not interested in any further follow-up. Thorbjørn Jagland never visited the White House, even though he met Obama at several international events. The Republicans were still doing everything they could to oppose Obama. For many of them, the prize illustrated the fact that Obama did not first and foremost represent American values, but instead was a spokesman for a global community they did not really like. Even many of Obama's supporters also thought the prize was a mistake. As such, the committee did not achieve what it had hoped it would.

Obama's Nobel speech was impressive. He had written a lot of it himself, on the plane to Oslo. He and speechwriter Jon Favreau worked on it right up until the ceremony started. Favreau later admitted that they had almost not had the speech finished in time. Obama's point of departure was very serious. He was waging two wars; yet now he would receive the Nobel Peace Prize. A proper answer was required as to how this was possible. Obama gave a realistic description of the dilemmas faced by a US president. He himself was waging war in both Afghanistan and Iraq. He had been against the latter; he had supported the former, and he was now facing a significant increase in the number of US troops in Afghanistan. The first part of his Nobel speech was directed at the American audience, which expected to hear that he, despite the Peace Prize, would defend the USA's interests. He was absolutely doing this. He praised Gandhi and King, 'but as a head of state sworn to protect and defend my nation, I cannot be guided by their examples alone. I face the world as it is, and cannot stand idle in the face of threats to the American people. For make no mistake: evil does exist in the world. A non-violent movement could not have halted Hitler's armies. Negotiations cannot convince Al-Qaeda's leaders to lay down their arms. To say that force may sometimes be necessary is not a call to cynicism—it is a recognition of history; the imperfections of man and the limits of reason.' This was a direct and honest speech.

Then, in the second part of the speech, Obama switched to speaking about what would be required to ensure a more peaceful world: effective non-violent mechanisms had to be developed; peace had to be based on human rights, which also had to include social and economic conditions. His conclusion was strong: 'Clear-eyed, we can understand that there will be war, and still strive for peace. We can do that—for that is the story of human progress; that's the hope of all the world; and at this moment of challenge, that must be our work here on Earth.'

Even many critics of the Peace Prize were impressed. At the banquet, I discussed the speech with Obama's speechwriters. It was brilliant to meet them. The chief speechwriter, Jon Favreau, was only 28 years old. We agreed that this was probably the second-best speech the President had ever given, after his speech in Cairo earlier in 2009. We also agreed that his inauguration speech in January 2009 had not really lived up to expectations. When Obama re-joined his wife immediately after the ceremony, Michelle said: 'Did you have to go there?' It seems she thought the speech had been too direct, a defence of the wars he was waging, but the President felt he had to give an honest answer to a difficult question. In a well-known picture from the ceremony, I wave my index finger at Obama as he greets the committee members immediately after giving his speech. Of course this was not a criticism, but an expression of my interest. I congratulated him on an honest and interesting Nobel speech, and it is a bad habit of mine that I often brandish my index finger when I am expressing interest in something.

Having a current US President to visit is no joke. He came with a lot of baggage—several planes, helicopters, and his own cars in addition to his large delegation. They prefer to follow a standard arrangement from which deviations cannot be made. Up to three groups of people were sent ahead to assess all conceivable premises and they asked about most things. However, they did not answer our questions. Among other things, we asked which names should feature on the diploma, which seems a simple enough question. However, we received no response. It was his middle name, Hussein, that was the potential problem. In the end the solution was to put Barack H. Obama.

Of course, we wondered when the President would arrive, how extensive the programme would be, who would accompany him, and so on. No final confirmations were made before 7 December, two to three days before Obama was due to arrive. It was a strange situation. Every day hoards of journalists called me to find out whether there was any news on the programme. Every day I had to say we did not have any final confirmations to share. And on this went, day in, day out. The people sent to check everything before Obama arrived were largely respectful. When I complained about one member of the security staff, we saw no more of him. Some of them were somewhat indiscreet. The Secret Service also accompanied former US presidents wherever they went, as evidenced in the many stories about women and Bill Clinton.

The laureate normally stays in Oslo for three full days. Obama stayed for twenty-six hours. Some people said this was an insult to the host, but the committee understood that he could not take part in a full programme. When we first met the President, we found him quite personable. For me it was a dream come true to meet a current US president. There was a lot I wanted to discuss with him. He had been well briefed and knew who all the main players were on the Norwegian side. When he spoke, he looked you right in the eyes and answered your questions honestly. I almost had to pinch myself. Were we really conversing with the US President in such a manner? We had been told he might come across as a bit distracted. We did not see much evidence of that. The same applied to Michelle. She and my wife, Aase, got on well. They had a lot to talk about, about politics and about Chicago and about raising children. Aase and I both knew Chicago well since our son, Erik, had recently taken a sabbatical there with his family and we had visited them.

In Jodi Kantor's book *The Obamas*, the Obamas tell their version of the story of their visit to Oslo. They were clearly anxious about what sort of reception they would have since they knew many people had criticized the prize. The book reveals that they were positively surprised. The conclusion was clear: 'the trip came as a big surprise, a brief, happy fantasy for the President, a Nordic alternative reality where the citizens were enlightened and thoughtful, the discussions were contemplative, and everyone was a fan.' The torchlight procession, in which as many as 15,000 people participated, made a big impression: 'It was difficult to think of a time since the inauguration that the Obama family had received such a shower of gratitude.'

For the first and only time, the laureate's speech at the banquet was broadcast on television. The US President could not speak without the world hearing what he had to say. There was wall-to-wall coverage of the visit for its duration. Almost everything that happened was shared with the world. However, Obama needed some time put aside to check in with the White House in Washington, DC. He used my office at the Nobel Institute as a meeting room for internal discussions and contact with the American capital. My lovely office had this function for around forty minutes.

There is always a lot of interest in attending the Nobel banquet. Several people complain about not being invited. Some also complain about the seating arrangements. In 2009, absolutely everyone wanted to be there.

Even people who had been critical of the prize to Obama insisted on being there. Normally three to four government ministers were invited. The Nobel Committee is appointed by the Norwegian Parliament and therefore has obvious links to it. Despite this, the committee needs to maintain a certain distance from the government. It became clear that at the very least the party leaders thought they should be invited, but the committee stood its ground. In the end almost every single guest had to justify their presence. For example, why was Valgerd Svarstad Haugland at the banquet? She was not involved in politics any more, after all. However, she was an active member of the board at the Nobel Peace Center.

During the banquet, I sat David Axelrod next to Gro Harlem Brundtland. I was sitting at the same table. This was supposed to be a celebration, but Gro was disappointed when she found out that David did not know who she was. He knew everything about American election campaigns, but not necessarily that much about international politicians. Gro turned to me in shock: 'He doesn't know who I am!' David knew he had made a fool of himself. He whipped out his mobile phone and was soon reading Gro's CV. But the damage was done.

There was a Nobel Concert in 2009 as well, although Obama did not have time to attend. However, he met the artists separately and did his best to help with comments and interviews. Every year the laureate can request an artist who we then invite to the ceremony and concert. We had of course asked which artist the President wanted there, but this was among the many things to which we never received any response. However, the organizers of the concert had seen a video where Esperanza Spalding had performed at the White House, apparently with success. We decided that she would be the President's choice. Esperanza was not very well known at that time, a nice and unassuming woman with an amazing talent for music, so it was nice to be able to help her out. She was also inspired by jazz, so we had some of 'my' music at the ceremony. Her announcement as the President's choice lit a fire under her career. The Obamas seemed to think this had been a nice touch.

In a way, all of Norway participated in Obama's visit. The media interest was enormous. After it was all over, many people approached me to congratulate me on how well it had all gone. Even in the depths of Nordmarka forest, I met people who wanted to offer their praise. It was as if Norway had had to sit a major and important exam and passed.

Obama's delegation teemed with well-known names. Some of them were exhausted after missing out on most of their night's sleep on the plane.

The adviser with whom I became best acquainted was Denis McDonough. Denis had joined Obama's team during the first phase of the election campaign in 2007. He kept getting promoted and became assistant security adviser a while after he had been in Oslo. He was from Stillwater, Minnesota, and I knew Minnesota well after living there as an exchange student and visiting the state several times. In 2013, he became Obama's chief of staff. It was quite clear to the other Americans that Denis was someone who checked in with the President several times a day. In 2010, Aase and I met Denis for breakfast at the White House. It was quite an experience. We were the only guests in the breakfast room, which was run by the US Navy. After seeing Denis, I met Norm Eisner, one of Obama's legal advisers. We discussed various things in connection with the prize money, which Obama had donated to a number of humanitarian and idealistic organizations. Norm was an informal sort of person; he should of course have seen us out after the visit was over. He did not. When Aase and I came wandering along the corridor and met the security people at the exit without an escort, this astonished them. I expect Norm would have had to answer for that.

What situation did Obama find himself in after the ceremony? It was impossible for him to live up to the enormous expectations he faced after his election in 2008. It was almost inconceivable that a black man had been elected President. Only three African-Americans had ever been elected senator, and Obama was one of them. Black people were a clear minority in all fifty states, and now one of them was President. From day one he was met with massive resistance from the Republicans, who did everything they could to prevent him from being re-elected. He also assumed responsibility for a financial crisis that was the biggest since the 1930s. Nevertheless, he was re-elected in 2012.

Despite the major challenges, Obama's economic policy has proved to be surprisingly successful. The USA got back on its feet a lot quicker than Europe following the financial crisis, and its growth has been strong recently. Nevertheless, it took a long time for these results to reach most people. Obama adopted a healthcare reform that brought the USA more into line with other industrialized countries; his environmental policy was better than expected considering existing domestic policy. But what of his foreign policy, which had been the most important element in the context of the Peace Prize? Obama was determined to withdraw US troops from Iraq and largely from Afghanistan as well, but did not entirely manage this. Things always happen that put paid to the best plans, particularly when you are the

US President. He kept the USA somewhat in the background during the Western intervention in Libya, and after much hesitation he did not send ground forces into Syria, though air forces were sent in as part of the fight against ISIS. He used drones on a much larger scale than Bush did, and he proved unable to close the detention camp at Guantánamo Bay, something he promised he would do very early on. He achieved rapprochement with both Cuba and Iran. Obama did not meet all expectations, but I would maintain that he has nevertheless made the world a slightly better place to live. Perhaps that justifies his Nobel Peace Prize, even in retrospect?

Liu Xiaobo (2010)

There were three questions that had to be answered before the Norwegian Nobel Committee could decide to award the Nobel Peace Prize to a Chinese dissident. Firstly, they had to consider whether any prize should be given to a Chinese person at all. China's development was in many ways heading in the right direction. Would a Peace Prize have a positive or a negative impact on the status of human rights in China? Secondly, it was well known that the Chinese dissident environment consisted of many different factions who had strained relationships with each other. The committee could not risk a prize to a dissident being attacked by other oppositionists. Thirdly, any prize would raise deep moral questions. Could the committee vote in favour of such a prize when they knew that the short-term effect might be that the laureate and other dissidents would find themselves in even direr straits?

The Norwegian Nobel Committee had established an honourable record when it came to fighting for democracy and human rights. The committee directly opposed Hitler through the prize to Carl von Ossietzky. It challenged the Kremlin through the prizes to Andrei Sakharov (1975) and Lech Wałęsa (1983). None of these people were able to come to Oslo to receive their prizes, but few prizes have garnered as much respect as precisely these three. The prize to Ossietzky in particular was controversial even within Norway. Two of the committee members, including Minister of Foreign Affairs Halvdan Koht, withdrew from the committee, and the king stayed away from the award ceremony.

There have now been many human rights prizes: just in my years as committee secretary, since 1990, there have been prizes to Aung San Suu Kyi,

Rigoberta Menchú, Nelson Mandela and F. W. de Klerk, Kim Dae-jung, and Shirin Ebadi. Every year human rights activists from various countries such as Cuba, Vietnam, and Latin American and Arab countries are suggested. But more and more we wondered: what was the committee to do about China? Was it afraid of criticizing superpowers? Would it only support dissidents in smaller countries? This unease among the committee members increased gradually during the 2000s.

China had experienced miraculous economic progress since 1978. Its gross national product increased by 10 per cent every year. First China's GNP surpassed Germany's, and then Japan's. In 2010, only the USA remained ahead of China. No major power had grown so quickly over such a long period as China had done since its reform policy was introduced in 1978. In the announcement of the prize for 2010, the committee also stated that 'over the past decades, China has achieved economic advances to which history can hardly show any equal. The country now has the world's second largest economy; hundreds of millions of people have been lifted out of poverty.'

The committee even concluded that 'scope for political participation has also broadened.' Some forms of expression became somewhat freer than they had been previously, particularly compared to the difficult years during the Cultural Revolution from 1966 until 1976. China's contact with the outside world increased dramatically. Nevertheless, there was no doubt that China was a dictatorship. There was one party, the Communist Party, which made all the decisions about the country's politics and economy. Those who did not respect the party's leadership ended up in prison. In 1989, the student protests in Tiananmen Square and around the country were brutally suppressed. The party regularly demonstrated that it was prepared to use any means necessary to control the country's development—what had happened in the Soviet Union and in Eastern Europe would definitely not happen in China. Economic modernization took place at record speed, but political modernization never came. Even before the Peace Prize was awarded in 2010 there were signs of a stricter policy being introduced as regards human rights activists and those opposed to the party, in the South China Sea, and in the general foreign policy. China was becoming increasingly self-aware in the international arena.

The committee sought advice from international experts on China. Many of them were sympathetic to the committee's intentions, but were nevertheless sceptical. Giving the prize to a Chinese dissident would be perceived as a direct challenge of those in power. They would suppress any unrest. The short-term effects would undoubtedly be negative. No one could be sure what the long-term effects would be. Nevertheless, the Nobel Committee became increasingly uneasy. Why should they make such a big exception for China? Other authoritarian nations were criticized, and Nobel prizes were awarded, but the committee did nothing where China was concerned. True enough, the committee had awarded the prize to the Dalai Lama, and it was no coincidence that this happened in 1989, when the authorities in China had demonstrated their will to protect the party's power monopoly so brutally. Still, Tibet was a special area; a prize to the Dalai Lama had several different dimensions. If you were to address the situation in China itself, the prize would have to go to a representative of the vast majority of Han Chinese.

Although the committee came to a positive conclusion on the first point about a prize being awarded to a Chinese advocate for human rights, the other questions remained to be answered. Who was the right choice? In 1999, there was an article in *Dagbladet* which said that I had apparently had the misfortune to announce that two Chinese dissidents would receive the prize that year. Wang Dan and Wei Jingsheng were the most likely choices. The former was one of the most renowned student leaders from 1989; the latter was a key figure in the so-called Democracy Wall in Beijing in 1978, where he had polemicized against Deng Xiaoping. *Dagbladet's* article was pure fabrication, but it still had consequences. The Chinese Ministry of Foreign Affairs complained to the Norwegian Ministry of Foreign Affairs about how something like this could have happened. The rumours had even led to an official protest! Then there were protests from many different Chinese dissidents around the world. The committee had chosen the wrong dissidents. Wei in particular had become a controversial figure by virtue of several strange statements. If the Peace Prize were to be awarded to a Chinese dissident, the committee had to at least have the support of most of the dissident environment. Even though everything was based on insubstantial rumours, and the prize for 1999 went to Doctors Without Borders, there was a lot to learn from the events.

For a long time Liu Xiaobo was just one of many Chinese dissidents, though some people were dismissive of him and thought he was too inspired by the West. He trained as a literary scholar in China, but also spent time abroad in Oslo, in Hawaii, and at Columbia University in New York. When the democracy movement spread in 1989, he returned home to

China. He and some friends went on a hunger strike to protest against the martial law and issued a political manifesto in six points, written by Liu, against dictatorship and in favour of democracy. Non-violence was a key part of their message, but this got them nowhere. Liu was later sent to a labour camp for 'spreading rumours and libel'. He became president of the Chinese PEN Center and was unbelievably productive. Over the years he wrote almost 800 essays, 499 of them after 2005. He was one of the main architects behind Charter 08, which was published on 10 December 2008 to mark, as it states in the document's introduction, '100 years since China's [first] Constitution, the 60th anniversary of the promulgation of the *Universal Declaration of Human Rights*, the 30th anniversary of the birth of the Democracy Wall, and the 10th year since the Chinese government signed the *International Covenant on Civil and Political Rights*'. Charter 08 was eventually signed by several thousand people in China and abroad.

On 25 December 2009, Liu was sentenced to eleven years' imprisonment and two years' deprivation of political rights for, as the judgment stated, 'inciting subversion of state power, the socialist system and the democratic dictatorship of the people'. Liu has always claimed that the judgment violates China's own Constitution and key human rights. But by virtue of this judgment Liu went from being one of several key dissidents to being *the* symbol of the fight for human rights in China. He stood out as the most obvious candidate among the dissidents.

The committee's third point was whether it was morally possible to justify giving the Peace Prize to a dissident when it was highly likely that the prize would have negative consequences for both the laureate and the dissident environment in general. But the dissidents knew they had been nominated for the prize, and no one understood better than them what the likely consequences would be. There was at least one example of a dissident who did not want the prize for fear of potential consequences. Luckily the committee was in a situation which meant we had good contacts who were able to report that most of the oppositionists viewed the prize favourably. The committee never doubted that Liu Xiaobo wanted the prize and that he was prepared to suffer the consequences this might have.

The Chinese had been concerned about the Nobel prizes for a long time. Their scientists aimed to win as many such prizes as possible as proof of the country's success and ascension. Several Chinese Americans had won such prizes; they were invited to visit China and celebrated as heroes. It was important to have these people and other Western prize recipients establish close links with Chinese universities. However, China only received the 'wrong' Nobel prizes. The prize to the Dalai Lama in 1989 in particular, but also the Nobel Prize in Literature to Gao Xingjian in 2000, had been harshly criticized.

I had visited China for a week in 1997 together with my wife after being invited by the Chinese People's Institute of Foreign Affairs. We were treated almost as if we were royalty. Traffic stopped for us as we whizzed around in Beijing and Shanghai. We met government ministers, renowned intellectuals, and experts in foreign policy. The people who accompanied us wherever we went were interesting conversation partners. There was also someone to make sure all our experiences were pleasant. When my wife wanted to look at some clothes in a supermarket right next to our hotel, she had to do it with an entourage of four men to keep an eye on her. I gave two lectures, one for young Chinese diplomats and one at Fudan University in Shanghai. The lecture in Shanghai had to be cut short by the president of the university because the students started asking questions about the prize to the Dalai Lama which were a bit *too* interesting. The president told me that he simply could not lose control of the situation in such a manner. Nevertheless, we were never in any doubt as to the intentions of the Chinese when it came to our visit. The authorities wanted to treat us so well that the Nobel Committee would never be tempted to ruin everything by rewarding a dissident. The Chinese Embassy in Oslo was certainly keen to maintain close contact with the Nobel Institute for a long time.

All of this changed abruptly in 2010. Both committee chair Jagland and I were visited on separate occasions by the Chinese Vice Minister of Foreign Affairs for European matters, Fu Ying. She had been the ambassador in the United Kingdom, spoke good English and was used to dealing with Western conversation partners. During a breakfast at the Chinese Embassy in Oslo, she made it quite clear that giving the Nobel Peace Prize to a Chinese dissident would be an unfriendly act. No specific names were mentioned. She gave two reasons for this attitude. Few, if any, Chinese people knew who these dissidents were. The people would therefore not understand if one of them received such a prize. The dissidents' views also clashed with basic Chinese notions of 'harmony and stability'. We struggled to understand how a prize to someone no one knew about would have such dramatic effects. Apart from this, the meeting was relatively relaxed. We talked about how China would meet many global challenges when the authorities insisted on full national sovereignty. I said that Beijing had already admitted the need for supranational solutions via the conflict-solving mechanism of the WTO. She replied that I did not know how right I was, because this mechanism had led to significant discussions at a high political level before it was approved.

The fact that both Jagland and I spoke openly about this meeting undoubtedly contributed to the warning lights starting to flash in Beijing. And not just in Beijing. They also started flashing at the Ministry of Foreign Affairs in Oslo. I knew the Norwegian ambassador in Beijing, Svein Sæter, well. He had often made it clear to me that a prize to a Chinese dissident would lead to major problems between Norway and China. What is even more remarkable is that Minister of Foreign Affairs Jonas Gahr Støre made the same message clear to Thorbjørn Jagland—two times of which I am aware. The first time was outside the UN building in New York. As far as Jagland understood, Støre said that the negotiations on a free trade agreement between Norway and China would grind to a halt and the dialogue on human rights would cease. The business sector's strong interests in China would be affected. Jagland informed the committee of this exchange of views. No one was in any doubt that this was an attempt to prevent a prize to a dissident. The committee found this inappropriate, although Jagland later downplayed this aspect to the media. The second time it happened was at a reception in Oslo City Hall. Støre reiterated the same points to Jagland. I was present at the same reception, and Jagland came over to me and told me what Støre had said. No one could be surprised that the Ministry of Foreign Affairs and the business sector had such views, but never before in my time as committee secretary had a member of the government conveyed such views to the committee so directly. The Chinese ambassador invited prominent Norwegian politicians such as Erna Solberg and Bård Vegar Solhjell to visit. Several business leaders and politicians called committee members to warn them against such a prize. The outcome was of course the polar opposite of what these people wanted. If the committee had been in any doubt before, it was certain now. It would not have been proper for the committee to change its mind due to pressure from Chinese and Norwegian authorities.

After the announcement of the prize to Liu Xiaobo, Beijing was so furious that the authorities implemented a number of measures to weaken the Nobel Committee's message. They did all they could to prevent the Chinese media from publishing the news that Liu had been awarded the Peace Prize. They established a new prize, the Confucius Peace Prize. It was awarded first to a former vice president of Taiwan, who did not want it, before they gave it to a seven-year-old girl. This was not unlike Nazi Germany's establishment of a new German prize to prevent Germans from receiving Nobel prizes after the prize to Ossietzky. Two or three attempts were made to hack the Nobel Institute's databases. Luckily they did not manage to do so. Even though we had help from national authorities to trace the perpetrators, we were never entirely sure who they were—but of course there was very good reason to suspect the Chinese.

The Chinese put a lot of pressure on all countries with embassies in Oslo to stay away from the Peace Prize ceremony. The ambassadors usually came to this ceremony. Many of them quickly accepted our invitation in 2010 as well. Then the Chinese made this a matter to be settled at the highest level. The prize was interference in domestic Chinese matters 'by a few clowns', as the Chinese authorities referred to the committee. Was it best to support the Chinese or risk offending them? Several ambassadors got in touch with me in the hope of obtaining information that might solve this dilemma. The situation changed from day to day as countries made new decisions. All we could do was take stock and send out bulletins on the most recent developments. The end result was that forty-seven countries were represented at the ceremony, while nineteen stayed away. The nineteen who declined our invitation gave many different reasons for doing so. Every year there were some ambassadors who were not present for some reason or other, but this year it was largely countries that did not like Western interference in domestic affairs, countries ranging from Russia to Kazakhstan, Saudi Arabia, Cuba, and Vietnam to Pakistan, Sri Lanka, and Sudan. Ambassadors from several of these countries told me directly that they were very unhappy the Chinese had put them in such an awkward position. Some of them had prominent candidates whom they wanted to receive the prize, or dissidents whom they did not want to receive it. The EU pressured Serbia and Ukraine into coming. They had no choice if they wanted to have good connections with the EU. The Philippines said no; they had to take into account the fact that five Filipinos they hoped to bring home had been sentenced to death in China for smuggling drugs. This was international politics up close.

Since neither the laureate nor any representative of the laureate could be present—the Chinese authorities made sure of that—it was a ceremony quite out of the ordinary. Jagland gave his customary presentation speech. This was the only customary thing about it. Of course there was music, but even here each of the artists had to decide whether they were prepared to offend China or not. If they attended, they would not be allowed to enter China. Several big international names said no to our invitation. Instead of the laureate's lecture, Norwegian actress Liv Ullmann read Liu Xiaobo's final statement in connection with his trial in December 2009: *I Have No Enemies*. It was a strong speech. A large picture of Liu was hung on the wall at Oslo City Hall.

When it became clear that Liu would not be able to come, the committee discussed what it should do. At first, it did not want an empty chair solution. That was too theatrical. However, in my many conversations with East Asian media representatives, it became increasingly clear that we would have to draw attention to Liu's absence. More and more people talked about having an empty chair. The day before the ceremony I strongly recommended to the committee that we have an empty chair onto which the medal and diploma could be placed. This is what happened. The empty chair was a dramatic image that made it around the world. In China, it suddenly became impossible to search for the words 'empty chair' online.

All in all, the Nobel Committee felt that it had done well in a difficult situation. The angry Chinese reaction had in fact strengthened the argument in favour of the prize. It became clear to many people that the situation in China was simply not as positive as they had thought. Paradoxically, the Chinese Constitution protects basic human rights. Article 35 states that: 'citizens of the People's Republic of China enjoy freedom of speech, of the press, of assembly, of association, of procession, and of demonstration.' Article 41 starts as follows: 'Citizens of the People's Republic of China have the right to criticize and make suggestions regarding any State organ or functionary.' It is no wonder that party leader Xi Jinping later warned against 'constitutionalism' in China. The party's security interests are held above the Constitution at all times.

China wanted to punish Norway for what the Nobel Committee had done. No one could be allowed to oppose an increasingly powerful China in such a manner. Political meetings between the two countries were cancelled until further notice. The import of salmon was greatly reduced. Other contact was also limited, but import and export nevertheless gradually picked up again somewhat. Academic contact remained largely undisturbed. The number of tourists visiting from China increased significantly, despite reports about certain problems.

Of course, the committee was aware that there would be problems as regards Norway's relationship with China, and that these would persist for a while. There was no detailed discussion in the committee about which reactions precisely could be expected and how long they would persist. No one had any way of knowing. I am personally surprised that the sanctions were maintained for so long. It is serious that the Norwegian government does not have contact with China on a political level. We can live with restrictions on the export of salmon. There are many other countries that are happy to buy Norwegian salmon. There are also back roads into China, such as via Hong Kong, for example. Norwegian industry did not get involved in this debate for a long time. It was unpopular to oppose the prize to Liu. Fish exporters who argued against the prize were more or less hung out to dry on television. The criticism gradually increased, but it is not a given that all the Norwegian exporters would have won their contracts even without the Peace Prize in 2010.

Through the Peace Center and the Peace Prize Concert, the Nobel side of things is dependent on income from various sponsors. None of our sponsors expressed even the least pleasure over the prize to Liu. Several of them limited the exposure of their Nobel involvement compared to what was normally the case. But they honoured their agreements. They deserve credit for that. However, there is no doubt that the Peace Prize for 2010 has made sponsor work more difficult than it otherwise would have been. No one wants to pick a fight with China.

However, the Norwegian Nobel Committee also has clear interests it needs to safeguard. The committee likely felt that the prize to Liu will join the ranks of prizes through which the committee has openly spoken out against authoritarian regimes. The Norwegian Nobel Committee will speak when others hold their tongues. If the committee were to defer to the Norwegian government or Norwegian business interests, there would be no point to it.

The committee told the Chinese it was unfair of Beijing to punish Norway and the Norwegian government for what an independent Norwegian committee did. Støre's warnings to Jagland demonstrated that the government was against the decision the committee had made. However, publicly the Norwegian government does tend to speak appreciatively about the decisions made by the Nobel Committee. This was also the case in 2010. Prime Minister Jens Stoltenberg chose his words carefully, but it seems he was in favour of the prize to Liu. This made it easier for Beijing to punish Norway as a nation for what an independent committee had decided. However, it must be added that the notion of an 'independent' committee is something the Chinese and many others have a lot of trouble understanding.

Towards the end of 2016, the Chinese sanctions against Norway were lifted. The joint Chinese–Norwegian statement did not contain any direct denunciation of the Peace Prize to Liu Xiaobo, though the prize was blamed for the strained relationship and the Norwegian government promised that in the future it would do its best to respect 'China's core interests'. In connection with this, the Nobel Committee reiterated its support for the 2010 prize.

No one can be sure what the future holds for China. As a historian, I prefer to concentrate on the past—it is much simpler. However, there is little doubt that from a long-term perspective, the fight for human rights has been very successful. More and more nations are becoming more democratic, though Russia, Nigeria, Venezuela, and Thailand illustrate the complications that can arise. There is no straight line from increased prosperity to democracy, though prosperity undoubtedly increases the possibility of democracy. There are two large areas that to a greater or lesser extent have resisted this democratic wave. The first is the Muslim part of the world, though progress has been made in a few countries. And then there is China. China is a country that simmers and seethes. The number of so-called 'mass incidents', protests against the authorities on a greater or lesser scale, has increased dramatically even though most of them have been local. The party in power has achieved very positive results economically, and it has also been in a position to build up national pride over the results achieved. However, the party is also responsible for huge mistakes such as the Great Leap Forward, during which as many as forty million people may have lost their lives, and for the Cultural Revolution that the Chinese look back on with horror and fear.

On 13 July 2017, Liu Xiaobo died of cancer while still in prison. When the economic growth starts to slow and the regime has less to show for itself, it is not inconceivable that the time will finally have come for political reforms, even if these will hardly be along traditional Western lines. This will not happen in the near future. It took twenty-one years for Aung San Suu Kyi to come to Norway to hold her Nobel lecture. I think we will see a somewhat different China in fifty years, politically as well as economically.

The European Union (2012)

On 12 October, the Norwegian Nobel Committee announced that the Peace Prize for 2012 would be awarded to the European Union (EU). The grounds for the award were as follows: 'The union and its forerunners have for over six decades contributed to the advancement of peace and reconciliation, democracy and human rights in Europe.' This decision was very surprising. It was well known that through the years there had been committee members who thought the EU should receive the Peace Prize. However, it was also known that there had always been opponents to such a decision on the committee. The EU was discussed by the committee many times, but there was always at least one member who protested against such a decision. Sometimes there were two members against it; sometimes even a majority. When there was a majority in favour of the EU, the majority might be able to push through a decision. However, although no members had power of veto, the majority was never prepared to do this. It would have been too much of an upheaval if one or more members had left the committee. The committee was divided because the Norwegian people were divided. Or to be more precise, the Norwegian people had voted against Norway joining the EU twice, once in 1972 and once in 1994.

However, in 2012 the entire committee was prepared to vote in favour of a prize to the EU. There was still at least one member who opposed Norwegian membership of the EU, former leader of the Centre Party Gunnar Stålsett, but this was not about Norway joining the EU. That question had been settled for the foreseeable future. This was about whether the EU had contributed to promoting peace and reconciliation in Europe. Stålsett was a deputy on the Nobel Committee for Ågot Valle, who had fallen ill at the end of 2011. Valle would never have voted in favour of a prize to the EU, something she subsequently made clear to the media as well. However, Stålsett came to a different conclusion. During the interwar years the Nobel Committee had awarded several prizes for work to promote peace and reconciliation in Europe. This happened on an official level, such as when foreign ministers Aristide Briand and Gustav Stresemann received the Peace Prize for 1926, and on a more public level such as when Ferdinand Buisson, also a politician, and historian Ludwig Quidde received the prize for 1927. All four of them were linked to the French–German reconciliation.

We all know how that went. After the optimistic 1920s, everything fell apart in the 1930s and into the Second World War.

In 1950/51, the European Coal and Steel Community was established, and in 1957 the European Economic Community. It was at this point that French–German reconciliation became a reality. Some of the people at the heart of this work, in particular Jean Monnet, but also Konrad Adenauer, were nominated to receive the Nobel Peace Prize, and the expert statements were positive. But it never seems to have been deemed appropriate to award any of them the Peace Prize. During the 1950s, Norway—both its government and its people—showed little interest in European integration. From the 1960s on, the conflict about Norway joining the EEC overshadowed the discussion about the merits of the new organization.

For most people who have studied and written about various aspects of European integration, it remained a paradox that the great transformation of Europe from a continent of war into a continent of peace never resulted in a Peace Prize. The prize to Willy Brandt in 1971 was well deserved, but it had little to do with European integration, more with *Ostpolitik*. In my countless lectures on the Peace Prize around the world, I increasingly noted that the lack of a Peace Prize to the EU was a sin of omission in the history of the prize. True enough, it was nothing compared to the lack of a prize to Mahatma Gandhi, but it won clear second place. I pushed my authority as committee secretary as far as I could, then a bit further still, when making these statements. But I thought the main point was so obvious it stood the test. I was never really criticized by the committee members for this, not even by those who were known opponents of the EU.

The parties in the Norwegian Parliament sometimes issued a positive message about the EU, such as in 2007 when the Standing Committee on Foreign Affairs unanimously stated that: 'It is the opinion of the Committee that the EU has played an important, stabilizing role in Europe in the last half century, and that the EU has contributed to economic development and international contact. The EU has influenced and promoted democracy in many former dictatorships, and continues to have a positive impact on the democratic development of several nations through its expansion.'

This ought to have been enough to justify not just one but several Peace Prizes. There are few, if any, people or institutions that have had such a positive impact on the European continent, but as long as the issue of Norway joining the EU was on the national agenda, such overall assessments quickly faded into the background of ongoing Norwegian politics.

The EU should have received the Peace Prize for the French–German reconciliation, which more than anything else contributed to transforming Europe from a continent of war into a continent of peace. The two countries had fought three wars against each other in seventy years, two of them world wars. Then they decided to cooperate. They started with coal and steel, which formed the basis of their national arms. In a surprisingly short space of time, they expanded this basis from coal and steel to the economy in general. Of course there were many factors that contributed to the French–German reconciliation: the USA's and NATO's overall role was important, as were the Cold War, economic progress, and relatively stable domestic policy. The integration partly reflected such conditions, but it was also important in and of itself. As President of the European Council Herman Van Rompuy stated in his Nobel lecture: 'Of course, peace might have come to Europe without the Union. Maybe. We will never know. But it would never have been of the same quality. A lasting peace, not a frosty cease-fire.'

As stated in the committee's grounds for the award in 2012: 'Today war between Germany and France is unthinkable. This shows how, through well-aimed efforts and by building up mutual confidence, historical enemies can become close partners.' There was something highly optimistic about the French–German reconciliation. When two such historical enemies can be reconciled, it should in principle be possible for anyone else to do the same. Van Rompuy touched on this during his Nobel lecture: 'So what a bold bet it was, for Europe's Founders, to say, yes, we can break this endless cycle of violence, we can stop the logic of vengeance, we can build a brighter future, together. What power of the imagination.'

The EU could also have received the Peace Prize for its contributions to strengthening democracies in Southern Europe. Greece and, to an even greater extent, Spain and Portugal, had more or less authoritarian governments for many years. The introduction of democracy in the 1970s largely took place due to internal factors, but democracy was also a pre-requisite of them joining the EU. In turn, their membership bolstered the democratic institutions. Greece joined the EU in 1981; Spain and Portugal followed in 1986.

The incorporation of Central and Eastern Europe into the EU was also very important. As stated in the committee's grounds for the award: 'The fall of the Berlin Wall made EU membership possible for several Central and Eastern European countries, thereby opening a new era in European history.'

After the Cold War ended, a new wall could have been built in Europe between the rich West and the poor East. Mutual membership of the EU made this difference a lot smaller than it otherwise would have been. The EU demanded that the new member states be democracies, which strengthened government reform in a region with somewhat modest democratic traditions. Regional and local conflicts also had to be resolved before these countries could join the EU. President of the European Commission José Manuel Barroso quoted Karol Wojtyła, who became Pope John Paul II, in his Nobel lecture: 'Europe was able to breathe with both its lungs'.

The EU has forced significant changes in Turkey. Since as far back as in the 1960s, there has been contact between Turkey and the EU with a view to developing a closer relationship. In October 2005, Turkey started the formal negotiations required to join the EU. 'Negotiations' is hardly the correct word, since Turkey did not have much choice than to accept the EU as it is. In Turkey, human rights have been strengthened, the Kurds have gained a somewhat freer position, and the role of the military has been weakened, though the situation now, again, seems more negative. The EU has achieved greater changes than some of the Turkish human rights activists who have been nominated for the Peace Prize. Now, when the possibility of membership has been reduced, we see that the reform policy in Turkey has also ground to a halt.

Finally, countries that used to be part of Yugoslavia have undoubtedly implemented fundamental reforms in order to improve their chances of joining the EU. Slovenia was relatively unproblematic. Croatia joined the EU in 2013 after the country helped bring national war criminals before an international court. Serbia is implementing reforms even though the most difficult issue, the status of Kosovo, remains to be solved. Macedonia and Montenegro are also candidates for membership.

Naturally, the EU was far from perfect. There were clear objections to a Peace Prize to the EU in addition to the more internal Norwegian assessments. The economic situation was very difficult, particularly for Greece, Italy, and Spain. Major demonstrations were being held in all three of these countries against retrenchment and difficult times following the financial crisis in 2008. In this situation, a prize to the EU could almost be perceived as a provocation. Jagland's response to this was clear: 'In the light of the financial crisis that is affecting so many innocent people, we can see that the political framework in which the Union is rooted is more important now than ever. We must stand together. We have collective responsibility.

Without this European cooperation, the result might easily have been new protectionism, new nationalism, with the risk that the ground gained would be lost.' It was important to hold on to the overall perspective of peace and reconciliation. The EU had not solved all of the troublesome territorial issues concerning the Union either. The difficult situation in Cyprus persisted, for example. The means of combining integration with control from democratically elected bodies remained a problem for the EU.

And it was not that easy to justify the decision to award the prize in 2012. The EU could have won the prize almost any year, so why in 2012 specifically? The real explanation for this was internal: in 2012, the decision could also be rooted in what was problematic. The EU needed 'a shot in the arm', as Kofi Annan put it in a conversation I had with him. You might also emphasize recent development in the EU's relationships with nations in former Yugoslavia. The announcement said: 'The admission of Croatia as a member next year, the opening of membership negotiations with Montenegro, and the granting of candidate status to Serbia all strengthen the process of reconciliation in the Balkans.' The long historical perspective of Europe's transformation still dominated.

In connection with the prize to the EU in 2012, the committee also discussed whether chair Thorbjørn Jagland might in any way be considered to have a conflict of interest. The main argument was that he, as Secretary-General of the Council of Europe, could have had his hands tied by the EU. With help from Berit Reiss-Andersen, committee member and prominent lawyer, the committee quickly concluded this was not the case. The Council of Europe had forty-seven members, the EU twenty-seven. They also received their income from entirely different sources. The cooperation of the Council of Europe and the EU on specific projects in some areas—such as in Kosovo and in Ukraine, for example—could not be enough to disqualify Jagland from taking part in the committee's deliberations.

The award ceremony on 10 December was dominated by the presence of nineteen heads of state and government from most of the European countries. Chancellor of Germany Angela Merkel considered the Peace Prize of crucial importance to the history of the EU and stressed that as many of them should be present as possible. Most of them loyally did as asked. It was a symbolically important moment when specific reference was made to Merkel and President of France François Hollande in Jagland's speech, and with their hands in the air they received the applause of those present. Jagland also delivered his most inspired Nobel speech. In his historic presentation, Mikhail Gorbachev and Lech Wałęsa were mentioned for their work to lay the foundations for the liberation of Central and Eastern Europe. Reference was also made to Helmut Kohl because he had taken responsibility for the enormous costs of uniting East and West Germany. As previously mentioned, Kohl himself had been a serious candidate for the Peace Prize by virtue of his contributions to both German reunification and European integration.

The Nobel Committee left it to the EU to decide who would play which roles during the various events in Oslo. Of course the EU wanted the organization to appear as efficient as possible. This was not that easy when every tiny detail had to be approved by those higher up. Cyprus, which at that point held the six-month presidency of the EU, played no part in the events and stayed away from the ceremony. The European Parliament, which was represented by its president, Martin Schulz, a very jovial German, was given various smaller tasks. The key tasks were to be performed by the President of the European Council, Herman Van Rompuy, and the President of the European Commission, José Manuel Barroso. They shared the Nobel lecture, each taking half—a constructive contribution to European efficiency. Van Rompuy could at times seem a little boring, but he had a lot of interesting things to say when you were just listening. Barroso was much more animated and always on the move. The Nobel programme was not enough for him; he wanted to see the opera house and the art museums as well.

The fixed CNN programme was dominated by Jonathan Mann's preoccupation with demonstrating how inefficient the EU really was and how severe its problems were. He said almost nothing about why the EU had received the prize. However, he received tit for tat from the three representatives of the EU (including Schulz).

Two torchlight processions were held that year, one against the EU and one in favour. There were concerns on the 'yes' side that they would be overshadowed by the 'no' side. To everyone's surprise, the opposite was actually the case, though there were still not masses of people. The committee interpreted this as at least some of the Norwegian people having realized that this was not about Norway's relationship with the EU, but the historical transformation of Europe from a continent of war into a continent of peace.

7

Conclusions

The Past

All in all, I think the Norwegian Nobel Committee has a solid record from the twenty-five years I was committee secretary. I would argue that no obvious mistakes were made during these years, though of course some decisions might be questioned. That is how it will always be. No individual or institution only makes perfect decisions, and if there is to be any criticism of any of the laureates, the committee secretary must of course accept his part of this criticism.

In this context, it is likely that the 2004 prize to Wangari Maathai will be discussed more than most others. Maathai combined work on human rights and environmental protection. This combination might be considered a good thing, but experience suggests a sharper focus is important for a successful prize. In this case, there were two very different focuses. Maathai was undoubtedly a human rights activist, but she had limited political support in Kenya. Eventually she became best known as an environmental activist, focusing on planting trees, which is quite a specific action. The environment became the most important aspect of her work. When the committee finally decided to award the first prize for environmental work, it is far from obvious that Maathai was the best candidate. There were many other candidates who could have been considered as well.

Two Norwegians have received the Nobel Peace Prize: Christian Lange in 1921 and Fridtjof Nansen in 1922. It was brave of the committee to award a prize to a Norwegian two years in a row. Since then, many Norwegians have been suggested as candidates for the prize, but few, if any, have quite fit the bill. In my time as committee secretary, no Norwegian came close to receiving the prize. Not even Gro Harlem Brundtland. When we first started considering environmental issues, there were very good arguments in favour of Gro. Many people considered her the world's leading green politician. Sissel Rønbeck, the Labour Party's representative on the Nobel Committee, was not a big admirer of Gro. Gro was not a big admirer of Sissel either. There was no discussion of Gro's candidacy, which seems strange. The committee was obviously afraid to award the prize to a Norwegian; it smacked of provincialism, but Gro had strong international criteria.

It also has to be said that, in hindsight, Xanana Gusmão should have been considered more carefully in connection with the prize for 1996. Gusmão was in prison in Indonesia, but the committee had previously awarded and would subsequently award prizes to people who were in prison, so this was no definitive obstacle. He was the clear leader of the fight for independence in East Timor, and when the committee considered the politics of the matter and not just the moral side of things via the prize to Belo, it became clear that the consideration of Gusmão should have been completely different. Subsequent events also emphasized his status as the clear leader of East Timor. There was something clearly tactical about the consideration of the prize to Ramos-Horta. He was free and able to keep the political struggle going around the world, but it was undoubtedly Gusmão who was in charge.

I have also wondered a lot about whether the committee should have included Canadian Minister of Foreign Affairs Lloyd Axworthy in the land-mine prize for 1997. What was characteristic of the fight against landmines was the close cooperation between some governments, the International Campaign to Ban Landmines, and the many independent organizations that supported a landmine ban. Without the activist governments, there would never have been any landmine treaty. Canada played the key role in this for a long time. The frustration associated with Axworthy's attempts to compromise with the USA in the finishing stage of the work on the treaty prevented a prize being awarded to him, but this might not necessarily have been the right decision. The committee could have chosen up to three laureates, so it would not have been difficult to include him.

No one knows what the future holds. When the committee awards a prize, it is difficult for it to predict what might happen next. Of course the committee has no control over the laureates once they have received the prize. It is not possible to take back a Nobel Prize once it has been awarded. The question marks are particularly significant as regards young laureates. We can only hope the future will be kind to and bring out the best in Tawakkol Karman and Malala Yousafzai.

The most controversial prize during my years as committee secretary was undoubtedly the prize to Barack Obama. The prize to Liu Xiaobo was strongly criticized by China, but the committee was praised by many other parts of the world. When it came to Obama, the criticism was deafening on the American right, whereas sympathy was greater in other parts of the world. Obama has remained more popular in many other countries than in the USA. The committee supporting a president who made himself a spokesman for that which had been at the heart of the history of the Peace Prize should perhaps not have been as surprising as it was. But the criticism of the prize to Obama did not only come from a very vocal American right. Many others, even among his supporters, thought the prize was premature. The committee's hope that the prize would bolster Obama in his future work did not really bear fruit. Obama himself and his supporters almost never refer to the prize. This is a clear sign that it has not given him extra political strength. Whether this means Obama should not have received the prize is another matter entirely.

The Future

The greatest advantage of the Peace Prize in recent decades is how global it has become. It is striking to see how each prize to a new region or a new country leads to more attention for the prize. It is in the nature of the scientific Nobel prizes that they are mainly awarded to wealthier countries that are able to finance renowned universities and expensive laboratories. It is different for the Peace Prize, and also partly for the Prize for Literature. Contributions to peace and literature can be made by many more people who are more independent of the economic/scientific infrastructure. We saw a striking example of this in 2014, with the awards to Kailash Satyarthi and Malala Yousafzai. Suddenly the prize was being awarded to the citizen of a country in the process of becoming the world's most populous nation—India. A great deal of attention was also turned towards the more controversial and complex issues in Pakistan. Although the Peace Prize has gone to all the continents of the world apart from Australia in recent decades, there are still many regions and countries with few or no Peace Prize laureates. Of course, the prize should not be distributed mathematically across the world, but few things, if any, would be more crucial to securing the prestige of the Peace Prize than more and more areas and countries being drawn into the prize work.

The comparative advantage of the Peace Prize must be consolidated and further expanded.

The Norwegian Nobel Committee has always held that there are many different roads to peace. At times, it can of course be confusing that Yasser Arafat and Mother Theresa have received the same prize. Nevertheless, I think people around the world know that there are different roads to peace and that different traditions have to be honoured. Attempts to link the Peace Prize to just one tradition would only limit and weaken the position of the prize. Awarding the Peace Prize more or less exclusively to those working within the peace tradition in the narrowest sense is not only a restricted way of interpreting Alfred Nobel's will, but it would soon lead to the Peace Prize losing its unique role. Most of those working within this tradition are relatively unknown in a global context. It is entirely acceptable to award the prize to lesser-known names on occasion, but if this were to become a common occurrence, interest in the prize would soon wane. A collective jaw drop now and then is fine, such as in the case of Józef Rotblad and Muhammad Yunus, but if this were to become the norm, the prize would experience problems.

The various roads to peace have been surprisingly stable from the first year of the prize. International organization is probably the most frequently recurring of all recurring themes in the history of the prize. Particularly in smaller countries, but also among liberals in large countries such as the USA and the United Kingdom, there has been unwavering faith that we can organize our way to a better and more peaceful world. The insistence of the school of scientific realism that international cooperation is nothing more than the sum of national interests where nobody is prepared to let others define their security has never really diminished the dream of global common security.

In the years before the First World War, almost all the Peace Prizes were awarded to people or organizations affiliated with the Inter-Parliamentary Union, the International Peace Bureau, or to work to strengthen international law. (The two most important exceptions were the humanitarian prize to Henry Dunant in 1901 and the realpolitik prize to Theodore Roosevelt in 1906.) It is not far-fetched to imagine that efforts to achieve a better organized world will continue to be recognized via the Peace Prize, whether this concerns new UN bodies and leaders, new international courts, or new international non-governmental organizations. It always helps when the Peace Prize contributes to success. But much remains to be done. It is in no way certain that, in the foreseeable future, nations will be in a position to put their security in the hands of organizations in which they themselves are a minority. However, much has been achieved since the first Peace Prize in 1901.

The second recurring theme throughout the history of the Peace Prize is the fight for democracy and human rights. A lot of progress has been made in this area as well, though not necessarily because of the Peace Prize, but general progress has bolstered the Peace Prize. The first modern democracies emerged in the nineteenth century, and the first democratic wave culminated at the end of the First World War. During the interwar years, everything went in the opposite direction. In 1942, there were only twelve democracies left in the world. The second wave of democratization came after the Second World War. India was the major breakthrough in the third world. The third wave came between 1974 and 1990, when more than thirty countries in Southern Europe, Latin America, and Eastern Europe became democracies. Since then it has been a bit spasmodic. It is new that over half of the world's population now lives under more or less democratic rule. There are major challenges in the Muslim world, despite progress in Indonesia, and even in Malaysia and Tunisia. Turkey made some progress as well, but has since backslid. And then of course there is China.

In the long run there is reason to be optimistic on behalf of democracy and human rights. Things take time; decades fly by, but the desire to be involved in determining our future is deeply rooted in most of the world's population. The Norwegian Nobel Committee should continue to be a key player in these issues.

The Norwegian Nobel Committee has awarded humanitarian prizes since as far back as 1901. This theme has been somewhat overshadowed by the two just examined, but humanitarian prizes will continue to be awarded. Again, the success of this work is striking. The number of people in poverty has been dramatically reduced, particularly in China, but not only there. The UN established its Millennium Development Goals. One of the most important of these was halving world poverty. We have now done this. Life expectancy has increased significantly, the education situation has improved, and women have gained more rights. There is a lot for the Nobel Committee to consider in this area as well.

The area for which the Nobel Committee has the least to show is, as specified in Alfred Nobel's will, 'the abolition or reduction of standing armies'. The number of nuclear nations has increased far slower than was expected in the 1960s, but Israel, India, Pakistan, and North Korea nevertheless now have nuclear weapons. Time and time again the Nobel Committee has awarded Peace Prizes to people and organizations fighting to ban nuclear weapons. But a lot still remains to be done in this area. It might be claimed that the fights against landmines (prize in 1997) and against chemical weapons (prize in 2013) have enjoyed somewhat greater success. These are weapons of which the world might actually be able to rid itself, though there is still a way to go.

In recent years, the Peace Prize has included the environment in its approach. It is not difficult to argue that the environment is linked to peace, and there will certainly be more environmental prizes in the future. It is not easy to conceive of entirely new areas that might be considered by the Nobel Committee. Instead they might consider more limited fields. Of course it is conceivable that journalists might receive the prize for their activities. In such a case, it is important to differentiate between accurate journalism and sensationalism. Two authors (Bertha von Suttner and Elie Wiesel) and three journalists (Alfred Fried, Norman Angell, and Tawakkol Karman) have already received the Peace Prize. However, this was more for their message than for their jobs.

Many different academics have received the Peace Prize (physicians: Schweitzer, International Physicians for the Prevention of Nuclear War, Doctors Without Borders; physicists: Sakharov and Rotblat; political scientists: Kissinger; historians: Quidde). Sooner or later a peace researcher will receive the Peace Prize even though the field is somewhat complex today. The same goes for philosophy (Kant would have been a strong candidate had he still been alive today). Musicians should not be ruled out in today's media world either. Some pop stars have a high profile within international politics (Bono, Bob Geldof, Sting). During the 2000s, several such names were actually considered, but the conclusion was nevertheless that these artists were better suited to receive Grammys than Nobel prizes. The Peace Prize must not become too popular either.

The various roads to peace have proven to be steadfast over time. This will probably remain the case in the decades and centuries to come as well. There will undoubtedly be some surprises. The geographical diversity will only increase. This is important and as it should be.

The most important thing for the future success of the Peace Prize will undoubtedly be making good decisions when it comes to the selection of laureates. There is no simple formula for what constitutes a good decision, but it has been found that controversy and success need not be incompatible.

Some controversial prizes have proved successful, but not all of them. (I am thinking, for example, of the prize for 1973 to Henry Kissinger and Lê Đức Thọ, which was undoubtedly controversial but not particularly successful.) Only awarding controversial prizes would not be any road to success either. All in all, the Nobel Committee has functioned a lot better since 1901 than could have been expected. The members have had their similarities and differences, and many different approaches, but the result of this has been surprisingly good.

Literature

INTRODUCTION

The leading presentations of the Nobel Peace Prize are Irwin Abrams, *The Nobel Peace Prize and the Laureates: An Illustrated Biographic History 1901–2001* (Nantucket: Science History Publications, 2001) and Øyvind Stenersen, Ivar Libæk, and Asle Sveen, *Nobels fredspris. Hundre år for fred. Prisvinnerne 1901–2000* [The Nobel Peace Prize, A Hundred Years of Peace. Laureates 1901–2000] (Oslo: Cappelen, 2001, also English edition). For a new American, conservative interpretation of the Peace Prize, see Jay Nordlinger, *Peace, They Say: A History of the Nobel Peace Prize, the Most Famous and Controversial Prize in the World* (New York: Encounter Books, 2012).

A constructivist interpretation of the Peace Prize can be found in Roger P. Alford, 'The Nobel Effect: Nobel Peace Prize Laureates as International Norm Entrepreneurs', *Virginia Journal of International Law*, 49:1, Autumn 2008, 61–153. A realistic interpretation can be found in Ronald R. Krebs, 'The False Promise of the Nobel Peace Prize', *Political Science Quarterly*, Winter 2009–10, 593–625.

A classical, general political science interpretation within the school of realism can be found in John J. Mearsheimer, 'The False Promise of International Institutions', *International Security*, 19:3, 1994–95, 5–49. Responses to Mearsheimer from representatives of various other schools, represented by Robert O. Keohane and Lisa L. Martin, Charles A. Kupchan and Clifford A. Kupchan, John Gerard Ruggie, and Alexander Wendt, and Mearsheimer's response to all of these, can be found in *International Security*, 20:1, Summer 1995, 39–93.

The history of international cooperation is best recounted in Mark Mazower, *Governing the World: The History of an Idea* (New York: Penguin 2012) and Akira Iriye, *Global Community: The Role of International Organizations in the Making of the Contemporary World* (Berkeley: University of California Press, 2004).

Liberal internationalism from a Norwegian perspective is best described in Bjørn Arne Steine, 'Fred, forskning og formidling. Internasjonale studier i Norge og Sverige 1897–1940' [Peace, Research and Dissemination. International Studies in Norway and Sweden 1897–1940] (PhD, University of Oslo, 2016) and in Torbjørn L. Knutsen, Halvard Leira, and Iver B. Neumann, *Norsk utenrikspolitisk idéhistorie, 1890–1940* [A History of Norwegian Foreign Policy, 1890–1940] (Oslo: Universitetsforlaget, 2016). Several of the Norwegian quotes in Chapter 1 were taken from the last book.

ALFRED NOBEL AND HIS WILL

The best biography about Alfred Nobel is still Erik Bergengren, *Alfred Nobel: The Man and His Work* (London: Thomas Nelson, 1962). Work on a new biography is now finally underway at the Nobel Foundation in Stockholm. The letters exchanged by Alfred Nobel and Bertha von Suttner can be found in Edelgard Bidermann, ed., *Chère Baronne et Amie—Chèr monsieur et ami. Der Briefwechsel zwischen Alfred Nobel und Bertha von Suttner* (Hildesheim: Georg Olms Verlag, 2001). Bertha's own story can be found in her *Memoirs of Bertha von Suttner: The Records of an Eventful Life*, Volume 2 (Boston: Ginn and Company, 1910). An interesting contemporary account of the peace movement is Anna B. Wicksell, *Fredsrörelse på 1890-talet* [Peace Movement in the 1890s] (Stockholm: Verdandi, 1901).

Another account worth a read is Anne Synnøve Simensen, *Kvinnen bak fredsprisen. Historien om Bertha von Suttner og Alfred Nobel* [The Woman Behind the Peace Prize. The Story of Bertha von Suttner and Alfred Nobel] (Oslo: Cappelen Damm, 2012). Fredrik S. Heffermehl's interpretation can be found in his *Nobels vilje* [Nobel's Will] (Oslo: Vidarforlaget, 2008).

Per Jostein Ringsby, '40 års kamp for fred. Tre fredsforeninger i Skandinavia 1882–1922' [The 40-Year Struggle for Peace. Three Peace Societies in Scandinavia 1882–1922] (PhD, University of Oslo, 2010) is useful reading about the peace movement in Scandinavia. Oscar J. Falnes, *Norway and the Nobel Peace Prize* (New York: Columbia University Press, 1938) is still useful as well.

THE LAUREATES, 1901–1914

The laureates are best described in the works of Irwin Abrams, *The Nobel Peace Prize and the Laureates* and Øyvind Stenersen, Ivar Libæk, and Asle Sveen, *Nobels Fredspris,* mentioned earlier. The Nobel Committee's presentation speeches and the laureates' acceptance speeches can be found in Frederick W. Haberman, ed., *Nobel Lectures: Peace, 1901–1925* (Amsterdam: Elsevier, 1972). Otherwise there is a list of all proposed candidates and all consultant reports in the internal publications at the Nobel Institute, organized by decade. These are made publicly available to those interested after fifty years. I had access to all these reports and even wrote some of them myself in my years as committee secretary. Due to secrecy rules, I cannot, however, include these reports as references. Martin Ceadel, *Semi-Detached Idealists: The British Peace Movement and International Relations, 1854–1945* (Oxford: Oxford University Press, 2000) and Sandi E. Cooper, 'Peace and Internationalism: European Ideological Movements Behind the Two Hague Conferences, 1889–1907' (PhD, New York University, 1967) have been most useful for information on the history of the peace movement. David Cortright, *Peace: A History of Movements and Ideas* (Cambridge: Cambridge University Press, 2008) is also of interest.

Øyvind Tønnesson, 'With Christian L. Lange as a Prism: A Study of Transnational Peace Politics, 1899–1919' (PhD, University of Oslo, 2012) is a useful study of Christian L. Lange's work. The best discussion of Norway and arbitration can be found in Roald Berg, *Norge på egen hand. 1905–1920* [Norway on Its Own. 1905–1920].Volume 2 in *Norsk utenrikspolitikks historie* [The History of Norwegian Foreign Policy] (Oslo: Universitetsforlaget, 1995).

WHAT HAD THE PEACE MOVEMENT ACHIEVED IN 1914?

See William McNeill, 'Introductory Historical Commentary', in Geir Lundestad, ed., *The Fall of Great Powers: Peace, Stability, and Legitimacy* (Oxford: Oxford University Press, 1994), 3–21; Root's Nobel lecture can be found in Haberman, ed., *Peace, 1901–1925*.

Norman Angell, *The Great Illusion: A Study of the Relation of Military Power to National Prestige* (London: Heinemann, 1913) is famous. Cooper, 'Peace and Internationalism' is also useful.

For an excellent overview of the development in Europe during the 1800s, see Richard J. Evans, *The Pursuit of Power: Europe 1815–1914* (London: Penguin, 2016). The best work in recent history on the run-up to the First World War which covers the role of the peace movement is Margaret MacMillan, *The War That Ended Peace: How Europe Abandoned Peace for the First World War* (London: Profile Books, 2013). Christopher Clark's *The Sleepwalkers: How Europe Went to War in 1914* (London: Penguin, 2013) has little to say on this topic.

THE LEAGUE OF NATIONS

See also the references listed in the following section. The diary entries of Halvdan Koht (1920–36) and Fredrik Stang (1923–35) from the committee meetings are available at the Nobel Institute. Odd-Bjørn Fure, *Mellomkrigstid. 1920–1940. Norsk utenrikspolitikks historie* [The Interwar Years. 1920–1940. The History of Norwegian Foreign Policy], Volume 3 (Oslo: Universitetsforlaget, 1996) is the most important source of information on Norwegian public policy.

THE LEAGUE OF NATIONS AS THE NEW
INSTRUMENT OF PEACE

The laureates are described in Abrams, *The Nobel Peace Prize and the Laureates* and in Stenersen, Libæk, and Sveen, *Nobels fredspris*. For the speeches from the committee and the laureates, see Haberman, ed., *Peace, 1901–1925* and Frederik W. Haberman, ed., *Peace, 1926–1950* (Amsterdam: Elsevier, 1972). The internal consultant reports from the Nobel Institute are also important.

Zara Steiner, *The Lights That Failed: European International History 1919–1933* (Oxford: Oxford University Press, 2005) and Fure, *Mellomkrigstid. 1920–1940* have been most useful for general international and Norwegian history.

There is a lack of decent, up-to-date analyses of the Kellogg–Briand Pact. Robert H. Ferrell, *Peace in Their Time: The Origins of the Kellogg–Briand Pact* (New Haven: Yale University Press, 1952) is still relevant.

Åsmund Svendsen, *Halvdan Koht. Veien mot Framtiden. En biografi* [Halvdan Koht. The Road to the Future. A Biography] (Oslo: Cappelen Damm, 2013) is most interesting for information about Halvdan Koht. Koht's notes from his Nobel work can be found at the Nobel Institute. Elisabeth Thue, *Nobels fredspris—og diplomatiske forviklinger* [The Nobel Peace Prize—and Diplomatic Complications] (Oslo: Norwegian Institute for Defence Studies, 5/1994) is informative as regards the Ossietzky case. Patrick Salmon, *The Ambiguities of Peace: The Nobel Peace Prize and International Relations Between the Wars*, The Norwegian Nobel Institute Series, 2:2 is useful.

AFTER 1945: THE DOMINANCE OF THE UNITED NATIONS

For information on the laureates, see Abrams, *The Nobel Peace Prize and the Laureates* and Stenersen, Libæk, and Sveen, *Nobels fredspris*. For the laureates after 1990, see Geir Lundestad, *Fredens sekretær. 25 år med Nobelprisen* [Secretary of Peace. 25 Years with the Nobel Peace Prize] (Oslo: Kagge, 2015). See also the internal consultant volumes at the Nobel Institute and Frederic W. Haberman, ed., *Nobel Lectures. Peace, 1951–1970* (Amsterdam: Elsevier, 1972), Irwin Abrams, ed., *Nobel Lectures. Peace, 1971–1980* (Singapore: World Scientific, 1997), and Irwin Abrams, ed., *Nobel Lectures. Peace, 1981–1990* (Singapore: World Scientific, 1997). New books in this series were then published every five years until 2005: *1991–1995, 1996–2000,* and *2001–2005* all edited by Irwin Abrams.

Committee chair Gunnar Jahn's private diary entries from the Nobel Committee for the years 1945 to 1966 are now available at the Nobel Institute. Aase Lionæs, *Tredveårskrigen for freden. Høydepunkter i Nobelkomiteens historie* [The Thirty-Year War for Peace. Highlights in the History of the Nobel Committee] (Oslo: Aschehoug, 1987) gives her cautious account of her years on the Nobel Committee. Another committee chair, Egil Aarvik, has provided his perspective in *Smil i alvor. Fragmenter av et liv* [Smile Seriously. Fragments of a Life] (Oslo: Gyldendal, 1985). A third, Gunnar Berge, has written his version in *Til kongen med fagbrev* [To the King with Guilds Certificates] (Oslo: Aschehoug, 2011).

A short and precise introduction to the history and organization of the UN can be found in Jussi M. Hanhimäki, *The United Nations: A Very Short Introduction* (Oxford: Oxford University Press, 2008). Thomas G. Weiss and Sam Daws, eds., *The Oxford Handbook on the United Nations* (Oxford: Oxford University Press, 2007) goes into much more detail. Mazower, *Governing the World* is also useful. Brian Urquhart, *A Life in Peace and War* (London: Weidenfeld & Nicolson, 1987) is an exciting account from inside the UN system. For a recent example of criticism of the UN's bureaucracy and inefficiency, see former Deputy Secretary-General Anthony Banbury, 'I Love the U.N., but It Is Failing', *New York Times*, 20 March 2016, SR5.

Knut Frydenlund, *Lille land—hva nå? Refleksjoner om Norges utenrikspolitiske situasjon* [Small Country—What Now? Reflections on Norway's Foreign Policy] (Oslo: Universitetsforlaget, 1982) gives an important Norwegian perspective. The quote from Thorvald Stoltenberg about the UN is from his and Per Anders Madsen's *Frokost med Thorvald. Sju samtaler om verden, livet og kjærligheten* [Breakfast with Thorvald. Seven Conversations about the World, Life and Love] (Oslo: Kagge, 2017).

Jakob Sverdrup, *Inn i storpolitikken. 1940–1949* [Inside International Politics. 1940–1949], Volume 4 in *Norsk utenrikspolitikks historie* [The History of Norwegian Foreign Policy] (Oslo: Universitetsforlaget, 1996), Knut Einar Eriksen and Helge Pharo, *Kald krig og internasjonalisering. 1949–1965* [Cold War and Internationalization. 1949–1965], Volume 5 in *Norsk utenrikspolitikks historie* [The History of Norwegian Foreign Policy] (Oslo: Universitetsforlaget, 1996), and Rolf Tamnes, *Oljealder. 1965–1995* [The Oil Age. 1965–1995] (Oslo: Universitetsforlaget, 1997) give the Norwegian part of the history of international politics after the Second World War.

The story about Roosevelt's medal in the Roosevelt Room is based on my own visit to the White House. The story about Johnson and the Nobel Peace Prize is from Randall B. Woods, who wrote the biography *LBJ: Architect of American Ambition* (Cambridge, MA: Harvard University Press, 2007). Nixon's interest in the Nobel Peace Prize is documented in sources in the National Archives, College Park. For Khrushchev's interest in the Peace Prize, see Olav Njølstad, 'Da Khrusjtsjov ville ha fredsprisen' [When Khruschchev Wanted the Peace Prize], *Aftenposten*, 4 November 2003, updated online on 19 October 2011.

TEN PORTRAITS

The portraits are based on my *Fredens sekretær* [Secretary of Peace]. A number of the laureates have written their memoirs/accounts of their lives either to strengthen their candidacy for the Peace Prize or after they received it. Here is a selection: Aung San Suu Kyi, *Freedom from Fear* (London: Penguin Books, 1991), José Ramos-Horta, *Funu: The Unfinished Saga of East Timor* (Trenton, NJ: Red Sea Press, 1986), Arnold S. Cohen, *From the Place of the Dead: The Epic Struggles of Bishop Belo of East Timor* (New York: St. Martin's Griffin, 1999), Shirin Ebadi, *Iran Awakening: A Memoir of Revolution and Hope* (New York: Random House, 2006), Wangari Maathai, *Unbowed: One Woman's Story, A Memoir* (London: Heinemann, 2006), Al Gore, *An Inconvenient Truth: The Planetary Emergency of Global Warming and What We Can Do About It* (New York: Rodale, 2006).

John Allen, *Rabble-Rouser for Peace: The Authorized Biography of Desmond Tutu* (New York: Free Press, 2006), Matthew Evangelista, *Unarmed Forces: The Transnational Movement to End the Cold War* (Ithaca: Cornell University Press, 1999), and Nina Suomalainen and Jyrki Karvinen, eds., *The Ahtisaari Legacy: Resolve and Negotiate* (Helsinki: Tammi, 2008) are also useful.

SOME CONCLUSIONS

Some of the material in the first part of Chapter 7 is based on my book *Fredens sekretær* [Secretary of Peace]. The references to the political science literature can be found above in the first section.

List of Peace Prize Laureates

Year	Laureate	Country	Rationale
1901	Henry Dunant	Switzerland	For his role in founding the International Committee of the Red Cross
	Frédéric Passy	France	'[For] being one of the main founders of the Inter-Parliamentary Union and also the main organizer of the first Universal Peace Congress'
1902	Élie Ducommun	Switzerland	'[For his role as] the first honorary secretary of the International Peace Bureau'
	Charles Albert Gobat		'[For his role as the] first Secretary General of the Inter-Parliamentary Union'
1903	William Randal Cremer	United Kingdom	'[For his role as] the "first father" of the Inter-Parliamentary Union'
1904	Institute of International Law	Belgium	'[F]or its efforts as an unofficial body to formulate the general principles of the science of international law'
1905	Bertha von Suttner	Austria–Hungary	For writing *Lay Down Your Arms!* and contributing to the creation of the Peace Prize
1906	Theodore Roosevelt	United States	'[For] his successful mediation to end the Russo–Japanese war and for his interest in arbitration, having provided the Hague arbitration court with its very first case'
1907	Ernesto Teodoro Moneta	Italy	'[For his work as a] key leader of the Italian peace movement'
	Louis Renault	France	'[For his work as a] leading French international jurist and a member of the Permanent Court of Arbitration at The Hague'

(*continued*)

Continued

Year	Laureate	Country	Rationale
1908	Klas Pontus Arnoldson	Sweden	'[For his work as] founder of the Swedish Peace and Arbitration League'
	Fredrik Bajer	Denmark	'[For being] the foremost peace advocate in Scandinavia, combining work in the Inter-Parliamentary Union with being the first president of the International Peace Bureau'
1909	Auguste Beernaert	Belgium	'[For being a] representative to the two Hague conferences, and a leading figure in the Inter-Parliamentary Union'
	Paul Henri d'Estournelles de Constant	France	'[For] combined diplomatic work for Franco-German and Franco-British understanding with a distinguished career in international arbitration'
1910	Permanent International Peace Bureau	Switzerland	'[For acting] as a link between the peace societies of the various countries'
1911	Tobias Asser	Netherlands	'[For being a] member of the Court of Arbitration as well as the initiator of the Conferences on International Private Law'
	Alfred Fried	Austria–Hungary	'[For his work as] founder of the German Peace Society'
1912	Elihu Root[A]	United States	'[F]or his strong interest in international arbitration and for his plan for a world court'
1913	Henri La Fontaine	Belgium	'[For his work as] head of the International Peace Bureau'
1914	*Not awarded due to the First World War*		
1915			
1916			
1917	International Committee of the Red Cross	Switzerland	'[For undertaking] the tremendous task of trying to protect the rights of the many prisoners of war on all sides [of the First World War], including their right to establish contacts with their families'
1918	*Not awarded due to the First World War*		

1919	Woodrow Wilson	United States	'[F]or his crucial role in establishing the League of Nations'
1920	Léon Bourgeois	France	'[For his participation] in both the Hague Conferences of 1899 and 1907' and for his work towards 'what became the League to such an extent that he was frequently called its "spiritual father"'
1921	Hjalmar Branting	Sweden	'[F]or his work in the League of Nations'
	Christian Lange	Norway	'[For his work as] the first secretary of the Norwegian Nobel Committee' and 'the secretary-general of the Inter-Parliamentary Union'
1922	Fridtjof Nansen	Norway	'[For] his work in aiding the millions in Russia struggling against famine' and 'his work for the refugees in Asia Minor and Thrace'
1923	*Not awarded*		
1924	*Not awarded*		
1925	Sir Austen Chamberlain[A]	United Kingdom	For work on the Locarno Treaties
	Charles G. Dawes[A]	United States	'[For work on] the Dawes Plan for German reparations which was seen as having provided the economic underpinning of the Locarno Pact of 1925'
1926	Aristide Briand	France	For work on the Locarno Treaties
	Gustav Stresemann	Germany	
1927	Ferdinand Buisson	France	'[For] contributions to Franco-German popular reconciliation'
	Ludwig Quidde	Germany	
1928	*Not awarded*		
1929	Frank B. Kellogg[A]	United States	'[F]or the Kellogg–Briand pact, whose signatories agreed to settle all conflicts by peaceful means and renounced war as an instrument of national policy'
1930	Nathan Söderblom	Sweden	'[F]or his efforts to involve the churches not only in work for ecumenical unity, but also for world peace'

(continued)

Continued

Year	Laureate	Country	Rationale
1931	Jane Addams	United States	'[F]or her social reform work' and 'leading the Women's International League for Peace and Freedom'
	Nicholas Murray Butler	United States	'[For his promotion] of the Briand–Kellogg pact' and for his work as the 'leader of the more establishment-oriented part of the American peace movement'
1932	*Not awarded*		
1933	Sir Norman Angell[A]	United Kingdom	For authoring *The Great Illusion* and for being a 'supporter of the League of Nations as well as an influential publicist [and] educator for peace in general'
1934	Arthur Henderson	United Kingdom	'[F]or his work for the League, particularly its efforts in disarmament'
1935	Carl von Ossietzky[B]	Germany	'[For his] struggle against Germany's rearmament'
1936	Carlos Saavedra Lamas	Argentina	'[F]or his mediation of an end to the Chaco War between Paraguay and Bolivia'
1937	The Viscount Cecil of Chelwood	United Kingdom	For his work with the League of Nations
1938	Nansen International Office for Refugees	League of Nations	For its work in aiding refugees
1939	*Not awarded due to the Second World War*		
1940			
1941			
1942			
1943			
1944	International Committee of the Red Cross	Switzerland	'[F]or the great work it has performed during the war in behalf of humanity'
1945	Cordell Hull	United States	'[For] his fight against isolationism at home, his efforts to create a peace bloc of states on the American continents, and his work for the United Nations Organization'

1946	Emily Greene Balch	United States	'Formerly Professor of History and Sociology; Honorary International President, Women's International League for Peace and Freedom'
	John Raleigh Mott	United States	'Chairman, International Missionary Council; President, World Alliance of Young Men's Christian Associations'
1947	Friends Service Council	United Kingdom	'compassion for others and the desire to help them'
	American Friends Service Committee	United States	
1948	Not awarded because 'there was no suitable living candidate'. (A tribute to the recently assassinated Gandhi in India.)		
1949	The Lord Boyd-Orr	United Kingdom	'Physician; Alimentary Politician; Prominent organizer and Director, General Food and Agricultural Organization; President, National Peace Council and World Union of Peace Organizations'
1950	Ralph Bunche	United States	'Professor, Harvard University Cambridge, MA; Director, division of Trusteeship, UN; Acting Mediator in Palestine, 1948'
1951	Léon Jouhaux	France	'President of the International Committee of the European Council, vice president of the International Confederation of Free Trade Unions, vice president of the World Federation of Trade Unions, member of the ILO Council, delegate to the United Nations'
1952	Albert Schweitzer	France	'Missionary surgeon; Founder of Lambaréné (République de Gabon)'
1953	George C. Marshall	United States	'General President American Red Cross; Former Secretary of State and of Defense; Delegate UN; Originator of [the] "Marshall Plan"'
1954	Office of the United Nations High Commissioner for Refugees	United Nations	'An international relief organization founded by the UN in 1951'

(continued)

Continued

Year	Laureate	Country	Rationale
1955	*Not awarded*		
1956	*Not awarded*		
1957	Lester Bowles Pearson	Canada	'Former Secretary of State for External Affairs of Canada; former President of the 7th Session of the United Nations General Assembly'; 'for his role in helping to end the Suez conflict and trying to solve the Middle East question through the United Nations'
1958	Dominique Pire	Belgium	'Father in the Dominican Order; Leader of the relief organization for refugees "L'Europe du Coeur au Service du Monde"'
1959	Philip Noel-Baker	United Kingdom	'Member of Parliament; lifelong ardent worker for international peace and cooperation'
1960	Albert Lutuli	South Africa (Born in Southern Rhodesia)	'President of the African National Congress', 'was in the very forefront of the struggle against apartheid in South Africa'
1961	Dag Hammarskjöld[C]	Sweden	'Secretary-General of the UN', awarded 'for strengthening the organization'
1962	Linus Pauling	United States	'for his campaign against nuclear weapons testing'
1963	International Committee of the Red Cross League of Red Cross Societies	Switzerland	For their work in the protection of human rights in the ICRC's 100 years of existence
1964	Martin Luther King, Jr.	United States	Campaigner for civil rights, 'first person in the Western world to have shown us that a struggle can be waged without violence'. King spent his time working in various areas of the civil rights movement; from equal education to economic enfranchisement of minorities. King also organized the March on Washington, where he gave his famous 'I Have a Dream' speech.

1965	United Nations Children's Fund (UNICEF)	United Nations	'An international aid organization'
1966	*Not awarded*		
1967	*Not awarded*		
1968	René Cassin	France	'President of the European Court of Human Rights'
1969	International Labour Organization	United Nations	For creating international norms for working conditions
1970	Norman E. Borlaug	United States	'International Maize and Wheat Improvement Center'; 'for his contributions to the "green revolution" that was having such an impact on food production particularly in Asia and in Latin America'
1971	Willy Brandt	West Germany	'Chancellor of the Federal Republic of Germany; for West Germany's *Ostpolitik*'
1972	*Not awarded*		
1973	Henry Kissinger	United States (Born in Germany)	'For the 1973 Paris agreement intended to bring about a cease-fire in the Vietnam war and a withdrawal of the American forces'
	Lê Đức Thọ[D]	Vietnam (North)	
1974	Seán MacBride	Ireland (Born in France)	'President of the International Peace Bureau; President of the Commission of Namibia'. 'For his strong interest in human rights: piloting the European Convention on Human Rights through the Council of Europe, helping found and then lead Amnesty International and serving as secretary-general of the International Commission of Jurists'
	Eisaku Satō	Japan	'Prime Minister of Japan', 'for his renunciation of the nuclear option for Japan and his efforts to further regional reconciliation'
1975	Andrei Sakharov[E]	Soviet Union	'[for his] struggle for human rights, for disarmament, and for cooperation between all nations'

(*continued*)

Continued

Year	Laureate	Country	Rationale
1976	Betty Williams Mairead Corrigan	United Kingdom	'Founder[s] of the Northern Ireland Peace Movement (later renamed Community of Peace People)'
1977	Amnesty International	United Kingdom	'[for] protecting the human rights of prisoners of conscience'
1978	Mohamed Anwar Al-Sadat Menachem Begin	Egypt Israel (Born in Russia)	'for the Camp David Agreement, which brought about a negotiated peace between Egypt and Israel'
1979	Mother Teresa	India (Born in Skopje, now Republic of Macedonia)	'Founder of Missionaries of Charity'
1980	Adolfo Pérez Esquivel	Argentina	'Human rights leader'; 'founded non-violent human rights organizations to fight the military junta that was ruling his country (Argentina)'
1981	Office of the United Nations High Commissioner for Refugees	United Nations	'An international relief organization founded by the UN in 1951'
1982	Alva Myrdal Alfonso García Robles	Sweden Mexico	'[for] their magnificent work in the disarmament negotiations of the United Nations, where they have both played crucial roles and won international recognition'
1983	Lech Wałęsa	Poland	'Founder of Solidarność; campaigner for human rights'
1984	Desmond Tutu	South Africa	'as a unifying leader figure in the campaign to resolve the problem of apartheid in South Africa.... Through the award of this year's Peace Prize, the Committee wishes to direct attention to the non-violent struggle for liberation to which Desmond Tutu belongs, a struggle in which black and white South Africans unite to bring their country out of conflict and crisis.'

1985	International Physicians for the Prevention of Nuclear War	United States	For 'authoritative information and by creating an awareness of the catastrophic consequences of atomic warfare. The committee believes that this in turn contributes to an increase in the pressure of public opposition to the proliferation of atomic weapons and to a redefining of priorities, with greater attention being paid to health and other humanitarian issues.'
1986	Elie Wiesel	United States (Born in Romania)	'Chairman of "The President's Commission on the Holocaust"'
1987	Óscar Arias	Costa Rica	'for his work for peace in Central America, efforts which led to the accord signed in Guatemala on August 7 this year'
1988	United Nations Peace-Keeping Forces	United Nations	'[for] their efforts [that] have made important contributions towards the realization of one of the fundamental tenets of the United Nations'
1989	Tenzin Gyatso, 14th Dalai Lama	India (Born in Tibet)	'In his struggle for the liberation of Tibet [he] consistently has opposed the use of violence. He has instead advocated peaceful solutions based upon tolerance and mutual respect in order to preserve the historical and cultural heritage of his people.'
1990	Mikhail Gorbachev	Soviet Union	General Secretary of the Communist Party of the Soviet Union and President of the Soviet Union, 'for his leading role in the peace process which today characterizes important parts of the international community'
1991	Aung San Suu Kyi[F]	Burma	'for her non-violent struggle for democracy and human rights'
1992	Rigoberta Menchú	Guatemala	'for her work for social justice and ethno-cultural reconciliation based on respect for the rights of indigenous peoples'

(continued)

Continued

Year	Laureate	Country	Rationale
1993	Nelson Mandela Frederik Willem de Klerk	South Africa	'for their work for the peaceful termination of the apartheid regime, and for laying the foundations for a new democratic South Africa'
1994	Yasser Arafat	Palestine (Born in Egypt)	'to honour a political act which called for great courage on both sides, and which has opened up opportunities for a new development towards fraternity in the Middle East'
	Yitzhak Rabin	Israel	
	Shimon Peres	Israel (Born in Poland)	
1995	Joseph Rotblat	United Kingdom (Born in Poland)	'for their efforts to diminish the part played by nuclear arms in international politics and, in the longer run, to eliminate such arms'
	Pugwash Conferences on Science and World Affairs	Canada	
1996	Carlos Filipe Ximenes Belo	East Timor	'for their work towards a just and peaceful solution to the conflict in East Timor'
	José Ramos-Horta		
1997	International Campaign to Ban Landmines	Switzerland	'for their work for the banning and clearing of anti-personnel mines'
	Jody Williams	United States	
1998	John Hume	United Kingdom	'for their efforts to find a peaceful solution to the conflict in Northern Ireland'
	David Trimble	United Kingdom	
1999	Médecins Sans Frontières (Doctors Without Borders)	Switzerland	'in recognition of the organization's pioneering humanitarian work on several continents'
2000	Kim Dae-jung	South Korea	'for his work for democracy and human rights in South Korea and in East Asia in general, and for peace and reconciliation with North Korea in particular'
2001	United Nations	United Nations	'for their work for a better organized and more peaceful world'
	Kofi Annan	Ghana	
2002	Jimmy Carter	United States	'for his decades of untiring effort to find peaceful solutions to international conflicts, to advance democracy and human rights, and to promote economic and social development'

2003	Shirin Ebadi	Iran	'for her efforts for democracy and human rights. She has focused especially on the struggle for the rights of women and children.'
2004	Wangari Muta Maathai	Kenya	'for her contribution to sustainable development, democracy and peace'
2005	International Atomic Energy Agency	United Nations	'for their efforts to prevent nuclear energy from being used for military purposes and to ensure that nuclear energy for peaceful purposes is used in the safest possible way'
	Mohamed ElBaradei	Egypt	
2006	Muhammad Yunus	Bangladesh	'for advancing economic and social opportunities for the poor, especially women, through their pioneering microcredit work'
	Grameen Bank		
2007	Intergovernmental Panel on Climate Change	United Nations	'for their efforts to build up and disseminate greater knowledge about man-made climate change, and to lay the foundations for the measures that are needed to counteract such change'
	Al Gore	United States	
2008	Martti Ahtisaari	Finland	'for his efforts on several continents and over more than three decades, to resolve international conflicts'
2009	Barack Obama	United States	'for his extraordinary efforts to strengthen international diplomacy and cooperation between peoples'
2010	Liu Xiaobo[G]	China	'for his long and non-violent struggle for fundamental human rights in China'
2011	Ellen Johnson Sirleaf	Liberia	'for their non-violent struggle for the safety of women and for women's rights to full participation in peace-building work'
	Leymah Gbowee	Liberia	
	Tawakkul Karman	Yemen	
2012	European Union	European Union	'for over six decades contributed to the advancement of peace and reconciliation, democracy and human rights in Europe'

(continued)

Continued

Year	Laureate	Country	Rationale
2013	Organisation for the Prohibition of Chemical Weapons	International	'for its extensive efforts to eliminate chemical weapons'
2014	Kailash Satyarthi	India	'for their struggle against the suppression of children and young people and for the right of all children to education'
	Malala Yousafzai	Pakistan	
2015	Tunisian National Dialogue Quartet	Tunisia	'for its decisive contribution to the building of a pluralistic democracy in Tunisia in the wake of the Jasmine Revolution of 2011'
2016	Juan Manuel Santos	Colombia	'for his resolute efforts to bring the country's more than 50-year-long civil war to an end, a war that has cost the lives of at least 220,000 Colombians and displaced close to six million people'
2017	International Campaign to Abolish Nuclear Weapons	Switzerland	'for its work to draw attention to the catastrophic humanitarian consequences of any use of nuclear weapons and for its ground-breaking efforts to achieve a treaty-based prohibition of such weapons'
2018	Denis Mukwege	Democratic Republic of Congo	'for their efforts to end the use of sexual violence as a weapon of war and armed conflict'
	Nadia Murad	Germany (Born in Iraq)	

[A] Elihu Root, Austen Chamberlain, Charles G. Dawes, Frank B. Kellogg, and Norman Angell were all awarded their respective prizes one year late because the Committee decided that none of the nominations in the year in which they are listed as being awarded the prize met the criteria in Nobel's will; per its rules the Committee delayed the awarding of the prizes until the next year, although they were awarded as the previous year's prize.
[B] Carl von Ossietzky's prize was awarded *in absentia* because he was refused a passport by the government of Germany.
[C] Dag Hammarskjöld's prize was awarded posthumously.
[D] Lê Đức Thọ declined to accept the prize.
[E] Andrei Sakharov's prize was awarded *in absentia* because he was refused a passport by the government of the Soviet Union.
[F] Aung San Suu Kyi's prize was awarded *in absentia* because she was being held prisoner by the government of Burma. Following her release from house arrest and election to the Pyithu Hluttaw, Suu Kyi accepted her award in person on 16 June 2012.
[G] Liu Xiaobo's prize was awarded *in absentia* because he was imprisoned in China.

Index

democracy (*cont.*)
  social 7, 18, 83
  spread of 94, 189
  strengthening of 181
Deng Xiaoping 171
Denmark 7, 32, 60, 200
deterrence 97
Dharamsala 95
diplomacy 39, 60, 161, 209
disarmament 6–7, 21, 51, 57, 59, 64,
    79–80, 85, 88, 96–7, 100–1, 105,
    109, 116, 189, 202, 206 *see also*
    arms control
  nuclear 8, 82, 96–8, 189–90, 207–8,
    210 *see also* under nuclear
    weapons
disease 84, 157 *see also* health
dissidents 169–73 *see also* activists
Doctors Without Borders 152, 171,
    190, 208
Doyle, Michael W. 151
Drummond, Sir Eric 45
Ducommun, Élie 30, 199
Dunant, Henri 3, 7, 19, 188, 199

East Germany 90, 108, 143, 184
East Timor 14, 92–3, 143, 149, 186, 208
Eastern Bloc, the 149, 182
Ebadi, Shirin 13, 94, 170, 197, 209
economic development 159, 170,
    180, 208
economic interdependency *see*
    interdependency, economic
economics 34, 70, 72, 76, 83, 90, 93, 95,
    114, 123, 146, 156, 164, 168, 170,
    178, 181, 208 *see also* economic
    interdependency *and* trade
education 18, 84, 210
Edward VII (King of the U.K.) 38
Egypt 11, 75, 96, 132, 153, 155, 206,
    208–9
Eisenhower, Dwight 76
Eisner, Norm 168
El Salvador 80
ElBaradei, Mohamed 82, 96, 98,
    160, 209
Elizabeth I (Queen of England) 62
Elizabeth II (Queen of England) 130
England 23
environment, the 85, 100–1, 186, 190

environmental policy 168
environmental work/protection 3, 101,
    185–6, 190, 209
equality 127
Eriksen, Knut Einar 197
Esquivel, Adolfo Pérez 13, 91, 206
d'Estournelles de Constant, Paul
    Henri 200
Ethiopia 63
ethnicity 117–18, 120, 207
eurocentrism 9
Europe 2, 30, 33, 44, 55–7, 70–1, 78, 81,
    83, 108–9, 168, 173, 180–1, 183–4,
    195, 209
  Central 14, 181, 184
  Eastern 14, 55, 78, 90, 94, 105–7,
    115–16, 170, 181, 184, 189
  integration of 9, 77, 116,
    180–1, 183–4
  Southern 181, 189
  Western 2, 53, 61, 86, 94
European Coal and Steel
    Community 180
European Convention on Human
    Rights 79, 205
European Court of Human
    Rights 79, 205
European cooperation 18, 181, 183
European Economic Community
    (EEC) 180
European Union (EU), the 9, 12, 72–3,
    122, 175, 179–84, 209
  Commission of 182, 184
  Council of 181, 184, 203
  Parliament of 119, 184
Evangelista, Matthew 197
Evans, Richard J. 195

Falnes, Oscar J. 194
famines 53, 201
FARC guerrillas, the 96
fascism 59
Favreau, Jon 164–5
Ferrell, Robert H. 195
financial crises 145, 168
Finland 45, 51, 209
Finnmark 92
First World War 43, 46, 51, 53–4, 69, 78,
    84, 195, 200
  outbreak of 37–8, 41, 49, 52, 147